Rex Barney's

Orioles Memories

1969-1994

To Mrs. Lydia Bennett & family, and to my doctors,
Sheldon Goldgeier, Charles Silberstein, and Bill Neill.
—Rex Barney

To Mr. Rex: Thank YOUUU for the pleasure
of working with you.
—Norman L. Macht

Rex Barney's
Orioles
Memories

1969-1994

with Norman L. Macht

Foreword by Mike Flanagan

Published by Goodwood Press, P.O. Box 942, Woodbury, CT 06798

Contents

If you like artist George Wright's work on the cover of this book, you can get a 24 by 36 inch poster of it — and help Baltimore-area children at the same time.

For your full-color poster, send a check or money order for $19.95 to:

George Wright
P.O. Box 1142,
Cambridge, MD 21613.

All proceeds go to the Orioles Children's Charities and Baltimore Reads, Inc.

Foreword

I received the call that every player longs for on August 31, 1975. The next day I would drive, way too fast, to Baltimore. It was my mother's birthday, and I was in a dream world. As I walked into Earl Weaver's office, however, he immediately brought me back to terra firma with the words, "Go to the bullpen, keep your mouth shut and listen to Palmer, Cuellar, Brooksie, Lee May, and Elrod."

After that I would arrive at Memorial Stadium around 3:00 to check and see if my number 46 was still in my locker. Once assured of that, I could go about my quiet day of observation. The clubhouse is quite empty at this time of day: batboys shining shoes, mail being handed out, and older players getting a rub, hiding injuries from younger eyes.

A tall, handsome man entered the clubhouse that day, as he would for years to come like clockwork. He walked over to the now legendary trainer, Ralphie, who I would grow to love as a son loves his father, and they began to talk baseball. I listened, or should I say eavesdropped, on their conversation, and realized that these two men knew much more about baseball than I did.

The tall man came over to me, extended his hand, and said, "Michael." I was surprised; no one ever called me Michael. It was "Mike" by my acquaintances, "Mikey" by my parents till I was 25, "Flanny" by teammates, and many other names by fans that I don't care to mention. There was a kindness in this man's eyes, sincerity in his voice, and power in the handshake. I don't remember what he said after "Michael." It doesn't matter. But I do remember that it was at that moment a long, tight bond would begin.

Some people will remember this man as the hard-throwing but somewhat erratic pitcher, and some as "The Voice of Memorial Stadium," but to me he sounded more like the voice of God coming from above the field, giving me confidence that it was going to be all right. I was fortunate to have that voice as my security blanket for the next 15 years, and for that I am still grateful.

Rex Barney, *thank you* for those quiet 3 o'clock chats, whether things were going good or bad. Most people stayed away when things weren't going well, for fear of saying something wrong or not knowing what to say. Not you, Rex. You were always there through the tough times, and always knew what to say to make it better.

As the years have passed, I've had time to reflect on my interpretation of what is "Oriole Tradition." I know now it's you, Rex, and it's Ralph, Bob Brown and the Tylers, Helen Conklin, and the numerous recognizable but unnamed faces that were always at the ballpark long before game time.

Take care of yourself, pal. To me and many others, you are a treasure. And just one more favor—always call me Michael.

To Friendship, with love and admiration.

Mike Flanagan

Preface

One of the advantages of my being lucky enough to be part of baseball for more than 50 years is that I got to see all the changes that have taken place.

One of the disadvantages of my being lucky enough to be part of baseball for more than 50 years is that I got to see all the changes that have taken place.

Overwhelmingly, the most significant change is the money. No question about it.

In the 1940s and '50s we didn't make any money. My peak salary was $28,000. But we *thought* we were making all the money in the world. Nobody knew any different. We took it as it came. We were not stars in a money sense, just guys who had a good summer job. We had to work at something else during the winter to eat.

These kids today are spoiled. And I think I would be, too, if I was playing now.

Several years ago a team held a grievance meeting in the clubhouse. You know what the big complaint was? They wanted more outlets for their hair dryers. And they got them.

At Memorial Stadium the Orioles constantly heard complaints from visiting clubs. Over what? They didn't have wall-to-wall carpeting in the visitors' clubhouse. Can you believe that?

The food spreads in both clubhouses after a game can sometimes resemble a catered wedding. Every club has to supply it for both teams. Ribs. Chicken. Steak. I've seen all that. If the visiting club doesn't like the menu, they'll go to the Orioles' player representative and complain. What do they do with that $59 a day meal money the traveling secretary hands out at the start of every road trip? They buy one big meal in the early afternoon.

When we were in Brooklyn and had to go across to Manhattan for a series against the Giants, that was not considered an away series. We got nothing—no carfare, train fare, meal money. You know that would never happen today.

We had no minimum salaries (it is now $109,000). No food in the clubhouse, unless you paid for it yourself. A hot dog, soda, package of crackers—whatever, it was all written down, nickels and dimes, and when you left town you paid up. No hair dryers. No carpeting in the clubhouse. When Jackie Robinson arrived in Ebbets Field he had a nail in the wall to hang his clothes.

I was part of the group who started the pension plan in the 1940s. We had to pay into it to be eligible. No more. Later I began to get $500 a month from it. For years guys like Ralph Kiner, Allie Reynolds and Early Wynn led the fight to get a raise for the founders of the plan. But the young players turned them down. One of the player reps who opposed it was Doug DeCinces. His reason? "They're finished. They don't do anything for us now."

Finally, in 1990, we got a big raise. A lot of old-timers needed that money more than I did. But players whose careers ended before 1946 still get nothing from the pension plan. That's why I'm active in BAT—the Baseball Assistance Team. If any old-timers need help, BAT is there to help them.

Today the average salary is more than one million dollars a year. I talk to Brooks Robinson and some of those guys who never really made the big money. They all say the same thing I say: if somebody offered me a long-term contract for an enormous amount of money, sure I'd take it. Why not? Wouldn't you? But nobody made us offers like that when we played.

Some players know how ridiculous their paychecks are. A few will admit it to close friends; more will admit it to themselves. They get paid twice a month during the season; I've seen some of them stare in near disbelief at the string of 0000s on each check.

Players' attitudes are different today. We were very proud and highly honored to be a major league player. We were the big shots of the sports world; there was no competition from other sports for the heroes' spotlight. We played hard to get to the majors and, more important, just to stay there.

I think money took that pride—and hunger—away. Not in every case, certainly. Not with every player. But with a lot of them.

Players today are individual corporations. There is less cohesiveness, and sense of team, of family, of togetherness, for want of a better word. On the trains we sat and talked to each other for hours. Some guys played cards. Today they get on a plane and slap on the headsets. On the road very few players have roommates; they go their separate ways.

Television has made a difference, too. There was none of this pouring champagne over each other after a pennant clincher or a World Series win. That's ridiculous stuff to an old-time player. And the high fives and making a big deal about anything from a home run to a sacrifice fly? There was none of that. If a guy hit a home run, maybe the next hitter waiting to bat put out a hand. Maybe. Otherwise you were called a showboat, showing up the other team, and that would earn you a pitch that sent you sprawling in the dirt.

The intensity level of the game is lower today. Sure, there are some who play just as hard as anybody ever did. But the general level of intensity is not there the way it was. Most guys are not worried about their jobs. With multi-year contracts, next year's salary does not depend on today's performance.

And here's another fundamental difference: fun. The players of the past had more fun than they do now. It's a business today. They forget that they are still playing a game. It takes some talent, but it is still just a game. That hasn't changed.

Managers have certainly changed. It used to be the manager was the highest paid guy on the team, and everything was "Yes sir" and "No sir". Now the manager is among the lowest paid, and nobody says "Yes sir" and No sir".

Guys like Al Lopez and Leo Durocher and Whitey Herzog and Gene Mauch and Eddie Stanky and Casey Stengel couldn't do the job today. I see Dallas Green with the Mets having a hard time containing his temper and his patience; I don't know if he can last.

Changes in the game itself? The godawful DH is one. I like to think that nine guys play this game and one of them is the pitcher.

The complete game pitcher is gone for good. It happens, but the fact that it is noteworthy when it happens is evidence of what I'm talking about. A starter starts 30 to 35 games and says, "I'm going to give them 200 innings this year." Big deal. What does that figure out to per start? You figure it out.

We used to start spring training the first week of January. We needed the time. We didn't work out all winter because we were selling clothes or pumping gas or doing something to earn a living. Today they come to camp in better shape than we did. And a lot of people think spring training is too long. But I've never known a player who didn't need the time. They better put in hours of hard work and running and exercising before or after the exhibition games. The players know it is not too long, even if they hate it.

Was there ever such a thing as a check swing when I was playing? I can't remember appeals to the first or third base umpire. I can't remember guys I pitched against doing any of that half-swing action. I don't remember yelling, "He swung", and looking to one of the other umps. The guy behind home plate called the pitch and that was it.

I've noticed that when a batter checks his swing and the umpire calls it a strike and the guy argues, the pitch was a strike almost every time, even if he didn't half-swing. Some umpires say that's one of the toughest calls to make. Steve Palermo told me it's the easiest, because the pitch is a strike anyhow.

Besides, as hitters we were taught, "If it's close enough to be called a strike, swing at it."

Despite all the changes I've seen in baseball, I am not one of those old-timers who says that every player was great in my day and better than any of today's players, or that modern players are all self-centered brats. Every year I see outstanding pitchers come along, and hitters I would not want to have to pitch against. And I meet many delightful, friendly, giving gentlemen in the game.

I appreciate the attachments I have among people in baseball, the old and the young. When I go to spring training for a few weeks with the Orioles in St. Petersburg, where the Cardinals also train, I see older Cardinal fans who remember seeing me pitch in Sportsman's Park. Guys I pitched against, like Stan Musial, and old teammates show up. And I renew acquaintance with players I watched during their entire careers, like Don Baylor, now the Colorado manager.

One day Baylor said to me, "Did you ever play here at Al Lang Field?"

I said, "In 1949 I pitched a few innings here when we came over from Vero Beach to play the Cardinals and Yankees."

"That's interesting," Baylor said. "That's the year I was born."

I prefer to think of myself as more of a link than a relic.

This book, though, is not about me and the old days. It is mostly about the Orioles and some of the players they have played against during the years I have been in Baltimore, beginning in 1968. I have gotten enormous satisfaction and pleasure out of jogging along the dusty trails of memory to weave these woolgatherings and share them with you.

Perhaps they will jog some memories of your own.

There is one other sidelight to baseball that has changed very little going back 50 years to when I started in Brooklyn. There has never been much of an admiration society between the print guys and the radio and television people. Maybe part of it is jealousy; the radio and TV have the story right now, especially the play-by-play guys, and they make a whole lot more money than the writers. It seems to be one of those long-standing things about baseball. They may not admit it, but I'm in the business and I can see it.

The writers think it is the easiest thing in the world to sit there and talk, but it's not. And I know writing is not easy. I'd love to be able to write, but I can't. I can talk and tell a story, but put it down on paper? No way.

What you are about to read, and—I hope—enjoy is just me talking. And if I make a few errors along the way, please forgive me. I made a few when I was pitching, too.

THANK Youuuu.

Rex Barney
June, 1994

1

Genius in the Dugout

T here are a few things about baseball that I know for sure.

1. *Nobody really knows this game.*
2. *There is nothing new.*
3. *A lot of good, successful managers either never played in the major leagues or had mediocre careers at best. To name a few, Earl Weaver, Sparky Anderson, Tom Lasorda, Tony La Russa, Buck Showalter, Cito Gaston, Tom Kelly, and among the old-timers Walter Alston, Joe McCarthy, Bill McKechnie. There is no connection between the ability to hit or throw a pitch and the ability to manage people.*
4. *Hall-of-Famers are often flops as managers.*
5. *Players make managers look like geniuses, not the other way around.*

The argument over how many games a manager wins or loses for his team over a season has been going on since the Cincinnati Red Stockings of 1869. I think managers can lose games for a team; I'm not so sure that they ever win one.

Hank Bauer had a long career as an aggressive, winning player. A rugged, flatnosed, ex-Marine, he was not as tough as he looked. He was a delightful guy who told it like it was, and was his own man at all times. When the club owner, Jerry Hoffberger, asked him to stay in Baltimore during the winter, Bauer said no way, he was going home to Kansas City.

Bauer was the last Orioles manager to enforce a midnight curfew on the road. He called each room at 12:15 for a bed check and fined errant players $100, a significant amount in the 1960s. One night in Minnesota he caught half the team out.

A former Yankee of the Casey Stengel era, Bauer knew how to play the game, but not always how best to communicate his lessons. One night in Anaheim, it took the Orioles seven throws to execute a rundown. Bauer said, "You gotta *submerge* on the guy. It should take only two throws. Run the man back to a previous base, and when the man covering it yells 'Now,' you throw it to him."

Bauer also told Jim Palmer, who had just given up a home run, "Just throw the ball. Don't think out there."

The players liked playing for him, but there seemed to be a pulling apart on the club after they swept the 1966 World Series. The next year they finished sixth. In 1968 Harry Dalton brought in Earl Weaver as a coach to replace Gene Woodling, and Bauer did not like Earl. He believed that Weaver had been brought in to take his job, and in mid-1968 that is exactly what happened.

Earl Weaver was a pretty good minor league player who could not make it in the majors. Earl used to ask me about Leo Durocher, because he wanted to style himself in Leo's pattern. And he did, to some extent.

One thing I give Earl credit for: he handled 25 players better than anyone I've known. He was like Durocher and Stengel that way. He used all 25 to their maximum, and made the 25th player feel as important as the number one. No matter how much the platoon players—Lowenstein, Roenicke, Rettenmund—complained about not playing enough, Earl managed to get them 200 or 300 at bats every year. I always thought one of the greatest jobs Earl did was mixing Lowenstein and Roenicke in left field. And he used Benny Ayala to great advantage. He made those guys.

But some people could not play for Earl. Bobby Bonner was an outstanding college player in Texas, but he got into all kinds of trouble, and a lot of clubs turned him down. The Orioles signed him and straightened him out. Then he became a born-again Christian. Turned his life around. Became very sensitive. A switch hitter, he was the player of the year two years in a row at Rochester. In spring training 1982 you never saw a better shortstop. Magnificent hands. Lot of range. But he couldn't function under Earl's screaming and profanity.

The season began and you could see Bonner tighten up out there. Could do nothing. Doug DeCinces had been traded and Cal Ripken had replaced him at third base. Bonner and Lenn Sakata alternated at short. Sakata was not an everyday player, and Bonner could not get the job done. That's when Earl said he was going to switch Cal to shortstop. Everybody from Hank Peters down fought him on it, but Earl said, "If you can find me a shortstop, I'll move him back to third. Until then, I'm moving him."

You know the rest of that story.

But Earl a genius? Any manager can be a genius when he has the kind of talent Earl had during those winning years.

Dick Howser and Billy Martin, another pair of winning managers, both told me, "If I had Earl's players, I bet I could do even better."

Earl's famous strategy was, "Give me a well-pitched game and a three-run home run." Hell, that was Connie Mack's and John McGraw's strategy a hundred years ago. Every manager will tell you that a well-pitched game is the first prerequisite to winning any time. But to read the Baltimore papers, you'd think Weaver invented it.

They also made a big thing out of those index cards he used. Every manager has some system like that, to keep track of matchups: who hits which pitchers well, and which pitchers get certain guys out most of the time. Once, in a playoff game, the other team put in a pinch-hitter. Earl sent a coach out to the mound just to delay the game while he ran back to his office and found the card on the guy's pinch hitting.

Weaver was also a hunch player, like Durocher. Sure, when a manager selects a pinch hitter who goes up and wins the game, the manager looks like a genius. Of course, he wasn't the one who hit the ball.

One thing I liked about Earl was that, if a player came up from the minors, he would play the rookie right away. He insisted that every minor league manager in the organization prepare their players the same way—his way—so they would fit right in when they came up to the Orioles. And they did.

This might sound strange, but I have never known a player that Earl Weaver liked, nor a player who liked Earl Weaver.

Respect, yes. The players did respect his ability as a manager, but as a person? I'd question that. Earl didn't really care if anybody liked him or hated him. Didn't make any difference. All he cared about was if they did their job. And when they did, hitting a game-winning home run or something, he seldom congratulated them. His attitude was, "That's what they get paid for." There were no Tommy Lasorda hugs in the Orioles dugout.

Weaver often sat on the bench with his feet tucked under him. Some people thought that was to make him look taller. Not so. It was to escape Rick Dempsey smacking him in the feet with his shinguards, and to keep players from kicking him or spitting tobacco juice on his shoes and ankles.

Dempsey threw him down the steps twice that I know of, for taking him out of the game. But Earl couldn't care less. He gave no quarter, either. If he didn't like you, but you were a little better than the other guy, you played.

Earl did not like Steve Stone. For whatever reason, he just didn't like him. He'd carry on about him, then when the writers came in and asked, "What about Steve Stone?" he'd say, "Aw, he's a good kid. You guys are always picking on him. Why don't you leave him alone?"

He'd protect his players when it came to the press.

Don Baylor and Bobby Grich, who were inseparable as roommates, were also indivisible in their dislike of Earl. Weaver and Mark Belanger never got along; Belanger never forgot that Earl had given up on him in the minor leagues and did not think Mark was a big league prospect. Weaver, on the other hand, didn't think Belanger was aggressive enough to play as well as he could.

Belanger would rip Earl: "Ever notice the rooster? Any time

we win, he takes the credit. But if we lose, it's our fault."

I don't know if that was true, but I do know you'd never hear Earl take the blame for a loss, not in a million years.

When the writers went into Earl's office after a victory, you'd hear Jim Palmer yell out, "Tell 'em how you won it, genius."

Twenty-game winners can do that.

But Earl did have his favorites: Rich Dauer, Paul Blair, Tony Muser. Muser was a jokester, the kind of guy who keeps everybody loose—if you're winning. He'd write on the blackboard: "Daddy's Favorites - Dauer, Blair. Daddy's unfavorites - Palmer." Stuff like that.

Weaver was very sensitive about his height—or lack of same (he was five foot eight). He might have had a little of that Napoleon complex they talk about—the short guy managing all those big strong athletes. There might have been some of that in him, and the Orioles seemed to have nobody under six feet tall. So naturally the guys picked on that to tease him. They called him Midget, Jockey, Mickey Rooney.

The Orioles were in Houston for an exhibition game in 1970. We're sitting in the dugout, just Earl and me, and he says, "I don't mind it when they call me midget and all these nicknames, but there's one name that really upsets me."

"What was that?"

"I'll tell you," he says, "but if you ever tell anybody else, I'll kill you. And I'll know it was you who said it, because I've never told anybody else."

"Well, what is it?" I could tell he was upset just talking about it.

"Toulouse-Lautrec," he says.

Whatever you do, don't tell him I told you.

One cold day late in the season, Boog Powell had permission to report late for a game. He's standing in front of his locker while the team's out on the field taking batting practice. I'm standing there talking to Boog and in comes Earl from the dugout, running through the clubhouse to get a jacket—and another pack of cigarettes, I'm sure.

"Boog, you're late!" he yells. "You gotta get going. We're hitting, and you gotta get your hitting in. Hurry up." And out he runs.

Boog looks at me and says, "You know something? I always knew dwarfs were crazy."

Weaver was never loose, and had very little sense of humor, so little it was invisible. That, of course, made it all the more tempting for players to put him on.

Another "Little Napoleon", John McGraw, got the same treatment from a few of his players. He had a catcher, Earl Smith, who used to bait McGraw like a crabber putting eel on a trotline. Smith would argue with him and call him "Muggsy" until McGraw got all puffed up and red-faced, while the other Giants buried their heads in their lockers to smother their laughter.

During the 1982 season, Weaver was being called a lame duck manager because he had announced that he was going to retire at the end of the year. They're in Boston, and club owner Edward Bennett Williams called a meeting in the clubhouse. He did that from time to time. He told the players, "We don't have a lame duck manager. We have a manager. Forget that lame duck stuff, and go out and win this game."

Rich Dauer stood up and said, "Let's go out and win one for the duck!" That broke up the meeting. They went out and got beat and from that day on, Earl would come into the clubhouse or get on the bus and the players would go, "Quack, quack, quack."

If you get mad at that kind of stuff, you're just asking for it even more.

The worst (or best) confrontation I ever saw came on a Sunday in 1982. Earl generally didn't feel too good the morning after; a day game after a night game was hard for him to handle. So on this particular Sunday morning Jim Palmer is scheduled to come off the DL and pitch that day. He's lying on the training table in the clubhouse and I'm standing there talking to him and in stomps Earl.

"You ready to pitch?" he barks at Palmer.

"No," Jim says.

Weaver calls Palmer all sorts of names, none pleasant, and starts to leave.

Palmer gets off the table. "Hey, wait a minute," he says.

Bending low at the waist like he's talking to a child, he starts cussing out Weaver, then suddenly stops. "I shouldn't do that," he says. "It puts me as low and as small as you are."

Things are turning a little nasty, like maybe there's something physical brewing. I edge away, as Earl and Jim are screaming at each other.

"I'll suspend you and you won't pitch the rest of the year!"

"You don't have to. I'll go up and tell them I want out of here. I don't want to play for you."

Palmer stalks out like he's headed for general manger Hank Peters's office, leaving Earl ranting and raving, "He'll never pitch for me again, that ———."

I go out and round a corner and there's Palmer standing there, laughing his head off. "I really got him going this time, didn't I?"

"Jim," I ask him, "why do you do that? The guy's going to have a heart attack."

"He doesn't know what he's talking about," Jim says. "I know if I can pitch or not. What does he know?"

But some of the arguments between Palmer and Weaver were not put on; they were the real thing. Take the slider. Earl Weaver loved the slider. He read somewhere that Ted Williams called the slider the hardest pitch to pick up coming from the pitcher. The rotation is almost the same as the fastball.

Palmer hated the slider. Some pitchers say it's easy on your arm; Palmer believed it kills your arm. He wouldn't throw it. (Palmer hated it all the more because Earl liked it so much.) He refused to throw it, and they'd argue about it, right in the dugout.

"It'll make you a better pitcher," Earl insisted.

"I'm not throwing any sliders," Jim told him. He rarely threw one.

Other pitchers had their own ways of dealing with it. Scotty McGregor tried it. One day when Scotty was pitching, Earl pulled him aside in the dugout and reminded him, "Make sure you throw the slider to this first batter. He can't hit it."

"Okay, Earl."

McGregor went out and threw a slider for ball one, then

threw a fastball and the batter hit it over the fence. When the inning ended, he told Earl, "I tried and I missed with it, so I thought I'd try something else."

And then there was Mike Flanagan's approach.

During one game, Earl said to Mike, "You gotta throw that slider in on Winfield's hands. He can't hit it."

"Okay, Earl."

He goes out and throws a fastball and Winfield swings and the ball is last seen leaving Memorial Stadium headed for Delaware. Flanagan goes back to the bench and Earl says, "God damn, Flanagan. I told you to throw him a slider."

Flanagan says, "It was a slider."

And Earl says, "I guess he's a better hitter than I thought he was. Don't throw him a slider anymore."

Baltimore fans loved Weaver, and still do. One of the things they liked most about him was his fussing and feuding and kicking up dust with the umpires. Some of the players thought that Earl's intimidating the umpires might backfire on them and cost them a close call the next time. You like to think that doesn't happen, but human nature tells you it can.

Guys like Weaver and Billy Martin believed that antagonizing the umpires can win a game for you down the line. Managers are always analyzing what other managers do, trying to learn something. But a lot of them, the so-called "nice guys," are skeptical about what you can gain from arguing with umps.

The late Dick Howser, one of my very favorite guys in baseball, whose record for winning matches anybody's, told me, "You show me how kicking dirt and yelling at an umpire and throwing your cap on the ground and getting kicked out of a game wins one game for you, and maybe I'll do it."

But the fans loved it.

Earl did some things I didn't understand. We were in New York for a Saturday doubleheader. In the first game Earl gets thrown out by umpire Jim Evans. Between games I'm talking to some New York writers and I bet them that, if Earl brought the lineup to home plate for the second game, he'd be thrown out before the game started.

Sure enough, he comes out with the lineup card and the

next thing you know—Whooom—Evans's arm goes up and Earl's ejected. But he doesn't leave. Evans takes out his watch. Earl grabs it and throws it against the wall and it breaks into a thousand pieces. Evans goes over and picks up the pieces. And Weaver gets a big hand from the fans for putting down the umpires. He also gets a big fat suspension; a week.

That may have been the week this happened:

A manager who's suspended is supposed to leave the ballpark before the game each day. Not Earl. He would sit in his office and watch the game on television. I'm working the game on TV. Bruce Hurst, the left-hander, is pitching for the Red Sox. We're on the air and I say, "I'll tell you one thing about Hurst. If the Orioles get anybody on first base, they better be careful. Hurst has a great move to first. He's picked off seven guys this year, including two in his last game." As I say it, Eddie Murray singles, and I say, "Eddie's gotta be careful, now. Hurst will be looking to pick him off."

After the game I see Earl and he's laughing his head off. He says, "You got on the air and you're talking about Bruce Hurst and I'm listening and Eddie gets on first and I pick up the phone to call Cal Ripken (Senior) in the dugout to warn him and I say, 'I'm watching television and Rex just said…aw he just got picked off.'"

I told Hurst that story and he loved it.

Earl could give the umpires hell, but he could also be pretty cute. One night Jim Palmer is pitching against the Twins. Larry Barnett is the umpire behind the plate. The night before, Barnett was at first base and they got into a row and he threw Earl out of the game.

Palmer's pitching and everything is ball one, ball two, base hit, and it doesn't matter where he's throwing it, he's not getting any calls. Chuck Thompson and I are doing the game and we can see in the Orioles dugout and we see Earl get up and start pacing around. He knows he can't argue ball and strike calls or he's automatically out of the game. But he's getting more and more exasperated.

Finally he comes out of the dugout and goes out to the mound. Most of the time these conferences go on until the umpire goes out to break it up, and they break it up themselves just as he gets out there. It's one way to show him up. This time Barnett waits and Weaver doesn't move and finally Barnett goes out there.

"All right, Earl, what are you going to do?" he says.

"What do you want me to do?"

"Are you going to leave this pitcher in? Are you going to the bullpen? Come on. Let's get the game going again."

Earl says to him, "This pitcher? Maybe you don't know who this pitcher is. Let me introduce you to this pitcher. His name is Jim Palmer. He's won the Cy Young Award three times. Where in the hell would you like him to throw the ball so you'll call it a strike? I don't care. He doesn't care. Minnesota doesn't care. I got guys in the bullpen can't do that, but this pitcher can. You tell us, where do you want him to throw it so you'll call strikes?"

After that Palmer got the close calls, and won the game.

The writers loved Earl. He'd hold court in the dugout while he watched batting practice and never stopped talking, except when one of his players deliberately stood in front of him to block his view. Didn't make any difference if he was saying anything or just a bunch of nothing. He loved the attention and the writers always came away with something to fill space.

Earl was not impressed by anybody. Pittsburgh had just beaten the Orioles in the seventh game of the 1979 World Series, 4-1. Earl and I are alone in his office and he's ranting and screaming and carrying on. All of a sudden, here comes some secret service guys. One of them says, "President Carter is here and he would like to say hello to you."

Earl is in no mood to say hello to anybody, not even the president of the United States. But he snaps, "Okay, bring him in."

They turn to me. "You're going to have to leave."

Earl says, "No. He stays."

The guy in the suit shrugs. "Okay."

President Carter comes in, and I knew Earl liked him immediately because he was a little shorter than Earl. They exchange a few words, then Carter makes a blunder. Someone in Pittsburgh manager Chuck Tanner's family had died during the

Series. Carter says to Weaver, "I'm sorry to hear about the death in your family. It must have been a lot on your shoulders the past few days."

Earl snarls, "You ought to go over to the other clubhouse for that." He talked that way to everybody, didn't make any difference.

Then one of the suits says, "Mr. Weaver, the president would like to meet your players."

"Okay, come on," Earl snaps.

They go into the clubhouse and somebody helps Earl climb onto one of the equipment trunks and Carter climbs up there.

"Hey, guys," Earl yells. The players are walking around, some of them naked, some with towels draped around them. The place is jammed like it always is after a World Series game. "I want you to meet the president of the United States. Mr. President, this is my team."

And with that, Earl jumps off the trunk and leaves. Carter is left standing there. He didn't know what to say, what to do. A few guys went up to him and shook his hand, but not many.

That was Earl.

Every ballplayer is superstitious, whether or not they admit it. Show me one who will step on the white lines. But none of the Orioles could hold a candle to Mr. Weaver.

One day he wrote out the lineup with a ballpoint pen. The O's won. The next night he used the same pen. They won again. If the pen ran out of ink before they lost, he would talk to it like a person, and throw it against the wall. "It's your fault if we lose!" I saw that.

He's sitting in the dugout and the Orioles are winning; if a player gets up and changes his place: "Go back to where you were. Quick!"

If he and some others took a cab to the ballpark and they won, the next day only those who had ridden with him the day before could get into the cab. If you hadn't ridden with him, you didn't get into that cab.

Jimmy Williams, one of his coaches, tells this story:

"We were in Oakland and had lost the first two games there. I walked into the clubhouse area where the manager and coaches dress and started to change my clothes. I'm sitting on the stool and Weaver is sitting behind me staring at me. I start pulling on my sanitaries and I hear his voice, 'Goddammit, don't you ever put the right one on first?"

"I turned around, startled. He said, 'You. Don't you ever put the right one on first?'

"I said, 'What do you mean?'

"He said, 'You put that left sock on first the last two days and we lost two games. Put the right one on first and see what happens.'

"I said, 'Okay.' So I took the sock off and put it on my right leg, and I think we won that night, too. But he was really serious about things like that."

The Orioles used to have a man, Vince Greco, who filmed all their games from behind home plate. Did this for many years. In the 1971 World Series, they won the first two games at home against the Pirates. The team was getting ready to get on the bus to the airport to fly to Pittsburgh. Greco's father had suffered a stroke and Greco did not want to go. But Weaver, being as superstitious as he was, wanted Greco to get on that bus. Greco's family was there and he was embarrassed by all the fuss. But that didn't stop Earl, who kept insisting that he get on the bus. After all, if he did not go with the team, they were sure to lose three in Pittsburgh.

The doctor who was treating Greco's father was there, too. Finally he told Vince, "Go ahead. There's nothing you can do here," so he got on the bus.

P.S. They lost all three in Pittsburgh, anyhow, and the Series in seven games. But Earl would do the same thing again, in the same situation.

In his 15th year, with four pennants and one world championship, Earl announced that he would retire after the 1982 season. That was the year they went into the final four-game series against Milwaukee trailing the Brewers by three games, won the first three to pull into a tie, but lost the finale when Robin Yount hit two home runs off Jim Palmer.

On his way out, somebody asked Weaver if he would miss the players.

"Nah," he snapped, "why would I miss those guys?" Then he added, "Wait a minute. Two guys. Paul Blair and Richie Dauer." And out he went. But not for long.

When Weaver retired, Hank Peters wanted John McNamara to replace him. I think Edward Bennett Williams wanted Frank Robinson. Cal Senior was in the running. So was Joe Altobelli, who had managed at Rochester and knew the personnel. He was a coach for the Yankees at the time.

While the front office was debating, McNamara was offered the job with the Angels. He called Peters and said, "I got this offer from California, but I prefer to go with you."

Peters tried to reach Williams, who was in Europe. They couldn't find him, so McNamara went with California. That's how Joe Altobelli became the Orioles manager.

The team he inherited was put together by Earl and Hank Peters. It was their team.

In the spring of 1983 a meeting took place at Scott McGregor's house in Florida. The newspapers were lamenting the departure of Weaver and how the Orioles would falter without him. Most of the players were at the meeting, where they vowed to show everybody they could win without Earl. And they did. But it wasn't easy.

In July they lost seven in a row. They brought up a kid from Rochester, Bill Swaggerty, and he stopped the losing streak pitching a win in Chicago. Soon after that I had my stroke and was in bad shape.

Palmer and Flanagan went on the disabled list. Tippy Martinez went into the hospital for an appendectomy. Rich Dauer and Sammy Stewart had some problems.

Once I was able to function, I would call the clubhouse from the hospital every day and talk to Altobelli. "What's going on, with all this bad news at once?" I asked him.

"You got any suggestions?"

He and Hank Peters decided to go with what they had and make the best of it. As it turned out, it was a blessing in disguise for Tippy. They had been using him just about every day (he got into 65 games) and his arm was ready to drop off. The rest he got in the hospital enabled him to finish the year strong.

Joe Altobelli was a sound manager. In the 1983 World Series he completely outmanaged Paul Owen of the Phillies. He delegated a lot of authority to his coaches, Jimmy Williams, Ray Miller and Cal Senior.

I thought that '83 Series was one of the worst I'd ever seen. The Phillies were so bad I could not understand how they won the National League Pennant. Pete Rose was finished. Mike Schmidt had one hit in five games.

But things turned bad for the Orioles in 1984. They finished fifth and Edward Bennett Williams soured on Joe. Altobelli was a good manager and a good person. But he did not have good communication with the media and the front office.

We were in Oakland and Joe and I were having breakfast together.

"You seem a little down," I said.

He grumbled something about the goddamned guys in the media.

"Joe, let me ask you something. Do you know you're a very exclusive person?"

"What do you mean, exclusive?"

"There are only 26 big league managing jobs in the world, and you've got one of them. You get paid very well, right? No complaints, right?"

"No," he said, "but handling the media and all that stuff..."

I said, "Joe, you've still got one of the best jobs in the world. So do I. I tell those writers, and I'll tell you, what I always tell myself: it beats working, doesn't it?"

He started laughing. "I guess you're right."

But when EBW said on the record for the newspapers that Altobelli was a cementhead, imagine how that makes you feel if you're Altobelli. And he hadn't even been fired yet.

How that happened is atrocious. They were in Detroit and Hank Peters told him it looked like he was going to be let go. He asked Joe to finish the series in Detroit and then come to Baltimore. So Joe did, and when he came into the office to find out where he stood, Peters couldn't tell him until he heard from EBW.

Joe went out to the racetrack instead of hanging around. The Orioles found him there and brought him back to the office and fired him.

"Bringing back Earl Weaver to manage the Orioles is the smartest thing I've ever done," proclaimed Williams in June of 1985, after Joe Altobelli was fired.

General manager Hank Peters had every intention of naming Cal Ripken, Sr. to replace Altobelli, but when he walked into EBW's office in Washington to clear it with him, there sat Mr. Weaver. The media later bought the story that Earl just happened to be in town, but he had been summoned there by EBW.

Asked why Weaver would want to come back, after all his success, Hank Peters said, "If you could rob the club owner of as much money as he did, would you come back?"

Earl tried to be the same old Earl, but it wasn't there anymore. The older players no longer respected him, and he could no longer handle them. And without the horses, he suddenly was no longer a genius.

George Bamberger, who had been Earl's pitching coach, was now the manager at Milwaukee. We were in Milwaukee right after Earl returned. Bamberger said to me, "I understand the midget's back. You know something about major league managers? We're all whores, and number four is a bigger whore than all of us put together."

The Orioles finished fourth in '85 and last in the division in '86. But the fans still idolized Weaver. Players and managers on other teams wondered how he did it. If any other manager in any other city had done as poorly as he was doing during that comeback stint, he'd have been booted out in a hurry. Yet in Baltimore, the minute Earl stepped out on the field he got a big ovation every time.

I don't think he enjoyed it at all the second time around. He was drinking pretty heavily. And when he was drunk, he became obnoxious. Nobody wanted to be around him when he was in his cups.

One day he was drinking a beer and smoking a cigarette in his hotel room, and a young writer suggested, "Earl, that smoking and drinking is going to kill you."

"Don't start," he barked. "That's all I ever hear. I enjoy both drinking and smoking, and I'm going to keep it up. So what if it kills me? Marianna (his wife) will probably be very happy. I might die early and she'll get all the money."

Another tale about Earl circulated about that time. Earl's in Florida and he and his wife are playing golf about every day and one day Marianna says to Earl, "If I die first, would you marry again?"

Earl thinks a minute and says, "Yeah, I guess I would."

"Would you live in this house?"

"Yeah, sure."

"Would you sleep in our bed?"

Earl's getting a little edgy now, but he says, "Yeah."

"I suppose you'd let your new wife use my golf clubs."

"No," Earl says. "She plays tennis."

Weaver wanted to quit before the 1986 season was over, but Edward Bennett Williams made him stay until the season ended. Then EBW announced, "Bringing Weaver back was the dumbest thing I've ever done in baseball."

Cal Ripken, Sr., the ultimate organization man, thought he was entitled to a shot as manager of the Orioles. But every time the job was open, they hired somebody else. Hank Peters had pushed for him before, and finally succeeded in hiring him in 1987. Senior did a good job, but he had a bad team to work with. He did not handle the media and all that stuff very well. He was from the old school, exactly the way guys were brought up in the game in the '40s and '50s and '60s.

I have never known a real player, a real baseball man, who did not like Senior. Other managers in the league recognized and appreciated his knowledge of the game. If I had owned the club at that time, though, I would not have made Senior the manager. I would have made him one of the highest paid coaches in baseball. Senior's most valuable as a teacher. Ask the guys on the Orioles today who taught them what they know. They'll all tell you: Senior. Managing in the minors he was great, because he had the time to teach the young players the game. But in the majors there is so much more to the job.

The Orioles have never been very gracious when it comes to firing people. When they lost the first six games of the 1988 season, Senior was fired.

John Hart was his third base coach at the time. Hart had been a catcher in the lower minors and realized he wasn't going anywhere as a player. He became a manager in the Orioles organization and worked his way up: Bluefield in 1982, Hagerstown, Charlotte, Rochester, where he was the International League manager of the year in 1986. When he joined the Orioles as a coach in 1988, he was led to believe that he was next in line, after Senior, for the top spot. It was a reasonable expectation.

On the day Senior was fired I walked into the clubhouse in the early afternoon and John Hart was there, alone.

"John," I said, "did you hear the news?"

"What is it?"

"Senior's gone, and Frank Robinson got the job."

His mouth fell open in disbelief. He said, "That ends me in this organization."

He went upstairs to see Roland Hemond, but of course there was nothing Roland could do or say about it. Edward Bennett Williams was enamored of big stars, big names. It was his decision all the way. He gave Robinson a big raise and a longterm contract; but the Orioles lost the next 15 in a row. End of the year, John Hart was gone. Today he is the general manager at Cleveland and has done an outstanding job there. Good man.

As I've said many times, big stars rarely make good managers. Frank was a super super player, tough, played hurt, played hard. But I didn't see much as a coach or manager.

The clubhouse often reflects the manager. The Robinson clubhouse had no personality. There was no interaction between him and the players. Some players told me they couldn't talk to him; he was not approachable. Like so many super stars who become managers, Frank could not get out of his players what he had gotten out of himself. It just cannot be done.

But the attitude in the clubhouse has very little connection with how they perform on the field. I don't buy that old line: "They can't win because of dissension in the clubhouse." No group of 25 players can go along together for eight months without disagreements. There have been some great teams who won a lot of World Series and fought among themselves all year long. But when they went out on the field, they all fought the other team just as hard.

The Orioles finished last in '88, but 1989 was a freak year. Everything fell into place and a lot of guys had that one good year; they lost out to Toronto by two games. They finished fifth in 1990, and were 13-24 in May of '91 when Robinson was moved upstairs and Johnny Oates took over.

I'll tell you right up front that I am prejudiced when it comes to Johnny Oates. He is one of God's chosen people. I've never met a finer gentleman, a better family man, a more dedicated baseball man.

I can't tell you how long I've been a fan of his. I knew him when he was a player with the Dodgers, and all through his managing in the Orioles organization, where he was a winner, and as a coach here and with the Cubs.

With the Dodgers he sat next to Tom Lasorda in the dugout and kept asking questions, learning, absorbing all the time. He still does that, talking to other managers. He has a great deal of respect for Sparky Anderson and Tony La Russa. He is friendly with Buck Showalter of the Yankees, who played for him when Oates managed Columbus. (Oates can look in a mirror and see Showalter, they are that much alike.) Organization people, all business.

Sparky Anderson told me, "I love him. He's got that look that you can read in some guys. Burns right through you."

Johnny knew he was never going to make it to the majors as a hitter. So he worked to excel at calling a game and working with pitchers, the most important job of a catcher. Pitchers liked him. He didn't talk to them only when he caught them, but between starts, too. And he built a 10-year playing career in the major leagues that way. Got into two World Series, too.

When he was still a coach with the Orioles, the Yankees wanted him, but I think he saw his future with the Orioles. He used to say to me, "I hope I get to manage this club," and tell me what he would do.

But I'm not sure Orioles fans were ready for him. They had all those years with Earl kicking dirt and stomping and yelling and throwing his hat, and they complained that Johnny didn't argue enough.

"He's too quiet in the dugout," they'd say, and they still do.

Well, the job of a manager and managing styles have changed. Look in the dugouts of winning clubs in recent years. How many successful managers do you see sitting there inning after inning, their arms folded across their chests, expressionless? You can't tell if they are ahead by 12 or down by 10. Cito Gaston...Gene Lamont...Tom Kelly...Jim Leyland...Tony La Russa...Jim Fregosi...Bobby Cox...and on and on.

Sure, they go out and argue once in a while. Oates does, too, but only when he knows in his heart that the umpire blew a call and blew it badly.

Managers around the league tell me two facts of life: in the old days, as I've already mentioned, the manager was the highest paid on the team; now they are among the lowest. The other thing is, there are so many playing jobs with expansion, and so few players of major league caliber, if you threaten to release a player, they say, so what, and sign with another team.

When there were eight teams in each league, a player's job was on the line. If he did not perform, good-bye. There were legions of good young players ready to take your place.

The days of Durocher and Frisch and that type of fire-eating manager are gone. Any manager who chewed out a player or slammed him up against the dugout wall would be gone in a hurry.

I went up to Philadelphia to see Durocher when he was managing the Cubs in the late '60s, early '70s. I saw guys doing things in the clubhouse I couldn't believe. I said, "Leo, where's this coming from?" Durocher pounded and pounded on us, if we had the talent, and made us winners.

He said, "I can't do what I did with you guys anymore. They'll go to the Players Association and I'm gone."

Johnny Oates is a player's manager; he'll back them to the hilt. In his own quiet, amiable way, he demands and gets the respect of the young and the veterans. Never shows them up. If he has something to say, he'll take the guy aside when it's all over with. He won't put up with any foolishness.

Everybody in baseball gives you the classic line: "My door is always open." And it's always closed. But not his. He talks to his players one on one a lot. He goes to them and asks if they are hurting or can play and they tell him the truth.

When Glenn Davis was with the team and the papers were full of stories—he's going to play, he's not going to play—Oates called him into his office and said, "I read this stuff and I listen to you; now here's the deal. If you don't play, we'll send you to Hagerstown to be rehabilitated. Make up your mind."

Davis got up to walk out.

Oates said, "Sit down. I don't want any agents, no wives, nobody else involved. You tell me now."

Davis said, "I'll play."

And he did, for a while. You can't let these guys run you.

If Oates butchered a play or made a mistake, he'd tell you, "I sure butchered that one." You never heard Earl or Frank say they butchered a play. No way.

Johnny asked me once, "Rex, do you second-guess me?"

I said, "Sure, I do, just like all the fans do every game."

He said, "I know they do, and you know every manager second-guesses himself all the time, and I know the coaches are doing it, too. And that's okay. But the one thing I really like is for the players to second-guess me."

I looked at him. "Why would you want that?"

"Because it means they are in the game," he said. "If they are thinking right along with me—and I may not make the right decision—and they are sitting there second-guessing me, that's all right with me. I can take that."

Not all the players are in the game that much. You seldom hear them talk about what the manager did during the game.

But to me there is something inaccurate about that word, second-guessing. It has a negative connotation, and it really isn't, not when you are thinking right along with the manager at the same time. Earl Weaver told me once, "You're not second-guessing, you're first-guessing, anticipating right along with me."

I think that's what Johnny meant when he talked about the players thinking along with him.

Oates took over a difficult situation in 1991. The Orioles were a sub-.500 team and a lot of changes needed to be made. He knew he could not look too far ahead. When he was new in the job, some writers started asking him about what he was going to do the next year in spring training, and he said, "I have no idea. I haven't got the job for next year. I've got it now; I know what I can do today. But I can't answer your question."

That's him; that's the way he is.

When he got a two-year contract through 1993, I asked him about having his first spring training as a major league manager.

"It's probably the most exciting thing that has happened to me in the game of baseball," he said. "I know I'm young, but I've put in a lot of years, and I love this game. Having my own ball club from the start of the year is what I've worked for. I hope I succeed. I may fail, but I've got my shot and I'm going to take advantage of it."

I'll tell you something that impressed me in one of the first games he managed. He started a left-hander, then relieved with a right-hander, then brought in the submariner, Todd Frohwirth. I'm sitting in the press box, thinking, "I know his philosophy: every pitcher he brings in gives them a different look. When he was a player, he hated to hit against three or four pitchers in a game, especially when they were all different looking. He is giving them a different look with every guy. That's good thinking."

The Orioles made up 22 games in the standings in 1992, and stayed in the race almost to the end in '93, although they did not have the best team by any means. That's the measure of a manager: does he get the most out of what he has to work with? And his peers thought so; they do the voting for The Sporting News Manager of the Year, and who won it in 1993? Mr. Oates.

What changes did I see in Oates over his first few years? He would get down on himself, and that was reflected and picked up by the team. I think he anguished more than he did the first year. But he went into the 1994 season with an up attitude. It was a pivotal year for Oates and general manager Roland Hemond. The new owners could say, "We gave you all these high-priced free agents, now what are you going to do with them?"

I hear that this team or that one doesn't have a leader. I don't buy that. The manager is supposed to be the leader. The manager's personality is reflected in the team. In Johnny's case, that attitude is calm confidence, knowing that you are well prepared to do the job.

2

On the Other Bench

During my 23 years as the Orioles public address announcer I have worked with all the American League managers and became very friendly with some of them. Being a former player has given me an entree and a rapport I might not have had. In some cases, I played against them. Some of them were in the Dodgers organization in my time. Bobby Valentine is married to Ralph Branca's daughter.

So when I go in to get the lineups, they often invite me to sit and visit, reminisce or listen in on their conversations with coaches or the general manager. They also know that what I hear about players won't go any farther.

Here are some of my impressions.

I've always been a Cito Gaston fan. I've never understood why the Toronto papers call him the worst manager in the league. All he does is win. He gets a kick out of my announcement of the Toronto lineup at Camden Yards. For two years I started out, "And for the world champion Toronto Blue Jays." The fans always boo, but it's the truth, isn't it?

Gaston will go longer with a starting pitcher than most managers, and he is one of the few who will go out to the mound to talk to his pitcher even when he does not bring in a new one, instead of sending the pitching coach every time.

A real gentleman who loves to talk baseball, Gaston has the respect of his players.

Tom Kelly of the Twins is a typical example of the guys who never made it as players but are excellent managers. Kelly is a down-to-earth guy who is so happy being a big league manager, he can't stand it. He comes to the ballpark early, jogs around the outfield a few times, then sits and visits. Loves to talk about horses.

He brings players into the office to inquire if there is anything bothering them. It is evident that they like and respect him. He won two World Series in the 1980s, but how many people know Tom Kelly exists? He told me, "I know people don't recognize me. Why should they? See those two guys over there?" He pointed to Kent Hrbek and Kirby Puckett. "They run the club. They set the standards."

Phil Garner—"Scrap Iron"—is tough, but well-respected in the clubhouse. He and Kevin Kennedy and Hal McRae and Mike Hargrove—all are very low key, easygoing, polite.

Tony La Russa didn't have much of a playing career, and is a great manager. But I think he gets carried away with believing all that stuff that's been written about his plotting and planning and strategizing. When he had a lousy team in 1993 at Oakland, he suddenly was not a genius anymore.

Every manager has scouting reports and computer printouts on everything that every player has done against every pitcher in every ballpark and under every meteorological condition, plus what they ate for breakfast. And managers do think ahead; they have to. But you can still get all those planets lined up and the expected doesn't always happen.

When any manager gets to thinking he's got the game figured out, he's in trouble. And the writers who make the battle of wits between managers sound like something as complicated as a world championship chess match with two giant brains thinking 64 moves ahead are exaggerating reality.

There's a lot of lawyer in Tony's decision-making process, and he is a lawyer. When he was managing the White Sox, they had a serious clubhouse, very little joking. He is more relaxed with the A's. He stayed optimistic with his bad teams, admitting they were bad, but looking to the future.

He's still the biggest pain of all to get the lineup out of early.

I liked Joe Morgan very much when he managed the Red Sox. He was from my time, and loved to play oldtimer games. I'd come into the office and he'd say, "I bet you don't know anything about Bob Ramazzotti." So I'd reel off whatever I remembered about Ramazzotti.

One time we argued over whether Augie Galan was a switch-hitter or strictly left-handed. Turned out we were both right. He had been a switch-hitter when Joe saw him, and batted lefty only by the time I saw him.

I liked Joe, but I could tell there was unrest on his club; some players did not like him for some reason. Maybe because they never heard of Ramazzotti.

When Ted Williams was managing Washington, I broadcast some of their games. I don't think Williams enjoyed managing; he knew nothing about the rules of the game and cared less. But the players were in awe of him. You could see them sitting on the bench staring at him. Nellie Fox was his number one coach and a great leveler for him. Fox didn't hesitate to tease and needle him.

Williams could be gracious, but he was never enamored of the press.

I remember one night in New York after the Senators got killed. We got on the team bus to go back to the hotel. Ted was sitting in the front seat—the manager's reserved seat—when I got on.

"Hey, Bush (he called everybody Bush), come sit with me."

On the way, he got restless, as usual. "Let's walk back."

We got off the bus and he said, "Let's go into this drugstore and have a malted milk."

We sat there and talked about the game, then walked to the hotel. I enjoyed every minute of it.

George Bamberger never wanted to be a manager. He was happy as the Orioles pitching coach when Harry Dalton called him after the 1977 season. Dalton had been the O's general manager; he was now at Milwaukee.

"I want you to manage the Brewers," Dalton said.

"Are you nuts?" Bambi laughed. "I never managed anybody

in my life."

"Come out and let's talk about it," Dalton said.

Bambi told his wife, "I'll throw such a high figure at him, he'll say no and I'll be back."

He threw the high figure and it was accepted, and he became a manager. He did a good job, finished second to Weaver in '79 with 95 wins, but shifted over to scouting for a few years.

Then Frank Cashen, another ex-Oriole front office man, offered Bambi more money than he could turn down to manage the Mets. That lasted less than two miserable years. Bambi returned to Milwaukee and served another two-year term there.

In 1981 Bambi was living in Baltimore and scouting for the Brewers. One day after a workout at Memorial Stadium during that strike-interrupted season, a bunch of baseball people were sitting in Weaver's office, swapping stories.

"Hey, Earl," Bambi said, "did I ever tell you about this new hearing aid of mine?"

"No, I didn't even know you were wearing one."

"It's great," Bambi said. "Opened up a whole new world for me. I don't have to strain or read lips, or pretend I know what people are saying. I get it all. If you ever have any problems hearing, you should get one."

"That's great, George. What kind is it?"

"Oh, it's about three-thirty," Bambi said.

Everybody laughed.

Bambi turned to me. "What are they laughing about?"

I said, "He asked you what kind it was."

"I told him it was three-thirty."

Alvin Dark managed the Oakland A's for Charlie Finley, which was a job and a half. Finley was one owner who ran his own team; he had no general manager for several years. Dark was his own man, made his own decisions without hesitation. But he always had to wait for Finley's call to be sure of his lineup. He never knew when Charlie O. might make some changes or trade somebody.

Dark knew the game, and the players respected him. He was a little aloof with the media.

Dick Williams was more of a politician than Dark. Dick

worked for Finley, too, but had enough and quit. He managed the Red Sox and Angels and Montreal and San Diego before landing at Seattle, where he finally lost patience with the modern players and got out of the game.

Williams is another oldtime Dodger, who came up in the time of Mr. Rickey and learned from Durocher, Dressen, Bragan and Stanky. One of the last of the great bench jockeys. His players respected him, but he put up a barrier between himself and them: I'm the manager, you're the player. If he praised a guy, he had something negative to say about him, too.

Dick used all the charts and stuff the scouts sent him, and went all out, good teams or bad.

Jimy Williams was all baseball, dead serious at all times. If he had a personal conflict with a player, as he did with George Bell in Toronto, it got to him more than the player. He did not have a lot of patience with faults or lack of enthusiasm or concentration. A good teacher, like Cal Senior, he was a better third base coach than manager; Bobby Cox called him the best third base coach in baseball. But he just couldn't handle the media and all that other stuff that goes with managing.

Don Zimmer is another old Dodger alumnus. Tough. A survivor. Beaned in 1953, he was unconscious for two weeks, couldn't talk for six weeks, had four metal "buttons" inserted in his head. When he got out of the hospital he weighed under 100 pounds, but he came back and played second base for the Dodgers in the 1955 World Series. Then he got hit in the face by a pitch and that ended his playing days. He's been in the game as a coach and manager ever since.

Zimmer knows the game and lets his coaches do a lot. He never handled the press and radio and TV guys very well, but he has a great sense of humor, often directed at himself.

Zimmer chews tobacco all the time. One day in Texas there was a close play at first base. John Shulock, the umpire, is another tobacco chewer. They're out there arguing and tobacco juice is flying. Shulock says, "Get that chew out of your mouth," and Zimmer reaches in and takes out the wad and throws it on the ground. He says the wrong thing and Shulock runs him, but instead of leaving, Zimmer drops to his hands and knees.

Shulock says, "What the hell are you doing?"

"I'm looking for my teeth," Zimmer says. "I threw my bridge out with the tobacco."

He was managing Boston in Yankee Stadium on a nationally televised game when he got into an argument and the umpire threw him out. He said something else to the umpire and, instead of disappearing from sight, he went back in the dugout and sat down. The next time I saw him I asked what that was all about.

"I really hadn't done anything so terrible," he told me. "So I said to the umpire, 'Before you throw me out, I want you to know my wife and children are here today, and this game is on television and millions of people are watching, and it's embarrassing to me to be thrown out of the game.' And the umpire bought it and let me stay in the game."

Zim is the kind of guy whose baseball friends will go out of their way to help him. He is a coach at Colorado now.

Gene Mauch and I started together when we were both 18 at Durham in 1943. You could tell even then that he was destined to be a manager. He was a winning manager with a lot of clubs, but never got to a World Series in 26 years, so he'll go down as never winning the big one.

A very strict, surly guy, his contact with the players was remote. He wasn't the nicest guy to get along with. He had the respect of players and coaches, because he had a brilliant baseball mind, but he was not a friend to any of them. He guarded against that.

A lot of people didn't like the way he managed. He liked the bunt, the sacrifice. But he would take chances and try things. He tried Mr Rickey's five-man infield a few times: bring one of the outfielders in behind second base. He did it once in Baltimore and it worked. Tried it another time and the hitter got a ground ball past the first baseman and it didn't work.

I try to get the lineups from the managers at least four hours before game time. Everybody told me, "Mauch's tough. He won't give it to you until maybe 15 minutes before game time." That was the reputation he had.

The first time he came to town with Minnesota in 1976 I

went into his office early as usual and we had a great visit and I came out with the lineup. The press guys said, "How'd you get that?"

I said, "I asked for it."

I didn't tell them Mauch and I had roomed together in Ma Gregory's boarding house in Durham when we were kids. Those old connections come in handy.

Mauch was another guy who seldom said something nice about a player without adding something negative. But he went all out on two young players he had: Wally Joyner and Butch Wynegar.

Whitey Herzog was a manager from the old school who could not take the changes he saw in the game. He'd say, "This modern-day baseball. I love the game and everything about it, but there's a lot I don't like these days. It may be getting to me."

I didn't put a lot of stock into what he said; there was no way he would get out. But he did.

A lot of baseball people thought that Whitey handled his pitching staff better than any manager in the world. And I agreed.

A great talker, clubhouse guy, very friendly; you know where you stand with Whitey. No BS. If you deserve a pat on the back, you'll get it. If you don't, you won't get it.

I thought he would be a great general manager.

Personally, Dick Howser was my very best friend among all the managers I have known. A little guy, and perfect gentleman, he could be tough and his players respected him tremendously.

I first saw him at Vero Beach when the Dodgers brought him and Herb Score in for a tryout. In those days if they wanted to sign a kid out of high school, they would find out who his closest friend was and invite him too. Score was the one they wanted; Howser was his high school buddy. The Dodgers turned down both of them.

Howser began his managing career with the Yankees in 1980. He and Gene Michael and I were together one night in Baltimore after the Yankees had lost a game. Steinbrenner called, raising hell about the loss. "Why didn't you do this…why didn't you use this guy…tomorrow you make sure you do this and that…"

When it was over I asked Dick, "What do you do about

that?"

He said, "Nothing. I do it my way." Never argued with umpires, didn't think it ever won a game for anybody.

The Yankees lost the playoff that year, and the story was that Steinbrenner fired him. Not true. The owner blamed third base coach Mike Ferraro for losing the playoff and wanted to fire him. Howser quit rather than fire his coach. He coached at Florida State until Kansas City hired him near the end of the '81 season.

Howser would have preferred to stay with the Yankees, but he was not about to be intimidated by anybody. I was very happy for him when he won the 1985 World Series, but his health broke down and he barely made it through the next All-Star Game before he had to quit. He died from a brain tumor less than a year later.

I remember Dick as a kind, gentle man. When I was recuperating from my stroke, I had to take medication intravenously every two hours, so I could not go out. He arranged with Chuck Thompson to ask the doctor to double up the medication so they could take me out to dinner. That's the kind of thoughtful friend he was.

Ralph Houk, the major, that tough old marine chewing on a cigar. A congenial throwback to the suit-and-tie days, he felt more at home with former players and old marine buddies than he did with the media. A sound baseball man, tough when he had to be, he was completely dedicated to whatever organization and general manager he was working for.

Houk could kick up a fuss on the field, but he was always careful to take off his glasses and put them in his shirt pocket before he threw his cap and kicked the ground. One day Earl Weaver was kicking and caught a spike and almost fell. The next day Houk said, "Tell Earl to come see me if he wants to learn how to do that. I've never fallen."

Bob Lemon and I had a connection: we threw the only two no-hitters in 1948. Lem is great company, but I had my doubts about him as a manager. He handled pitchers well, but I thought he let the coaches do too much. I thought he would have been better with a young team, developing players; that was his strength, rather than game strategy.

Bobby Cox is a hands-on manager, mixes with his players a lot, talking to them. He knows every player personally, their problems and the good things in their lives, while maintaining the necessary separation a manager needs. He and his coaches in Toronto—Jimy Williams and Cito Gaston—were a close group.

I was surprised when he left Toronto, but I guess he got a better deal in Atlanta as the general manager. At the time I thought, "With Chuck Tanner as the Braves' manager, that's a great combination." Tanner's a gung ho, up kind of guy, like Lasorda and Sparky. I was wrong; it was not a winning combination. Cox replaced Tanner in the dugout and the Braves have been winning lately.

Lou Piniella ranks right up there with Billy Martin and Buck Showalter among Yankees managers during Steinbrenner's reign. A true Yankee, he knew the players and had their respect.

When Piniella came into the clubhouse, you knew he had arrived. "What's up? What's happening?" He's a player's manager; they relate to him. He'd blow up quick after a game, screaming and yelling in the clubhouse. But he'd also take the blame: "My fault. What a dummy. Why did I do that?"

Everything he did was action. A good hitter, Lou was an adventure whenever a fly ball was hit his way. I saw him get thrown out on a close play at first base one day in Memorial Stadium. He sat down right there in the dirt, beating on the ground like a little kid because he was out. I could see myself doing that as a five-year-old when my mother wouldn't let me do something. Who else would do that?

He was inquisitive, asked a lot of questions, and studied the scouting reports closely, because he had never managed and knew he was a little shallow in that department.

He never should have been fired by the Yankees, who moved him into the front office. Later he said, "When I managed the Yankees, I was regarded by Steinbrenner as one of the dumbest people in baseball. When I put on a three-piece suit and became general manager, I was the smartest person in baseball. Figure that out."

Lou's a devout horse player and owns some trotters. A fun guy. If you don't like Lou, there's something wrong with you.

I first knew Jim Frey when he played for Toledo in the American Association and I was broadcasting in Charleston, West Virginia. He coached for the Orioles and several other teams, and managed Kansas City in the 1980 World Series. A scholarly type of guy, he also managed the Cubs to the 1984 playoffs. Highly respected throughout baseball, but he would almost get too chummy with his players. He's a gentleman and a good guy; I often see him here in Baltimore.

Harvey Kuenn was a fine gentleman who never took himself too seriously. When his Milwaukee Brewers won the 1982 pennant, he admitted, "Anybody can manage this team, with all that talent." A lot of managers wouldn't say that.

Harvey lost a leg in an accident and took it in stride.

"No umpire can make me hurry up when I walk out to the mound," he told me. "That's why my pitcher in the bullpen will always be ready by the time I get out there."

We did an interview once on television, and he was chewing a big wad of tobacco the whole time. We're no more off the air than he says, "Rex, next time make sure I take this tobacco out. I don't mind people seeing me chew it, but I was worried about spitting it all over you."

I had been thinking the same thing.

John McNamara seemed to me to self-destruct. With Boston and Cleveland, he generated a lot of enthusiasm, then seemed to go downhill. He was a little aloof from his players and depended on his coaches.

Jeff Torborg is a nice guy who did not finish last. An excellent catcher who caught no-hitters for Sandy Koufax and Nolan Ryan, Jeff is a handsome, bright, articulate guy who never leaves anything undone.

When he was under contract to George Steinbrenner, the Seattle Mariners were interested in hiring him as their manager. Steinbrenner gave them permission to talk to Jeff, and he got the job. Then Steinbrenner changed his mind and would not let him go.

Bobby Valentine was regarded as one of the great prospects of all time. He could hit and he could fly. Then he broke his leg.

As a manager at Texas, he delegated authority to his coaches more than other managers. But he was the boss. In spring training of 1992 he predicted his Texas team would win the west division by scoring enough runs to overcome questionable pitching. They didn't, and that might have cost him his job.

In recent years there has been a big deal made out of how managers are becoming more one-on-one with players, using a more personal approach. Sparky Anderson has been doing that since before a lot of today's players were born.

Sparky is another example of the not-so-good player becoming a great manager. I knew him when he was George Anderson, an infielder in the Dodgers organization, one of those 900 kids looking for his name on the bulletin board at Vero Beach.

Through the years he has had more face-to-face contact with players than any manager. When he has to be, he can be very tough. When Jack Morris had some early success at Detroit, he got a little "headstrong" in Sparky's words. Morris told Sparky what to do with the ball one time when Sparky took him out of a game.

"I can't let that go on," Sparky said. "I can't let the other players see that. So I had a little talk with the young man. He's just highly competitive.

"I'm the manager and they are the players. That's what they've got to realize. Whatever I do is for them. The better they are, the better I am. That's what I've got to realize."

Sparky never complains about anything. He does not get involved in longterm contract negotiations or any other distractions.

"My job is to try to keep those 25 guys in the game at all times, and that's all. I believe they have problems like you and I do, and I try to find out what they are. You've got to understand what they're thinking and where they're coming from."

Nothing escapes him. He talks to everybody—players, trainers, batboys, everybody. He knows every clubhouse kid by name, and takes each one of them out to lunch every year. He once went to a clubhouse boy's home for dinner. Count the managers who would do that on one hand, one finger.

Anderson has one other characteristic: he believes that whoever he has playing for him at that time is the best at that position ever. Catchers? When he had Johnny Bench at Cincinnati, it was "Bench is the best catcher in baseball." When it was Lance Parrish, Parrish was the greatest ever. Shortstops? Dave Concepcion was the greatest fielding shortstop he ever had. Then it was Alan Trammell.

I've heard other managers say, "You want to know who has the greatest players? Go over to the other side and talk to Sparky; he's got them all locked up in one little clubhouse."

I find nothing wrong with that; he wants whoever is playing for him today to be the best, and in his heart he means it.

Why they fired him at Cincinnati I'll never know. He is now the elder statesman of managers. He does not know what "burned out" means, loves what he is doing as much as any man can, and will never quit.

"I live a life I never imagined," he says. "I go first class, best hotels and food, make a lot of money, go home every winter and paint my house and play with my grandkids and play golf in California, and then isn't it terrible I have to leave all that and go back to Florida for spring training. Isn't that a tough life?

"If they take this Detroit uniform off me, I'll go someplace else and work. I ain't quitting."

I can understand that. I stay in the game and don't want to leave it, either.

Buck Showalter is all baseball, no fooling around. He wouldn't ask you how you were if it killed him. He has a handle on things and will do a good job with the Yankees if Mr. Steinbrenner will leave him alone. The Yankee clubhouse won't be a zoo anymore with Buck in charge.

Gene Lamont is a very inquisitive gentleman. Another guy who never made it as a player and is a laid-back, stoic presence in the dugout. Nobody knows he's around. All he does is win.

On the other hand, you always knew when Billy Martin was around. Other managers had a great deal of respect for him. "You'd better be ready when you play his team," they'd say, "because he'll think of something."

I can't really tell you why Billy Martin and I became friends. I remember reading about this skinny little kid form the wrong side of the tracks, who came to the Yankees from Oakland, where he had played for Casey Stengel. Casey loved him, but for a few years there Billy never talked to Casey. That's how he was.

I've often said about him: "With a very good team like the Yankees, Billy's a good ballplayer. With the other, not-so-good teams he played for, he was just a fair player."

He mixed right in with that Yankee crew: DiMaggio, Berra, Whitey Ford. They liked his aggressiveness.

Getting the lineups was an adventure with Martin. He was by nature surly and nasty, especially with the press. He had a reputation for never showing up until ten minutes before the game. And, like anybody else who ever worked for Steinbrenner, he knew he'd get a last-minute call from the boss at the hotel or the ballpark. He wouldn't take calls at his room or his office, but if I called he'd give me his lineup.

And he was the only manager I ever dealt with who did not want to see the Orioles' lineup. "Right-hander or left-hander pitching?" That's all. His advance scout, Al Cuccinello, would send him voluminous detailed reports, and he'd never look at them. Other managers would have all those charts and reports and still ask for another opinion. Not Billy. He knew what he was going to do. It didn't matter what the other guy was doing.

Every team he went to he just burnt it up. He'd self-de-struct, and lose enthusiasm. I could see it in him. He really worked a game, the umpires, players, every angle. A lot of that was show: "Let's go...let's beat this club..." But it was also intended to light up the players and the fans. I saw Billy lose that. Late in the season, they might still have a chance to win, but that fire and energy was gone.

I took a lot of teasing about my friendship with Billy.

"How can you be a friend of that guy?"

My answer is, I think I knew a different Billy Martin. My parents taught me it's how people treat you and how you treat them. I never had any problems with Billy. He had one problem in his whole life: drinking. If he didn't drink, he may have become the best manager in the game. Some days he wouldn't eat, just drink. I didn't like that. Even when I was drinking, I used to argue with him about it.

Many teams stayed at the Cross Keys Inn, which was close

to Memorial Stadium. It had a dining room, coffee shop, bar and lounge. Some players didn't like it because it was so far from downtown. But it was close to Pimlico racetrack, which a lot of players appreciated.

Some managers make the hotel bar off-limits to players. "The hotel bar belongs to the manager, coaches and executives," they say. "The players can find plenty of places in the neighborhood." I think it's a good rule. But Billy associated with his players. He fought for them, argued for them, and related to them, and most of them liked him. But he never went near the clubhouse.

The manager of the bar was Mr. Yoo, a little Oriental guy the size of a jockey, who has been there since the place opened. He runs the place when he is not out fishing. He knew every player who was allowed in there by name, but he knew nothing about baseball. Billy loved Mr. Yoo, who had no idea what Billy Martin did.

Billy liked to have a good time, and he could handle his drinking until he was provoked. He was such a skinny little run-down-looking runt, things happened to him. Any reference to his skinniness touched him off. He didn't start out looking for a fight, but he never walked away from one, to his regret, and he lost most of them.

I was living at Cross Keys at the time, and one night Billy and I went into Mr. Yoo's bar after a game and Billy bought a round for everybody. There was a young couple sitting there. The girl said, "Are you Billy Martin?"

"Yes, ma'am."

"I'm a big fan of yours."

They chatted and she introduced her husband and said they had been married just a short time, and Billy said to Mr. Yoo, "Give this couple a bottle of champagne."

Then the girl said, "You certain are a skinny little guy."

Billy said, "You're right, lady, and you got a fat ass."

They're all laughing. Then Billy asked the girl to dance, and I thought, oh oh, here it comes.

They danced and he must have made some remark because they came back to the table and she said to her husband, "You know what Billy Martin said to me?" and she told him, and the husband got up and challenged Billy, and Billy said, "Okay, let's go."

Well, they stared each other down and nothing came of it. But it made the newspapers.

The next night is Saturday and Billy's a little depressed; the Yankees aren't playing well. We're back at Mr. Yoo's bar, sitting there minding our own business. Two New Yorkers wearing Yankee caps come in and spot Billy.

"Hey. Billy Martin!"

They shake hands and he signs something for them, and one of them says, "Billy, you ought to go into the next room. Your pitcher, Ed Whitson, is in there and some Yankee fans are giving him a bad time."

There had been some stuff in the papers about an argument between Whitson and Martin.

"You ought to do something to help him," they say.

So Billy goes in the other room and speaks to the fans.

"How about letting up on this guy? I've been giving him a bad time and he's had a little rough going. Leave him alone."

The fans say, "Okay, Billy," and start to leave.

Whitson stands up, drunk. "I don't need any little so-and-so fighting my battles," and he kicks Billy in the groin.

Billy goes down, but he gets up and flattens Whitson with one punch. In come the security people and clear out the place.

They go to their rooms, both on the third floor. A few minutes later, Whitson bangs on Billy's door.

"This isn't over. Let's go downstairs."

I had seen everything up to now; what happened next I heard from the Cross Keys manager and from Billy.

They went outside in the driveway. Whitson swung and missed. Billy swung and connected. Billy swung again. Whitson ducked. Billy fell and broke his arm. That ended the fight.

Back in his room Billy called me.

"Can you come get me and take me to the hospital?"

"Sure, what's the matter?"

"I think I broke my arm."

I took him to Sinai, they put it in a cast, and I took him

back. This was Sunday morning and we had a day game, so we each got maybe an hour's sleep. He showed up at the ballpark about 11:30—looked awful, smelled awful, felt awful.

I went into his office and wrote out the lineup for him. Then he said, "Okay, let 'em in."

There must have been 8,000 reporters out there, plus Clyde King and Woody Woodward from the Yankees' front office.

Billy told me, "When they question you, just tell the truth."

I didn't think anybody would ask me anything, but a few days later here came some detectives hired by Steinbrenner to investigate the incident at Cross Keys. I told them the same story I'm telling you. And I added, "I'm not defending him. I'm just telling you what happened, as I saw it."

Certainly I didn't condone the things he did. He knew that, but we remained good friends, over and above all that. Behind his reputation I knew him as a good, decent guy, but that didn't make headlines.

When I had my stroke and came out of the coma, Billy called me every day—twice from the Yankee dugout before a game started—to make sure I was all right. This was the mean, bad Billy Martin. He said, "I think you're always going to blame me for what happened to you." But I did myself in; I didn't need any help.

Billy did a lot of benefits and charity events. He also was a great student of the Civil War. Maybe he imagined himself as one of the generals, and that's where he got some of his tactics.

Yogi Berra has long been one of my favorite people. We go back a long way together, too. I've know him since we played against each other in Legion ball and we both broke in in the Piedmont League in 1943. He always kids me about being much older than he is. The difference is under five months.

Yogi is a smarter baseball man than people give him credit for. The managers he has coached for know better. Billy Martin used to say, "I couldn't function without him." Dick Howser told me, "He's the number one guy." Joe Altobelli said, "There's nobody who knows more than he does."

I asked him once in an interview, "Yogi, what do you do as a coach?"

"I am the executive coach."

"What does the executive coach do?"

"He sits next to the manager, and the manager asks him questions about different things."

Like a lot of the alleged Yogi quotes, when you stop to think about it, they make a lot of sense.

I don't know why Yogi got fired as a manager, especially after winning pennants. I do know he is definitely his own man. I've heard he was one guy who would talk back to Stengel with the Yankees. He was a one-on-one manager. If a player was not getting the job done, he did not hesitate to lay it on the line. Coming from Yogi, they would accept it.

Yogi was the exception to my theory that great players do not make great managers.

Nothing seems to bother him. If he was a manager and they fired him or demoted him to being a coach, he would accept it and do the job. But George Steinbrenner did something to him that turned him away from the Yankees to this day. I know him as well as anybody in the world, and I would never ask him about it. He won't even show up for an oldtimers game in Yankee Stadium.

Newspapermen who had known Yogi as a player idolized him. They always seemed to be a little softer on him. And he was nice to them. He would answer their questions patiently, never sound off if he thought they were dumb questions. But when they left, he might say, "What a jerk that guy is."

About the time Earl Weaver announced his retirement, and Joe Altobelli was being considered for the job, Yogi was in town, too. I lined up both of them to do television interviews. Altobelli went first.

"Joe, would you like to manage the Orioles?"

"Sure. I know all these kids from managing at Rochester."

It was Yogi's turn. He said to me, "Don't ask me any dumb questions."

The Yankees were also about to name a new manager. On the air, I said, "Now, Yogi, I want a definite answer. Would you like to manage the Yankees?"

And Yogi said, "Maybe."

I almost split.

Yogi never looked like a ballplayer. I remember when Mike Boddicker came up to stay with the Orioles. We were in Yankee Stadium one afternoon and Mike said to me, "Hey, Rex, who's that over there?"

"That's Yogi Berra."

"Aw, come on. That can't be Berra. Look how he walks. Look at the physique on him."

"Michael, that's Berra."

Yogi trotted out to throw some BP; he looked as if he was going to fall apart.

"How in the hell could he ever do anything?" Boddicker said.

"All I know is, he's always looked like that, and walked like that. Just be glad you're not pitching against him. That garbage you throw, he'd hit it anywhere you threw it."

Yogi still thinks like a hitter. He told me, "When we went into Detroit, if I had two broken legs, I'd play. I could hit a home run on my knees in that park."

There will be a lot of heartbroken hitters if Tiger Stadium gets torn down.

When I saw Yogi in December 1991, he said, "I hear that new Baltimore ballpark has a short right field fence. I might have to make a comeback."

Like Stan Musial, Yogi was popular in every ballpark he played in. And he remains to this day beloved by everybody who knows him. People who worked at the Cross Keys Inn when the visiting teams stayed there voted him their favorite player. Always a gentleman; never refused an autograph.

No matter how many Yogi stories people tell or make up, I assure you he's no joke when it comes to baseball and being a beautiful human being.

I've talked about a lot of managers I thought did a good job. So why do managers get fired so much? Good question.

Loss of control is one reason. A guy loses control, maybe because he just loses interest. No telling why. Some guys I can't see ever losing interest. Sparky's one of them. Tony La Russa. He took the White Sox from nothing and won a division title.

But when Ken Harrelson took over as general manager, Tony knew he was gone.

Sometimes the personalities don't mix. The manager and general manager or president don't get along. Dick Howser got fired because he wouldn't agree on something with the owner. I think Gene Mauch was fired because he fought the general manager. Mauch probably knew more than the GM, but that didn't matter. They don't have to like each other, but they have to respect each other.

There's a lot to be said for stability and continuity. The Dodgers moved from Brooklyn to Los Angeles in 1958, and they've had how many managers in the 37 years they've been out there? Two. Unbelievable.

Jim Lefebvre's advice to a young manager is, "Whatever you do, whether you like it or not, back your general manager a hundred percent. You get more cooperation that way. The GM may talk about a deal you don't like. You'll have your input, but he may decide something different. Tell him, 'If that's what you want, I'll back you one hundred percent.' Otherwise, you're gone."

One time Gene Mauch got fired at California because he left a pitcher in too long and it cost him the playoff against Milwaukee and Gene Autry let him go. But every club he went to, he improved. Took them off the bottom and moved them up. Do they lose interest when they succeed (although Mauch never got them to the World Series)? Or do the front office people lose interest in the manager?

I don't know why Yogi Berra got fired anywhere. The standard line is, "We think somebody else can do better."

I don't understand that theory, especially if they've won, like Yogi did. In 1964 Johnny Keane won the pennant in St. Louis and Yogi won with the Yankees. So what happened? They both got fired, and Keane managed the Yankees the next year. Can you explain that? I can't. And how about 1960, when Detroit and Cleveland traded managers in mid-season, Jimmy Dykes going to Cleveland and Joe Gordon to the Tigers? Both teams finished right where they were when they made the swap. Is that ludicrous?

There are two cliches: "Managers are hired to be fired," and "It's easier to fire the manager than 25 players."

Bucky Harris managed 29 years and was fired eight times. Rogers Hornsby managed six teams in 14 years.

The fans know that when a manager loses his job, it is because his players can't pitch or hit or field. And the manager knows that when he wins, it was the players that did the pitching, hitting, and fielding it took to win.

My favorite story about a guy being fired is not a baseball story. It's basketball. Charlie Eckman, a great basketball referee in the ACC, coached the Ft. Wayne Pistons to two world titles way back in ancient times. Fred Zollner, who owned the team, called him into his office and said, "Charlie, we're going to have to make a change in your department."

As Charlie tells it, "I was the department. There was nobody else but me. Why didn't he just tell me I was fired?"

If I had owned the Orioles 10-15 years ago, I would have hired Earl Weaver as my manager, because he had such a handle on things from the minor leagues up. I'd love to say Sparky. I'd like to say Tony La Russa or Gene Mauch. These guys stand out in my mind as good managers. Except for one thing—his drinking—I could hire Billy Martin in a second. Sparky and Gene Mauch can really help you on players.

As far as managing during a game, I'd take Sparky. He's more controlled. I'd probably also take Weaver. All right, if I have to pick just one manager, I'll take Earl for managing on the field, using all 25 guys. But, you know, I even have to hedge on that. If I had a mediocre club against a great club, I would take Sparky. He has more patience. Earl didn't have much patience.

Casey Stengel would be a terrible manager with a mediocre club.

Today, as I write this in 1994, Johnny Oates is my man. If I owned any other club in the American League, I would choose Buck Showalter.

3

The Flycatchers

The only great catches you ever hear about are the ones that take place in playoffs or World Series—the Willie Mays catch and Devon White's in 1992. They are re-played over and over as if they are the only ones that have ever happened. But you've got to stop and think that every day, some-where, in some ballpark, there are great catches being made.

The greatest catch I ever saw in Memorial Stadium was wit-nessed by maybe five or six thousand people on a cold, damp night by a guy who played all of 200 games in the outfield for the Orioles. His name was Larry Harlow, and if anybody remembers him in Baltimore, it is more likely because of the 24-10 game in Toronto in which he and Elrod Hendricks pitched for the first and last times in their major league careers.

Harlow was a tall, thin kid who could fly. Wore the glove on his right hand. He's playing center field this night, against the Tigers, and John Wockenfuss is up, right-hand hitter. Larry's play-ing a little shaded toward right center, and the ball is hit to left center. He takes off flying, leaps above the fence and hangs there, the post in the middle of his back, and catches the ball on the other side. And he's teetering on the top of the fence, couldn't go either way. He saw Elrod waiting to catch him behind the fence, but felt the left fielder pull him back onto the field. Scraped his ribs on the way down.

Damnedest thing I've ever seen. I hope those 6,000-odd people remember it. I know Larry does.

A great defensive outfielder, Harlow never could hit enough, but he played in the majors for six years.

I've seen a lot of great center fielders: Terry Moore, Duke Snider, Mays, Mantle, DiMaggio. Joe DiMaggio's the greatest I've ever seen, but Paul Blair, defensively, was as good as anybody. Without a doubt, the best the Orioles ever had.

There's another great catch I remember vividly. George Scott hit a screamer in Milwaukee. Ninth inning, game on the line. You know it's out of there in right center field. Blair is playing shallow as always. He takes off, but you know he's not going to get to the ball; it's over the fence. There's a gate out there that opens into the bullpen. Blair hit the gate, it flew open and he caught the ball out of the park. I thought George Scott would never leave the field. He just stood there for what seemed an eternity, staring. Not a routine catch, but almost for Blair.

Blair drove Earl Weaver crazy. Earl loved outfielders who played deep. Blair played as shallow as anybody ever did. Earl said, "I hate it. It drives me crazy. But I defy you to see the ball hit and see Blair make his first step. I've never done it. Even if I anticipate it, I never see it. If you see the bat hit the ball, he's gone by the time you look out there."

Blair put his head down and ran to where the ball was headed and got there. He anticipated so well, he seldom made diving catches. Like Cal Junior, he got where he had to be without looking spectacular doing it, because he anticipated and got a jump on the ball. He played close in behind second base, and nothing got over his head. He was the only outfielder Jim Palmer never tried to move. Jim knew Paul would ignore him, anyhow.

Not the greatest arm, but good enough. And accurate. Never missed the cutoff man.

Paul was severely beaned out in California and never again was the same hitter. He became plate-shy. You could see it.

Good disposition, well-liked, loved to play poker and gin rummy.

Blair hustled, but he needed a little fire lit under him. One day in spring training Frank Robinson did it, stood out there in the outfield and chewed him out. He needed something like that.

But Paul Blair was special, in the same way Joe DiMaggio was special in center field.

I love Al Bumbry. I think he's one of the nicest people I've ever known. Just a great person. But Al, bless him, missed more cutoff men than anybody, and didn't have a good arm. I used to say he played "Annie Over," the way he overthrew the cutoff.

Al's a little guy, five foot eight, and to this day he's probably in better shape than any active player. When they gave guys that fat-content test, he always had less than anybody. A platoon leader in Vietnam, he saw a lot of action, but refused to talk about it.

Al was not the center fielder Blair was, but he was a little faster, played deep and ran down everything. Whenever Palmer moved him, Al would move back when Palmer turned away.

The last excellent leadoff man the Orioles have had, he was fast, selective, adept at fouling off pitches, a good base stealer, and a .280 hitter.

They called him the Bee, and he was one of the most popular guys to play here. There were some bitter feelings when Edward Bennett Williams let him go. He was a coach with the Red Sox for six years, but returned in '94 to the Orioles organization as an instructor at Bowie.

Reggie Jackson is one of my favorite players—as a player. Whenever I say that, people start jumping on me, because they don't like him as a person. I can understand that. But as a player, you show me somebody who was much better than he was. He never, ever let down. He could hit a little one-hopper back to the pitcher, be out 60 feet of the 90 feet to first base, and still run as hard as he could. Sparky Anderson said three guys ran everything out: Pete Rose, Dave Winfield and Reggie Jackson. He never let up.

Reggie was not a great outfielder. He had a strong arm, but it was not very accurate. He'd throw the ball every which way. He concentrated on hitting and running the bases, and as an outfielder he was not as good as he should have been.

He played hurt a lot and never complained. In Memorial Stadium, in the bullpen beyond right field, there was an open part of the screen where you could see onto the field. I saw him hit that bar while making an unbelievable catch one night. The next day the groundskeeper showed me how that bar was bent almost into an L shape where he had hit it.

But Reggie had to have all the attention. If somebody else made the game-winning hit or play and the writers were crowded around that night's hero, Reggie would pipe up, "Didn't they see me? I'm the guy who moved the runner over, got him into scoring position."

Reggie got the most cheers and the most boos of anybody in Memorial Stadium. I asked him once, "Do those boos bother you?"

He said, "No, it goes on in every city. If 50,000 people boo or cheer, it's all the same thing. They're recognizing me."

He liked that. They were noticing him. He'd say to me, "Before I go up to bat, I like it when they boo me while I'm still in the on deck circle, so make your announcement real quiet."

All I had to do was say, "Number 44..." and they'd start booing.

I asked him, "What would bother you?"

"Silence when I went up to bat," he said. "That would drive me crazy."

Dock Ellis, a black pitcher, was pitching for Texas. Ellis drilled a white batter in the ribs while Reggie was in the on deck circle. Reggie called out to him, "I'd like to see you do that against one of your brothers." Then Reggie stepped in.

Poom! First pitch knocked the helmet off; glasses went flying. Reggie never reacted, just ran to first base.

Earl Weaver probably handled him as well as anybody. I was in the dugout one day when Reggie came out and looked at the lineup card. Earl's got him hitting fourth and playing right field. Reggie says, "I don't feel real good. How about being the DH tonight?"

Earl says, "All the money you make, you'll play right field."

And he played. Got a couple hits. Reggie's often said—not where Earl could hear him—that Earl's one of the best managers he ever played for. I can buy that. You knew he and Billy Martin would never get along. No way.

I think the other players felt Reggie let them down in '76 when he was late reporting. They believed if he had been here from opening day, they would have finished better. They may not have liked his personality, but they appreciated his talent. He could turn a game around with one swing. He was an intimidator.

Except to a pitcher like Scott McGregor. Mac couldn't blacken your eye with a pitch, but he handled Reggie like a genius. I'll never forget the day Reggie was with the Yankees and Scott struck him out three times, the last time in the ninth with the tying run on base. I can still see it: Reggie swinging from his heels and getting nothing and standing there with the bat, completely dumbfounded watching McGregor walk off the field. Because McGregor—you and I would want to hit. My daughter would want to hit. But Reggie couldn't touch him.

Gene Mauch managed him for a few years in California and pretty much summed up Reggie: "He was a pain in the ass, but you do get the player out of him."

Frank Robinson? There was not a better ballplayer in the game. One of the most exciting, knowledgeable players, he had no arm, but he cheated enough—playing shallow and playing the hitters—to get by.

The first time I saw Frank was in Columbia, South Carolina in the early 1950s. I was broadcasting the Mutual Game of the Day and once in a while we did a minor league game. Ernie White, a former Cardinals pitcher, was the manager.

"Tell me about your team," I said to him.

"I've got one kid. Major league hitter right now. But he'll never make it. Got great knowledge of the game, but he can't throw."

"What's his name?"

"Frank Robinson." I wrote it down.

"Where does he play?"

"He should be an outfielder, but he's playing first base because he can't throw."

"Why not?"

"His arm hurts so bad."

I could not imagine a guy playing baseball who couldn't

throw. But the first time he had a play at first base, he walked over almost to the pitcher and tossed the ball underhand. I thought, "Maybe he really can't throw." He got three hits that day. I remember that.

Years later I asked Frank about it.

Frank said he never could throw very well. "They sent me to every doctor. No operation would do. That winter I went home and swung a bat but never picked up a ball. I went to spring training and could throw a little bit."

If you ever saw him play, you know he had no arm. Frank played in Crosley Field in Cincinnati, which was not a big field, so he got away with it. In Memorial Stadium he knew how to play the hitters and got by. But how he played the game. Hit. Steal a base. Bury you if you made a mistake. Knew how to run the bases. Gave you everything he had at all times. He loved the game, but he was always a surly guy.

Since I had seen him as a skinny kid in the Sally League, I followed his progress in the National League. Great player, MVP and all that, but he was always rated fourth in the league among outfielders, behind Mays, Aaron and Clemente. When he came to the American League he took over.

Some people who know baseball says he's the best they've ever seen. I don't go that far. I've seen guys like DiMaggio, Musial, Snider who could do it all, and with so much class.

Robinson presided over the kangaroo court with the Orioles. He put a mophead on his head like a wig, took a bat and started beating on an old wooden box. He would fine guys for hitting a home run with the bases loaded—showing off. That kind of stuff helps to keep a team loose—when they're winning. It was fun, and it put him in with the other players more than any other one thing. They fined Chuck Thompson once for getting too excited on the air. Other clubs have done similar things, but I think having a player of the magnitude of Frank Robinson doing it made it a bigger thing.

I've never known Frank to have any superstitions. He tended to be a loner, although he and Elrod Hendricks have been fast friends for a long time.

Until Brady Anderson, the Orioles never had a really outstanding left fielder. Don Buford was steady, but no great shakes defensively. And Don Baylor had no arm at all.

Buford was a good leadoff man, switch-hitter, good power for a little guy (hit a home run on the second pitch of the 1969 World Series off Tom Seaver). He was typical of what they called a "Bible hitter"—thou shalt not pass. Up there hacking from the first pitch.

Back in the days when every player had a roommate on the road, Don had some odd ones. For a while he roomed with Chico Salmon, who could not sleep in the dark. Buford couldn't sleep with the lights on. Sometimes he would turn out the lights after Chico fell asleep. If Chico woke up during the night and it was dark, he got jumpy. Like newlyweds, they learned to adjust to each other and compromised, leaving a light on in the bathroom with the door cracked.

But Marcelino Lopez, a pitcher from Cuba, was too much for Don. Lopez insisted on lighting a long candle and burning it all night. Don said, "No way. Religion or no religion, I'm not sleeping in a room with a burning candle. The thing could tip over and burn up the place and there is no way we could get out of here."

They parted amicably.

Don is the type of guy you'd want in your organization as a coach or manager.

Don Baylor was another guy where God did us all a favor by putting such a nice guy into such a big, strong body. I have never seen a body like his. Scared of nothing or nobody, he could have picked up the world and thrown it over if he wanted to.

I have always had the greatest respect for him and Bobby Grich, the way they roomed together, black and white, in those southern towns in the minor leagues when it was not done. When they got traded apart, they both cried like babies.

Don could never throw, no matter how many times he came out early to the park with Weaver or Jim Frey and worked on it. But he was a born hitter and a good base runner. If he was on first, the second baseman or shortstop wanted no part of covering that bag. When he slid into a base, the world moved. He drove people into the outfield by sliding into them. Nothing malicious;

he was just so powerful.

They called him "Groove;" when he was in a groove, no-body got him out.

Baylor holds the record for being hit by pitches: 267. Maybe twice he charged the mound. Most of the time he never tried to get out of the way. Jackie Robinson used to do the same thing, but in those days the umpire would make him stay up at bat if it looked like Jackie did not make enough effort to get out of the way. That never happened to Baylor.

Very popular with the players, Don became a hitting coach and aspired to be a manager. I always thought he would be a good one, but I told him, "I know there are managers, like Lou Piniella, who walk right in without being a coach or anything, but if I were you, I'd manage in winter ball, like Frank Robinson and other guys did, to learn the trade. "

He did not think he should have to do that. As it turned out, he got the managing job with the expansion Colorado Rockies, and is in his second year at this time.

Although he did not like Earl Weaver, he admits that some of Weaver's ways come back to him as a manager. But he does not use one Weaverism he is fond of quoting: "If you feel like you're going to hit into a double play, strike out."

Joe Orsulak, to me, has got to be the perfect player to manage. A very popular guy, Slack had little to say, never complained, just showed up and did his job. I think everybody was sorry when he was no longer with the Orioles.

When we got Joe from Pittsburgh, he had not played regularly there. Vin Scully tipped me off that, if Joe stayed healthy, he would be one of our better players. He was right.

Joe would play every day if he found his name in the lineup, even with his arm problems and leg problems. He wouldn't complain. The trainer had to go to the manager and tell him, "Joe's hurt more than he's letting on."

I think he is a 120-game player. He hits better against right-hand pitching, but doesn't bail out against lefties.

Joe would do an interview, show up at the Orioles winter carnival, but he likes his privacy, likes to go fishing, doesn't need all that other stuff.

Curt Blefary was one of the few guys to come through here who did not fit the Oriole mold. A renegade, nonconformist, from Brooklyn (naturally), he wanted to be a New York cop after his playing days. I don't know if he did. His one great claim to fame is that he caught Tom Phoebus's no-hitter in 1968.

When Earl Weaver platooned Gary Roenicke and John Lowenstein, that was one of his greatest moves. They were like Gene Woodling and Hank Bauer on the Yankees. Combined, they had a fantastic year.

Roenicke and Lowenstein understood their roles and Earl's thinking, and neither one had ever been an everyday player, so they accepted the platooning.

Roenicke was a John Wayne: big, strong, swaggering walk like the Duke. He hit 20 home runs a few years, but he also hit some of the softest popups you ever saw. In the press box, if a batter hit a little 10-foot-high popup back to the pitcher, you'd hear, "There's a Roenicke popup."

He was one of the best defensive left fielders the O's ever had. One time the team had a lot of injuries and they brought up Benny Ayala. After Benny sits around for a few weeks, Weaver writes him into the lineup in left field and puts Roenicke in center field, where he had never played. Weaver says, "He's such a good outfielder, let's see how good he is."

They're in Minnesota, and Ayala hits two home runs and Gary makes some sensational catches. They both made Earl look good. He looked like the perfect ballplayer, but I don't think Gary ever lived up to his own or everyone else's expectations. One day he got hit by a pitch that broke his jaw, knocked some teeth out. He wanted to play the next day. After that he wore a helmet like a football helmet.

Lowenstein made every catch one-handed. We were in Texas and after the game a young writer asked him, "Who invented the one-handed catch?" John said, "Pete Gray," and walked away. We were laughing and the kid didn't know why until somebody told him that Pete Gray was a one-armed outfielder during World War II for the St. Louis Browns.

After John hit a home run that won a game, a writer asked him, "What did you hit to win the game?" John said, "I hit a home run. What did you think I hit?" That caustic sense of humor had to come out first, then he'd give the guy a proper answer.

One day he's on the bench and a relief pitcher comes in and John's called on to hit. "Anybody know anything about this pitcher?" he asks on the bench. "Yeah," somebody says. "I saw him in the minors. Great fastball, good curve, no changeup."

John goes up to the plate. The count goes to two and two and this guy throws a changeup that corkscrews John into the ground trying to hit it. He comes back to the bench and says, "Somebody better tell him he doesn't have a changeup. He doesn't know it."

One day he slides into second base at Memorial Stadium. Tremendous collision. He goes down and he's out cold. The doctor comes running out and starts working on him. Nothing. Out comes the stretcher. They roll him onto it and the doc is walking alongside it holding John's arm. The big crowd is hushed. Just as they get ready to go down the dugout steps, John sits up and waves two fists high in the air. The crowd goes berserk.

Later I asked him why he did that. He said, "Well, I had actually come to on the field and I sensed what's going on while they're carrying me off and I just felt I had to do something special."

John created his own nicknames: Brother Lo, Lolo. He's got a pet parrot that does nothing but cuss.

The Crow—Terry Crowley—was another guy Earl used effectively, primarily as a pinch hitter and DH. Crow used a little bat, almost like Little League size, but he made contact.

He and Belanger and Etchebarren loved the horse and dog tracks. The latter two were also big jai alai fans during spring training, but with Crow it was mostly the tracks.

Crowley was part of the Irish Mafia with Flanagan, Dempsey and Jim Dwyer. On the road those four were always together. I'd see them and say, "Okay, what government are you plotting to overthrow today?"

Now one of the best hitting coaches around, Crow is with Minnesota.

Dwyer was another pinch-hitter deluxe; he learned the art

from Crowley. They both came off the bench swinging. And they both liked to follow the horses.

Dwyer was a tough little Irish kid from Chicago, where his father owned a bar. He reported to Gene Mauch in the minor leagues carrying a cardboard suitcase and wearing cutoff jeans and thongs.

"Worst looking mess I'd ever seen," Mauch told me.

He earned the nickname "Pigpen," after the character in Peanuts. You could dress him in a $1,000 suit, send him to a $100 barber, it still wouldn't help. Always disheveled, looking like he'd just come into town by bumming a ride on a freight train.

But a quiet, popular guy, and a good guy to have on your club.

We got Ken Singleton from Montreal in the same deal that brought Mike Torrez to Baltimore. A big, heavy, slow guy, Ken got teased a lot about being the only black guy who couldn't run. But he could hit. Very selective, got on base a lot. He had a habit of bending down and picking up three pebbles and throwing them aside one at a time the first time he came up to bat in a game. He said, "That's to remind myself to get three good pitches to swing at." If he faced the same pitcher a second time, he did it again.

Kenny loved basketball. In the clubhouse he always had a rubber ball or rolled-up paper and he's dunking and hooking. Ask any baseball player; they'll all tell you they are better basketball players.

Singleton was great with kids, in or out of the ballpark. Always smiling, always teasing and going out of his way to pay attention to the clubhouse boys and batboys. There was a blond kid who looked like Jack Sikma, the pro basketball player, so Kenny called him Sikma. "Sikma" is now a bartender at The Prime Rib, and Kenny always asks about him.

Here's a coincidence: I used to visit my Brooklyn teammate, Ralph Branca, at his home in Mt. Vernon, outside New York City, when we were with the Dodgers. It was a big old house, room enough for the 13 Branca kids. Ralph's parents eventually sold it to Ken Singleton's parents, and Kenny grew up in that house.

A class act, with a nice family, Kenny wanted to stay in baseball. But coaching or managing did not appeal to him. He had a good voice and was very articulate, and I encouraged him to watch and learn from interviewers and practice it himself. He did, and he wound up broadcasting in Montreal.

Harold Patrick "Pat" Kelly was one of the wildest kids who ever lived, but he became a born-again Christian while he was playing and was devoutly religious. I don't know if there was any connection, but he began hitting home runs on Sundays. He also became known for going after fly balls in left field and pushing them over the fence. He did that a couple times and got kidded about it.

Weaver's his manager. Earl knew Pat was born-again, so he used a lot of profanity around him to agitate him. One Sunday Pat hit a home run and, rounding the bases, pointed up at the sky as if to say, "The Lord helped me." He came back to the bench and said to Earl, "You see what praying does for you."

Earl said, "What about the son of a bitch who threw the ball. He probably went to church and prayed harder than you. You mean the Lord plays favorites?"

Pat could never get ahead of Earl. One time he said, "When's the last time you prayed?"

"When I sent you up to pinch hit, that you'd get a walk."

I've never seen one of these born-again Christian players try to convert other players. Scott McGregor gave Pat Kelly all the credit for converting him, but said, "I went to Pat." Pat didn't force himself on anybody. Maybe a little "God bless you" and "May the Lord be with you," but nothing to offend anybody.

I don't know what starts a guy in that direction. Maybe they say, "I'm not getting anywhere with my life. I've got to try some other way." I don't know. I do know that not all those guys are sincere or devout in their thinking, like McGregor and Kelly, who are both ordained ministers now. But a lot of them are sincere. Storm and Glenn Davis, for example.

I think that stuff might have helped drive Dave Garcia out of baseball. When he was managing Cleveland, he said, "I'm sick and tired of hearing about how 'The Lord made me do it.'"

When I was doing the post-game star of the game interviews, and I'd say, "What a great game you pitched," I didn't want to hear, "Oh, the Lord was behind me." I'd rather hear,

"The team really helped me and I had a good night."

Did the Lord help them do it when they failed? I don't buy that. I was raised a strict Catholic, but the only thing I can remember saying is when I was 15 or 16, walking off the mound after winning the city high school championship. Some cheerleaders said, "You dirty Catholics. The only reason you win is because you pray."

I turned around and said, "Maybe you ought to try it. You might win."

I remember that. I didn't like what I said; what I believed was, "That isn't why we won. We're better than you."

Curt Motton played a little outfield and did a lot of pinch hitting for the Orioles during Weaver's pennant-winning years. Probably the biggest hit of his career came when he pinch hit for Hendricks in the bottom of the 11th of a scoreless playoff game against Minnesota in 1969, and drove in the winning run with a line single to center field.

Motton is called "Cuz" because he calls everybody "Cuz." I think guys do that because they can't remember anybody's name.

Motton's a guy who has turned his life around quite a bit. A little guy, he started drinking and gambling and all that kind of stuff. He tried to keep a job in baseball, but couldn't. I helped him get a job in Baltimore, but he didn't last long there. Then I think Pat Kelly got to him with Elrod's help and they straightened him out. He got back into the game, coached for the Orioles in 1991, and is now a scout for them.

I like Curt. I admire what he did with his life. I hated to see him wasting it, and he was. But no more.

Carlos Lopez came to the Orioles from Seattle. Took him ten minutes to get dressed in the on deck circle before I could announce him. Wrist bands, shin guard, headband, helmet, everything had to be on just so. Chuck Thompson once described his routine—every little movement—on the air.

One day Carlos is on first base and Jim Frey is coaching. Frey says to him, "Carlos, this guy has a great move to first. Be careful."

Carlos says, "Jeem, don't worry. I know baseball."

He no more says it than he gets picked off. That got to be a running joke. Sometimes when I see Jim Frey I say to him, "Jeem, don't worry. I know baseball."

Benny Ayala came from St. Louis. Had good power, but a terrible fielder. One of those guys who did just enough to stick in the majors. Whenever it looked like he was on his way out, he'd do something to win a game. Handsome kid, popular with the players.

Mike Young—another six foot two guy who could do it all, but never did it. Had flashes of brilliance—28 home runs in 1985—but faded each time. Eddie Murray tried to work with him. He should have been in the majors for 15 years, not five.

Merv Rettenmund was another one of my favorite type guys. Power hitter, could run, never got to play enough. He was always pestering Weaver to play him more. And every spring Earl would guarantee him he'd get his 300 at bats. And he did. But it was never enough for him. Went to three World Series, plus one with the Reds in 1975. Another guy who fit the mold.

What is this mold I keep referring to? When Sparky Anderson was managing the Reds, he told me, "I got two guys from your ball club, Rettenmund and Crowley. Two of the nicest gentlemen I've ever been around. They were educated well in that organization."

That's the mold I'm talking about.

Luis Mercedes had his chances, but one day early in 1993 Johnny Oates wanted him to pinch run and couldn't find him. He was in the clubhouse eating a sandwich. Right then it was so long Luis. I never believed he or Chito Martinez would be our right fielder.

Jim Fuller was a big, strong, nice man. He had one of the best arms in the history of the Orioles. Came up with the reputation of being one of the great home run hitters in the minor leagues. And he probably was. His problem was, he struck out more than he'd hit the ball. Hung around for a few years, got more chances than he probably should have. But if you ever saw this kid swing, you'd say, "I'm going to watch this guy. He can't miss." He had all the actions, all the moves, just couldn't hit the ball.

Another thing he did with the club—and in the early '70s you really needed this—he was the team barber. Jim cut everybody's hair, including mine. You couldn't beat the price; it was free.

Take a look at the years Tommy Davis had with Los Angeles. Frank Robinson said Davis's 1962 season was the greatest single year he's ever seen a player have. There was nothing he couldn't do. Hit, run, great arm. Then he broke his leg and was never the same. But he was a good hitter for three years here late in his career.

Tommy told me that his father was a cab driver in Brooklyn. He made Tommy go to Ebbets Field for a tryout. Tommy never thought he could be a ballplayer, but his father believed in him.

Juan Beniquez hit .300 in his one year with the Orioles. But he didn't fit the mold, temperamentally or physically. He was a bit of a clubhouse lawyer and was under six feet tall.

Ken Gerhart came up to me once and asked me if I had ever heard of a player named Lou Boudreau. That's when I got the message: I'm getting old. Nicknamed "Gomer" as in Gomer Pyle on the old Andy Griffith TV show, he wore old style bib overalls in the clubhouse.

Steve Finley was a good-looking rookie outfielder. In a spring game in Florida Steve Palermo is umpiring behind the plate. First time up Palermo calls a strike on him, a pitch just below the armpits. Finley calls time and steps out. "Mr. Umpire," he says, "is that your strike zone?" Not being smart, very quiet and polite. "Is that your strike zone?"

Palermo says, "Yes, it is."

Finley says, "I won't forget it."

Palermo told me later he had never had a player ask him a question like that. But this kid figures he's going to be in this league a long time and he wanted to file that information away.

Rich Coggins was one who just didn't have that great desire, the love or appreciation of the game. In that way, he was the opposite of Al Bumbry, but on the field he was a clone. Very quick, good defensive player. As the 1-2 hitters, Bumbry would lead off, get a single. Coggins a single. Men on first and third. Night after night. But it didn't last. He was through at 26.

Disco Dan Ford had a big year in '83. Could do everything, but was always hurt. Not really into the game.

Phil Bradley was a quarterback at Missouri. He could run and had a good arm. Phil had a run-in with the Phillies' manager while he was there in '88, but he finished the season strong and Orioles scouts liked him. He came over with a reputation of a bad guy in the clubhouse, but that did not sound right to me, not the guy I knew when he had been with Seattle. I knew him as a quiet guy, a fan favorite, who played hurt.

Then Frank Robinson sat him down for a few days during the 1990 season, and Bradley sounded off to Frank and took his case to the press: the Orioles didn't care about him, he had contract gripes, and so forth. Mistake. So the Orioles traded him for Ron Kittle. They took a lot of heat as a result. But it wasn't a great deal for either team. Bradley didn't make it with the White Sox; they let him go and nobody picked him up and he went to Japan.

Taking your business out on the street is a bad idea. But I don't consider that being a troublemaker in the clubhouse. The players didn't, either.

John "T-bone" Shelby was the perennial greatest player of all time who never fulfilled his billing. He could fly, but struck out a lot. Every time he hit a home run, he thought he'd hit nothing but home runs from then on.

His wife came to me one day and said, "Why do you always announce him as John?"

"'Cause that's his name," I said.

"Well, what about calling him T-bone?"

I said, "I don't like that name. I think it's degrading."

I'm not one for nicknames. My friends know that. When I'm talking to Flanagan or Devereaux, I call them Michael. Even on the air, I'll call Winfield David. I don't go for Flanny or Devo, those inside nicknames. But sometimes the fans wouldn't know who you were talking about if you used their real names.

Suppose somebody interviewed Edwin Snider; would anybody recognize that it was Duke? As he says, "How would that song—'Willie, Mickey and the Duke'—have gone over if it was 'Willie, Mickey and Edwin'?"

One of the very best-looking outfielders I ever saw was Fred Lynn when he was Rookie of the Year and MVP at the same time in Boston.

When he got to Baltimore later, he told me that baseball came too easy to him. "I was always outstanding in school, the big star, and I go to the major leagues and I'm still the big star and I thought, 'What a piece of cake this is,' but I found out it's not so easy."

He could do it all. A spectacular player.

Cal Senior had great respect for Lynn's work habits in spring training. Ankles taped every day, he went at it 100 percent, following his own plan. One spring they moved him to right field. I go out early to the ballpark in Miami and I see a screen set up at third base facing right field. Here comes Lynn with a bag of baseballs. He goes out to right field and practices throwing the ball against the wall and playing the rebound, then throwing to third from every possible place in right field. Learning a new position, nobody had to tell him what to do.

Larry Sheets was a first round draft choice ahead of Cal Junior. Power hitter, poor fielder. Twice in the minors he got homesick and quit. I questioned his commitment to being away from home and family, but he had some good years here, and later played in Japan. So I guess that shows how wrong I was.

Attitude counts for a lot in success. The Orioles have had a few outfielders who came up and had all the tools, but did not really care enough. Attitude plays a more important part than people think. Why do you see some unbelievably great athletes who have all this talent and don't do the job, while other guys with very little natural ability get the job done. Can it be attitude?

I see guys forget every day that they are basically playing a little boys' game. Roy Campanella was right when he said, "To play this game, you have to be a man, but you have to have a lot of little boy in you."

Some guys don't forget it. They know it beats working for a living.

4

Eddie
and Boog

For 25 of their first 35 years, the Orioles were blessed with two outstanding first basemen they developed: Eddie Murray and Boog Powell.

I've been an Eddie Murray fan since the first time I saw him when he showed up at spring training as a non-roster player and just lit up the sky.

Now I'm going to get a little—what do I want to say, not offensive, and certainly not defensive, maybe belligerent—but this is my book and I want to get this off my chest and on the record.

Every time some Baltimore writer called Eddie "a cancer in the clubhouse"—and they were still doing it even at the start of the 1994 season, when he had been away from the Orioles for five years—it sends my blood pressure through the roof.

First of all, nothing could be farther from the truth.

Second, it's a terrible phrase, a thoughtless, offhand reference to a disease that has caused so much anguish to so many people.

Third, some of the guys who wrote it never saw Eddie play, never talked to him once in their lives, and never bothered to ask any of the other players how they felt about him. They just flat out don't know what they are talking about.

If any of these guys can bring me a quote from somebody in the game that is negative about Eddie Murray, I want to hear it. The only people who ever knock him are media people. Why is that? I have never heard a player, coach or manager knock him. Ever.

I'd say it's because Eddie doesn't talk to the Baltimore media, and that offends them. That's all. Eddie's very touchy; he is not a trusting person. It has nothing to do with black/white stuff. He is just very self-conscious of everything he does, and is always wary and guarded. Once upon a time he did not like some columns written about him, and he did not trust writers after that. Eddie came from the Watts section of Los Angeles. Many of his friends were in jail or dead. He said, "If I didn't have this talent, there's no telling where I'd be."

I'm not saying he was right. He and I talked about it many times, and I would beg him to do a few interviews every year. But he refused. I understand it, but I don't condone it.

Eddie could never understand all the attention he got. To him, if he struck out four times and made four errors in a game, or he hit four grand slams in a game, he thought he was supposed to be treated the same. He never grasped the difference it made to the media, because to him he was the same guy whichever kind of day he had. He could not accept the adulation and stuff that went with the territory.

Let me tell you how Eddie and I got close. The Orioles were in Oakland. I was sitting by myself in a coffee shop in the hotel. Eddie came in and sat down with me and said, "I've been wanting to talk to you about Jackie Robinson. Can you tell me some things about him?"

So I told him some of the gory stories about how Jackie had been treated.

"I didn't realize that," Eddie said. "I had to play in Bluefield and Asheville and Charlotte and I thought I was treated badly, but nothing like that."

I loaned him a book about Jackie; he read it and told me, "I understand some things a little better now."

He was interested enough and thorough enough to look into it and learn. But nobody gives him that kind of credit. If certain people read this, they'll think I'm lying because I like Eddie.

I don't think he ever liked Earl Weaver. Earl tried to get him into conversations, but Eddie did not want to talk to him. There's only been one way to handle Eddie—and I told Jeff Torborg when Eddie went to the Mets: just leave him alone. Put his name on the lineup card every day—unless he tells you he can't play (and he'd have to have a broken leg to do that)—and he'll play and he'll produce.

Lee May was the Orioles first baseman when Eddie came up in 1977. So Eddie was the DH that year. The following spring they switched jobs. And who do you think taught Eddie more about how to be a big leaguer than anybody? Lee May.

Eddie was a very good first baseman. I never saw him fail to make the play. But his critics, the guys who couldn't handle his not talking to them, wrote, "He never gets his uniform dirty...he never dives for a ball...Eddie never does this...Eddie never does that..."

I see a lot of guys who get their uniforms dirty diving all the time, but they know they're never going to get to the ball most of the time. I'd rather not see them diving for a ball that they know they can't reach.

Anyhow, one night right after they had written all that stuff, Eddie stole third base sliding. He scored on a short fly ball and slid into home, got up with dirt all over his uniform and a big grin all over his face, as if to say, "Well, I hope everybody saw that."

But he wouldn't talk about it after the game.

No matter how many times I tried to get him to put an end to all that by holding two or three press conferences a year, he would not do it. Maybe it was because he tried it once. He became fairly friendly with Richard Justice, who wrote for the *Baltimore Sun*, then went to the *Washington Post*. Evidently Justice put something in the paper one day, supposedly quoting Eddie, and Eddie exploded inside and from then on he shut everybody off.

One of his complaints was, "There's only one newspaper. You talk to one guy and he tells other writers and they all write against you and that's it. You can't go to five guys, and maybe three get it right and two don't. You tell one, and that's it."

He didn't like that. I don't like it, either.

In the clubhouse, Eddie was one of the most popular players I have ever known here in Baltimore, as a man and a player, more so than the fans will ever know unless they take it from me. He was not a talker, not a clubhouse lawyer.

In California Eddie would come into the clubhouse with huge slabs of ribs his mother cooked. But that's not unusual. A lot of teams have somebody who brings some favorite recipe from his mom or a product they endorse to share. When Jim Palmer started doing commercials for Jockey, all the players received stuff without asking for it. Players are more giving than the media wants to let people know.

One of Eddie's close friends was Rick Dempsey. Remember Dempsey's band? Look at a photo of them; who's playing the drums, behind the dark glasses? Eddie.

But his closest friend on the team, and the one guy who could stifle all that "cancer in the clubhouse" garbage once and for all, was Cal Ripken, Jr. They hit it off from the moment Junior came up to the Orioles. Everything Lee May had taught Eddie, Eddie passed along to Cal: how to dress, how to act, what to do as a major league player. But don't ask Eddie about it; he'll say he didn't do anything.

When Eddie signed with the Indians in 1994, the first time they came to Baltimore, who were the two guys standing out near home plate visiting for about ten minutes after batting practice? Eddie and Cal. (Of course, that kind of fraternizing couldn't happen in the old days. Leo Durocher would be yelling, "Go ahead and kiss him!" and the umpires would report you and it would cost you 50.)

Otherwise, Eddie's closest friends connected with the Orioles were non-players: the trainer, Ralph Salvon, and the current PR director, Dr. Charles Steinberg.

Eddie was unbelievable with kids. I've seen him with the children of other players, and club employees. He was that way all around the league, with clubhouse boys and batboys.

"Uncle Eddie! Uncle Eddie!" They all ran to him. He always had time for those kids. On the field he'd go over and talk to kids in the stands. If adults came running for autographs, he'd probably turn and walk away. That's not right, but that's Eddie.

Some umpires called Eddie difficult, antagonistic, possessed of "fetishes about where umpires should be" on the field, according to Umpire Dave Phillips. Eddie was portrayed by a former American League umpire as "the kind of guy who is going to argue a called second strike in the ninth inning of a blowout game his club is about to wrap up."

He had what the *New York Times* called "celebrated antagonistic relations with (umpires) Ken Kaiser and Steve Palermo."

Sure, Eddie asked the umpires to move out of his line of vision when he was up at bat, and he did it more than other guys. But what's wrong with that? Steve Palermo told me Eddie never used profanity; you just had to understand him and leave him alone. Every Orioles manager remembers those funny looks Eddie would give the umps, but so what?

I did see Ken Kaiser throw Eddie out of a game because Eddie imitated him. He would stand there with his arms folded across his chest the way Kaiser did, or mimic Kaiser's tiny "out" motion with his thumb. Never said a word. But the ump claimed Eddie was trying to show him up.

Eddie would give me two interviews a year, one in spring training and one later in the season. I always left it up to him to decide when he wanted to do it. He wouldn't talk to any other radio or TV or press people, and of course that not only made him a bad guy, but it made me suspect, too. A lot of those media guys look down on me, but it doesn't bother me.

In 1988 it was obvious that Eddie was finished in Baltimore. The owner, Edward Bennett Williams, and he had a falling out. There's no question about that. Richard Justice wrote a column in the *Sun*, all quotes from Williams, just crucifying Eddie. Didn't like his attitude, his work habits, how he didn't work out in the wintertime. Just really nailed Eddie, who is very sensitive.

The next night I'm working Home Team Sports TV, and it's raining, so I go down to the dugout to interview the groundskeeper or anybody else I can find. We're off the air and Eddie is sitting next to me on the bench. After making sure the mike was not on, he said, "I want to ask you a few things. I understand that Mr. Williams is one of the most brilliant lawyers in the world."

"That's right."

"When Hank Peters or Joe Altobelli get on me about playing, I understand that. I accept that. But what gives that guy, who's been in baseball two or three years, the right to tell me what to do or how to do my job? I don't tell him how to be a lawyer."

He had a point.

On the last day of the season—his last as an Oriole—Eddie agreed to do his last half-hour interview with me for HTS. We met at 9:30 Sunday morning at Memorial Stadium. When word got out that we were going to be taping at that time, media people from all over were there to see it, and Williams came up from Washington. It was some scene.

Before we started, I told Eddie, "I might ask you some things you don't like but if I do, just tell me you don't care to answer that, or say 'No comment' and we'll go on to the next subject."

The HTS guys were screaming in my ear, "Ask him this...ask him that..." But I ignored them. I ask what I want to know, and what the fans want to know. Eddie answered everything I asked him, and never pulled any punches about anything.

He said that one of the things that bothered him was that the team kept bringing guys up from the minor leagues "and I read about how good they are, and then they get here and they don't do the job."

I asked him what other problems he had with the city. He mentioned a recent game in which Scott McGregor had had a bad first inning and the fans booed him. He said something like this: "Scott McGregor, who has given so much to this team and this city, and is such a nice man, got booed off the mound before the first inning was over. I don't understand that. And I don't think the fans understand or appreciate things like that. I could take it, but they should never do something like that to somebody like McGregor."

(The next day they wrote things like, "Eddie doesn't understand why they boo him.")

Now, game's over. Season's over. The media descend on him in the clubhouse. "Eddie! Eddie! How about talking?" And Eddie, he could burn your shorts off, the way he looked at you.

"No interviews."

"You talked to Rex for half an hour," they protested.

"He's a friend of mine," Eddie said. "You and I haven't talked in years and I'm not going to start now."

Some guys figured that HTS must have paid him to do my interview. The whole episode didn't make it any chummier between me and the rest of those guys. But that's okay.

That winter Eddie was traded to the Dodgers, later went to the Mets, and didn't talk to the newspaper guys there, either. Then, in the winter of '93, he and Dennis Martinez became free agents and signed with Cleveland. The Orioles wanted both of them in the worst way, but their agent, Ron Shapiro, steered them to Cleveland.

I got to spend about ten minutes with Eddie in Florida. I said, "I hear you've let up in Cleveland with the press guys."

"Yeah," he said. "I've gotten a little different reception there, and you know I like John Hart (Indians general manager who was in the Orioles organization)."

To me, Eddie is the ultimate DH; hits with power from both sides and drives in runs. He was the most durable, consistent clutch hitter and player and Orioles have had since Brooks.

And don't you think it was a thrill for me to announce him the first time Cleveland came to Camden Yards in May, '94? I knew the fans would give Eddie a big ovation and the "Ed-die Ed-die" chant. And don't you know that same old "cancer in the clubhouse" line was dragged out again in the newspaper?

So what was this "poison" doing when I saw him in the Cleveland clubhouse before a game? Sitting, relaxed, talking hitting, and laughing with the Indians' young players and the batboy and the clubhouse boy.

But when the Baltimore writers approached him, he said, "Go away. You know better than to ask."

That's Eddie.

Boog Powell probably loves life as much as anybody I've ever known, and that includes before, during and after his playing days.

Next to Eddie Murray, he is the best first baseman the Orioles have had.

He is so outgoing, and always pleasant to be around. I've often thought the good Lord took care of people like Boog by not making him mean and surly, somebody who would go into bars and beat up everybody.

On that last day at Memorial Stadium in 1991, when he walked out on the field and I was in the hospital watching on television, it was like the sun came out again. The fans chanted, "Boog Boog" like they always did. And he joked, "At the tail end of my career in Baltimore, I never heard many Gs on that 'Boog'."

He used to get some criticism; he had a thumb injury one time and couldn't play, and people would say, "Pellington of the Colts plays with a broken arm. Why can't a big, strong guy like Boog play with a bad thumb?" They forgot that Pellington didn't have to go up there and hit. With Boog, you could have taped up that thumb and made him a tackle on some team and he'd have done the job. But take a tackle and ask him to swing a bat with a bad thumb, and what do you think he could do? Nothing.

I used to tell other players that Boog was as close to Johnny Mize as anybody I'd ever seen, and a lot of them didn't know what I was talking about. They never saw Mize, who was the best-looking hitter I ever saw. Letter perfect. Boog was like that. MVP in 1970. They don't get much better than that.

The first time I saw Boog Powell he was playing in a high school championship tournament in Ft. Pierce, Florida. I was living in Vero Beach, about 14 miles away, so I went to the game. I saw a lot of scouts I knew, and I asked them, "What are you guys looking for?"

"The pitcher, George Mira," who was also some kind of quarterback.

But I noticed the big blond kid playing right field for Key West. John Wesley Powell. Hit a couple home runs in a preliminary game, but was only 2 for 13 or something in the tournament. Boog, they called him; one of his brothers had called him Booger from the time they were little. He was a lineman on the football team, too. When they needed a yard or two, they gave the ball to Boog, and he ran over the top of the other team.

Later Boog told me that tournament cost him $100,000. It seems Atlanta offered him a bonus of $120,000 if he didn't play.

They didn't want to get into a bidding war if other scouts saw him and wanted him. He turned them down and, after the tournament, they offered him nothing. The Orioles came up with about $20,000 and that's what he signed for. Baltimore fans couldn't have been happier.

Boog's official weight was 260, but I know he went to spring training weighing closer to 300 one year. I thought he was huge until Frank Howard showed up. Once Chuck Thompson and I were doing an exhibition game in Florida on radio. Boog was playing first base and Howard got on base. We looked at those two standing together and I said to Chuck, "Imagine what would happen if those two guys were mean."

Chuck laughed and said, "No, I don't want to imagine."

Both of them are the meekest, mildest, most likable gentlemen you'll ever meet.

Boog played the outfield when he first came up because the Orioles had a guy named Diamond Jim Gentile playing first. I was still with the Dodgers when they signed Gentile. The Dodgers wanted to make him an outfielder, but he didn't want to play the outfield. He wanted to play first base, but he had a problem—a guy named Gil Hodges was already there.

Paul Richards took an interest in him and picked him up for the Orioles. Jim was six foot three, and could stretch for throws better than anybody. A great fielder, unbelievable swing, lots of talent, handsome guy, but his own worst enemy. He just thought he should be perfect all the time. He would sulk and get down on himself when he didn't do everything well. He'd get so upset with himself, you'd be scared what he was going to do.

Jim took such a big swing, catchers used to catch a little farther back when he was up. He'd hit them on the back of the head with the bat on his follow-through. He had a callous on his own back from swinging the bat against it.

Jim could have had more of a career than he did, but was that some year he had in 1961? Hit .302, 46 home runs, 141 RBI. Hit two grand slams in one inning. You can't do much better than that. Maybe he tried to live on those laurels after that.

Lee May was the first baseman when I arrived in Baltimore. Lee had been in the National League for a long time before that.

He was well-liked around both leagues.

Then Eddie Murray arrived. Every year, year in and year out, every major league manager goes through hell during the last week of spring training. I'll bet that none of them sleeps during the last three days. How do you get down to 27 or 28 players, then have to cut some more to get to 25? The manager is the one who has to make the decisions and tell the players involved.

Earl Weaver told me the one thing he could not handle was releasing or sending a player down. I was in his office when Hank Peters came in and said, "If you are going to cut Lee May, you are the one who has to tell him."

Earl said, "I can't do it. You do it." Now this is that same coarse Earl Weaver who never gave a player a pat on the back or a kind word.

Peters said, "You're the manager. It's your job."

"Give me a few days."

"Okay, but you've got to do it."

That night in pregame practice, Eddie was taking ground balls. One came up and hit him in the eye. He couldn't play. Lee May's going to play. Hit two home runs. That ended the story about who's going to tell Lee May he's gone. They kept him the rest of the year.

I have so much respect for Lee May. Everybody did.

Among the other first basemen who played here briefly, Jim Traber was one of those guys who started out like a house on fire, then fell off. Frank Robinson summed him up best: he's a good player, but not as good as he thinks he is. When that appeared in the papers, it tore Jim up. He had a fair year, lined up a few endorsements, came to spring training out of shape. He had it made, he thought. Went to Japan and tried a comeback with Cleveland. Ever since Cecil Fielder did it, that seems to be the trend.

Johnny Oates was high on Randy Milligan. He could have made a trade for a pitcher, but he refused to include Milligan in the deal, because he was wary of Glenn Davis's condition. He was right about that. I felt sorry for Davis. He never did get straightened out here. I was hoping he would make the Mets, but he just didn't get the job done during spring training in '94. He signed with Omaha as a DH.

David Segui is a great kid. He faded in the last month of the '93 season because he had never played a full season every day. He is a little overanxious at the plate with men on base, and can be violent in the dugout when he strikes out with men on base. The whole dugout goes to the other end away from him; he is so intense, he'll throw bats and helmets around. I think if you had a batting cage open 24 hours a day, he'd be in it 24 hours a day. A good fielder but slow runner, he'll have to hit 20 to 25 home runs and drive in 85 runs to hold that position in the major leagues. I was happy to see him get a chance to play every day with the Mets. I like David very much and hope he does well.

5

2B or Not 2B

I n my opinion, the best second baseman the Orioles have had
was Bobby Grich. It's too bad it was for such a short time—
five years. Then they lost him as a free agent.

He could play second base, no question, very smooth in the
field. At the plate he hit a lot of home runs for a second baseman,
and could hit and run, hit behind the runner, whatever you
needed. A tough guy, but a popular one. You know how some
players just stand out above the rest. If you went to a game, hav-
ing never seen any of the players, and you saw these guys, you'd
think, "That guy out there looks like he's better than everybody
else." Not that Grich was, but boy, he was a ballplayer.

Bobby had great knowledge of the game, and didn't make
mental mistakes, or errors of omission, as Branch Rickey, my
mentor when he was GM of the Brooklyn Dodgers, used to say.

A very up person, friendly, and very Southern California,
with the blond hair, good looks, surfboard stuff. They used to
kid him about being a typical Californian; he never let it get to
him.

Grich was never a big Earl Weaver fan. He had a feeling
that Earl never really liked him, and held him back when he first
came up. I didn't think it ever made any difference with Earl
whether or not he liked you. If you were the best he had, you

played.

For a long time, the Orioles reminded me of the old Dodgers. Mr. Rickey got rid of the clubhouse lawyers and the troublemakers. The Orioles did, too. It's not because I'm prejudiced about the Orioles that I bring all this up. (I do admit to being prejudiced about the old Dodgers, but you know that.) I'm telling you the exact truth as I remember it about these guys. As we go over each one, it jogs my memory. And those guys in the '70s just fit.

Grich and Palmer became close friends. Nobody knows why; they just were. And I've told you about Grich and Baylor and how close they were.

Grich was followed by Richie Dauer, one of the most lovable, enjoyable kids I have known. I know this is getting to sound like a broken record, but, my God, Richie Dauer! He'll be 50 years old when he's 115. His enthusiasm for the game, for life— he's like a little kid.

He's about the only player Earl Weaver ever liked, but if you don't like Richie Dauer, there's something wrong with you.

His name is Rich. Everybody in the world calls him Rich except me. He heard one of the press box ushers call me Rexer one day, and he started calling me Rexer, so I said to him, "Okay, Richie." That started it. Many years later, he's coaching third base for Cleveland. The first night they come to Baltimore, I announce, "For Cleveland, coaching at third base, number 24, RICHIE Dauer." He just about collapsed.

Later he told me, "You're the only guy in the world I'd ever let call me Richie." I don't care; the name fits him very well.

Dauer couldn't run very well, but he'd give you everything he's got. Get hit by a pitch to get on base, do whatever it took. He helped everybody, kidded and teased, but could take it in return. A lot of guys can dish it out, but can't take it. He could. They called him "Whacko," and it was an honor for him to have that nickname.

Rick Burleson only played with us for about a year, after a long career as a shortstop at Boston and California. One of the toughest guys around, but a nice guy. I liked him especially. He and Jerry Remy played together at Boston; they could imitate me better than any other players. From the introductions to the temperature at game time, they had it down to perfection.

Burleson played hard his whole career. If he could throw you out by 30 feet or three feet, it didn't make any difference. He threw as hard as he could. But he had a bad arm when he came here; he went to the front office and told them, "I can't do it anymore."

Davey Johnson was a very good second baseman, too, from 1966 to 1972. He was one of the first guys I ever heard talk about computers. A brilliant guy, he went to some computer school here while he was playing. But common sense—not one drop. He could sit and talk about computers, and the percentage of balls hit to his left or right, and how to play baseball games out on the computer, but he didn't seem to have a grasp on everyday life.

Davey was a hypochondriac. Weaver would tell me, "If he comes in complaining, he'll probably give me the best night of his life." Davey always had something wrong with him: a finger, an arm, a hand. He got caught in the lawn mower, or he got bumped by a piece of furniture that fell over—something was always happening to Davey Johnson

They called him "Luke," after Luke Appling, Old Aches and Pains, who complained every day of his life while he played his way into the Hall of Fame. Like Appling, Davey always played, and he had some great years here. Popular with the players, who figured he'd end up as a coach or manager, which he did. Still using those computers.

Bill Ripken is a good player, but again that old saying, "Not as good as he thinks he is." Good defensive player. I didn't say great. He's one of those players who gives you everything he's got, but how much does he have? He dives after everything, gets big ovations for doing that. But if the play's not made it doesn't mean very much.

I used to do a show from the Hit and Run Club in Memorial Stadium. We had a little stage there, and I'd bring in a player or coach after a game and interview him, and the fans in there could ask questions. It was very popular with the fans. One time I asked Cal Junior to go on and I said, "How about bringing Bill with you?" Cal said, "Okay, but he's a little different."

And he is, the nonconformist in the Ripken family. No particular reason; he's just that type of guy. In the clubhouse he's very up, likes to kid around. He's the one who called Bob Milacki Big Bird. I've known Bill almost all his life. When the Orioles brought him up, he came to me and said, "Uncle Rex, now that I'm in the big leagues, how about calling me Bill instead of Billy. If you call me Bill on the P.A., everybody will pick it up."

So I did. But I asked his father, "What do you call him, Bill or Billy?"

Senior said, "I call him Motormouth." Affectionate description.

I remember when Bill was in the minors and I asked some scouts about him. They all told me, "He'll be a major league player, but may not have the talent to be an everyday player." That was a pretty good assessment. When he came up, we all hoped he could do the job. We were rooting for him. He hit .291 that one year (1990); that's pretty good for a second baseman. But one of his problems was, if he hit one home run, all of a sudden he was going to be like his brother. But he's never going to have power. If he can keep his head on and be more strict with himself, and know he's there to move runners over the best way he can, he could be a better player. But he's got to get that kind of discipline. It's hard for players to do those things today because they see all the big money going for power.

And then there was Baseball Billy Smith, first player to go to arbitration with the Orioles, in 1979. Nobody knows why. He couldn't do much. Pretty good defensive player, but nothing with the bat. Alan Wiggins started as an outfielder, wound up an infielder for San Diego. He could fly; that's one thing he could do. He acquired a terrible reputation, had drug problems, got suspended. The San Diego players did not want him back. Every club in baseball turned him down—except one. Mr. Williams wanted him; he thought the Orioles could straighten out his life. They couldn't. Wiggins was the last player I've seen get picked off with the hidden ball trick. Pete O'Brien's playing first base for Texas. There was a bang-bang play at first and Wiggins slid in and was safe. As he got up, he saw O'Brien's motion to throw the ball to the pitcher. But Pete kept it. Wiggins took a lead off the base, and O'Brien tagged him out. Can you imagine how embarrassing that is?

Nowadays players' schedules are so different from the old days. They don't have a lot of time at night to get into trouble. After the game they have a quick bite to eat, sleep until 10 or 11 in the morning, have a meal, go to the ballpark. Mr. Rickey used to say, "The worst thing that can happen to a ballplayer is to be on the road and have the game rained out. They can get into more trouble in one day and night than most people can in a lifetime."

Alan Wiggins certainly did. He died young.

Jerry Adair was one of the first second basemen I saw here. He was a very hardnosed guy, quiet and tough. A real team player, good guy to have on your club, but not much talent. Good, but not that good. Pete Stanicek was another of the Orioles' Stanford harvests. A good hitter, he would have been the second baseman today, but injuries and health problems cost him his career. Everybody was sorry he didn't make it.

Every winning team needs a guy like Lenn Sakata on the roster. A delightful guy, smiling all the time. Always a favorite in the clubhouse, he would help anybody, go out and pitch early batting practice if somebody wanted to hit. He was Hawaiian, and some guys called him Hirohito, but he didn't mind. Lenn always told me I was mispronouncing his name, no matter how I said it. He never wanted to be interviewed on the air.

When he first showed up with Milwaukee, I thought he was the batboy. Never saw such a skinny, emaciated-looking kid. Then they told me he was the second baseman, and I thought they were kidding. But he built himself up with weights and exercise.

If he played three or four days in a row, you'd see the greatest second base or shortstop you've ever seen. But he could not keep it up every day. Earl realized that. He said, "This kid can really help you. But you've got to know how to use him, because he can hurt you, too."

Lenn was one of the guys they tried at shortstop in 1982 when Cal came up as a third baseman and Bobby Bonner started at short. That's the only year Sakata played in more than 81 games. As a pinch hitter he was .333 lifetime. That's pretty good.

But I remember Lenn Sakata best for his part in one of the all-time legendary things that happened at Memorial Stadium.

The night was August 24, 1983. Sakata was unhappy, complaining about not getting enough playing time. A few days earlier, he had told his agent, Ron Shapiro, "Get me out of here." Shapiro went to the Orioles and told them how Sakata felt. They said, "We'll see what we can do when the season's over."

Now Toronto's in town. Cruz starts at third base, Dauer at second. Dempsey's catching.

In the seventh, Dwyer pinch hits for Cruz; Joe Nolan pinch hits for Dempsey, and takes over the catching in the eighth, while Dauer moves to third and Sakata comes off the bench to play second.

In the ninth Ayala pinch hits for Nolan, but the inning ends with the score tied, 3-3. Earl has no catchers left. Sakata had caught a few innings in spring training, as Earl wanted somebody to be able to go in in case of "emergencies." Now the emergency was here. John Lowenstein comes in from left field to play second, and Lenn's the catcher.

Sakata comes out in all that catching gear; he's so little it hangs on him like he's a three-year-old. Tim Stoddard is pitching. The first man up, Cliff Johnson, hits a home run and Toronto takes a 4-3 lead. When Bonnell singles, Earl brings in Tippy Martinez. Tippy comes in, looks at his catcher, looks around the infield, doesn't recognize anybody but Eddie Murray at first base. He promptly picks off Bonnell.

Collins pinch hits for Barfield and walks. He takes a wide lead off first, and Tippy picks him off.

Upshaw singles. Takes a lead. Tippy picks him off. Picked off three straight guys for all three outs in the inning. Later he said he "thought" he balked once. He thought—that means he balked. You can bet on it.

The next day I asked the Toronto manager, Bobby Cox, how he could get three guys picked off. He said, "I'll tell you one reason. Sakata was setting up so far behind home plate, he'd never get the ball to second base. I figured we could run all night. So I had them all taking big leads."

Sakata caught a total of six pitches in his one and only big league inning as a catcher.

But wait. If that was the end of the story, this would be Tippy's story, not Lenn's. In the last of the tenth, after Ripken homers to tie it again, who comes up with two on and two out and hits a home run to win it? Lenn Sakata.

Afterwards he said, "I didn't want to catch anymore, so I figured I'd better do something to end it."

6

Brooks and the Others

It may seem strange to you that I am starting out this discussion of third basemen by talking about Doug DeCinces, when the whole world knows that this chapter belongs to Brooks Robinson. But I think Doug's story might help to put Brooks in perspective.

Doug DeCinces was a very good third baseman in the wrong place at the worst possible time. Nobody was ever more underappreciated in Baltimore. It wasn't his fault; it wasn't the fans' fault. But you follow a Brooks Robinson and you're in trouble. I don't care how great you were, and Doug wasn't great, but he was a very good ballplayer, and the best third baseman in the league except perhaps for Graig Nettles.

Good arm, good hands, good power, knew the game. But I don't care if it was the most impossible play in the world, every time Doug went after a ball and didn't get it, people would start yelling, "Brooks would have had it." Doug went through life in Baltimore with that. His timing was terrible. If he could have been here five or six years after Brooks, he'd have been recognized as one of the best that the Orioles ever had. They haven't had anybody better since then.

The only guy the fans might have accepted in that position was Cal Junior. Doug was traded to California for Dan Ford because Cal was ready to take over. Then he moved to shortstop and, ever since, the hot corner has been like a revolving door. But at least I don't hear, "Brooks would have had it" anymore.

The players called DeCinces "The Horn." You could tell his nose had been broken a few times.

One of the greatest shows of affection I have ever seen was when Brooks retired and they had a day for him where they gave him a car and other stuff. At the last moment, here comes Doug DeCinces out of the dugout. He picks up third base—the bag—and takes it and presents it to Brooks without saying a word. The crowd went crazy; everybody got the message: "Here you are, Brooks. I'm the third baseman now, but this really belongs to you. You own it."

I like a lot of guys, as you can tell. You're probably tired of hearing me talk about how delightful and popular so many guys were. But Brooks Robinson is one I regarded as a saint of a person, on and off the field.

Brooks had been in Baltimore for about 10 years before I came to stay. I had heard a lot about him but had not seen him play. The first time I saw him I thought, "This can't be the guy I've heard so much about." I thought he was going to fall down walking. He had no coordination at all. I quickly found out that his first couple of steps were the quickest you could imagine. And that's all you need at third base.

I also learned that when Paul Richards had his first look at Brooks, he told Hall of Famer George Kell, "He's going to be a dandy, better than you were."

Does that tell you maybe Mr. Richards knew a little bit more about judging ballplayers than I did?

Brooks knew all about me. He told me, "I remember when you played for the Dodgers. The closest major league club to Little Rock was the Cardinals, so we used to go to St. Louis to watch them. I was a big Stan Musial fan. But there was a guy in Brooklyn I liked more than anybody—Bruce Edwards." He just liked the way Bruce did everything. Well, since Bruce was one of my favorites, too—he caught my no-hitter—that impressed me.

I didn't think I'd ever see anybody better at playing third than Billy Cox of the old Dodgers. But I learned to believe. Comparing those two is a terrible thing to do, because physically they were so different. Cox was a skinny little guy, slightly stoop-shouldered, but with an unbelievable arm. He'd throw every runner out by one step. Didn't matter if it was the world's slowest or the world's fastest—one step. He'd stand there and hold the ball, look at it, then throw the guy out. Drove Gil Hodges crazy. He caught everything that was hit near him, and made Pee Wee Reese's job a lot easier.

Brooks was just the quickest thing I've ever seen. Those first two steps did it all. But I teased him for years. He'd say to me, "A lot of people tell me about Billy Cox, but you're the only guy I know who played with him. Am I as good as Cox?"

And I always said, "Never. How could you be as good as Cox?"

In the famous "Brooks Robinson World Series" of 1970, when he made all those diving plays, catching everything in sight, throwing guys out, we were in the clubhouse after a game and he's surrounded by writers and he yells, "Hey, Rex. Better than Cox?"

I said, "No way. Billy Cox wouldn't be diving. He'd be catching them standing on his feet."

Brooks turned to the writers and shook his head. "He won't let me get ahead of Cox."

After another game in that Series the writers were looking for him. No Brooks. "What do you need him for?" I said. "You should be over there interviewing his glove. That's the thing that's doing the job."

Brooks would put up with that kind of humor. I knew he was better than Billy Cox, but I wasn't about to make it easy for him by admitting it to him. Until now.

During that '70 Series between Cincinnati and the Orioles, there was a day off after the first two games. The Reds used it to practice in Memorial Stadium. Lee May was with the Reds then, and I'm standing behind the batting cage while he's hitting. He hits a shot by third base and I hear him say, "Catch that one, Brooks, you son of a bitch."

Did he make an impression in those first two games, or what?

The Reds used artificial turf and the Orioles played on grass.

Before the Series somebody asked Brooks, "Do you think that will make a difference to you?"

Brooks said, "I don't know why. If you're a major league player, you should be able to play in the parking lot and be better than anybody else."

Pretty good theory.

There were only two times that I heard Brooks say anything that was the least bit on the bragging side. In Miami, spring training '71. They're showing the players the World Series films one night in the clubhouse. I'm standing in the back of the room. Dave McNally and Brooks are sitting in front of me. Curt Gowdy is narrating all those great Brooks plays. All of a sudden Brooks hits Mac and says, "You know something, Mac? I'm a hell of a player." And Mac says, "Yeah, you are." End of conversation.

Another time, he's in broadcasting. We're in Yankee Stadium. Just a pane of glass separates the radio from the television guys. Chuck Thompson and Brooks are doing TV; I was doing radio. We're shoulder to shoulder, except for that glass. Graig Nettles makes one hell of a play, but just misses throwing the guy out at first.

The inning's over, and Chuck says, "Brooks, that was some kind of play Nettles made."

Brooks says, "That's right, big boy. But I want to tell you one thing: there's only one guy in the world would have made that play, and you're sitting next to him."

Unknown to him, the mikes were live, and it went out over the air. Brooks was embarrassed. But he was telling the truth.

A couple years later in Texas Cal Ripken hit for the cycle, and Chuck asked Brooks if anybody else with the O's ever hit for the cycle. "Not that I know of," said Brooks, and Chuck said, "You did."

"I did?" Brooks said. "I must be pretty good."

He'd come into the press dining room: "Make way. Hall of Famer's here." All in fun. There is no pretense about Brooks.

Brooks always got to the ballpark very early. He answered all his fan mail, every bit of it. Come playoff time, World Series, he would get his tickets and stuff the envelopes himself and give them to people.

A lot of fans didn't recognize him when he came to the ballpark. He was always the worst-looking mess you've ever seen. Looked like he'd just painted four houses. Dark glasses, hat pulled down.

When the game was over, by the time the bullpen people got to the clubhouse, he'd be on his way out the door, showered, dressed and gone.

On the road he had friends everywhere. You'd see him sitting in the hotel lobby, talking to people. He had no interests outside of the game. Later he took up golf.

The game was the thing with him, yet when he got out of it, he never missed it. Just walked away from it. Very few guys can do that. He was in broadcasting for a while, but when that stopped, he didn't miss it. He was a player, nothing else. Great baseball sense, but didn't study the game. We've talked about some players you could see were going to be coaches or managers; you could see that he wouldn't stay in the game. He didn't talk baseball, was not into the strategy. Just did his job.

He might be hurt, but it was rough to get him out of the lineup. If you look up his record, you know he hardly missed a game. And that was just fine with the rest of the team, because if he was not in the game he was a nervous wreck and drove everybody else crazy. Paced up and down, kicked and carried on, screaming and yelling. They'd make him go to the bullpen or anywhere but the dugout, just to get rid of him.

He was that way away from the game, too. One time we pulled into the train station in New York, got off and went up to the street to get on the team bus to the hotel. No bus.

"Where's the bus?"

"Right down there at that red light."

Brooks says, "I can't wait for that," and jumps in a cab. Can't wait five seconds for anything.

If you sit down to eat with Brooks, he can demolish a six-course meal before you get your soup down. Could wipe out an entire carton of nachos during a commercial break.

One time he threw out the first ball at a World Series game. A writer asked him, "Brooks, after you throw out the first ball, could I talk to you for a few minutes?"

Brooks said, "Sorry. Before the ball hits the catcher's glove, I'll be in my car, gone."

We're driving from Baltimore to Washington one night to a meeting of the Major League Baseball Players Alumni Association. Brooks is now president of that group. Another former Oriole, Joe Durham, is driving. I'm in the back seat. Brooks is in front. Suddenly I hear this flip flop. Flat tire. It's the dead of winter, cold windy night.

"It's all right," Brooks says. "Don't worry about a thing."

We get out.

"I'll fix it," he says. "Joe, get the spare out. Give me that wrench. Rex, hold my toupee on. I don't want to lose that."

I'm glad it was dark, because if the world had seen us, we'd never have heard the end of it.

I think that phrase, "what you see is what you get," was coined for Brooks Robinson.

He had no superstitions of any kind that I know. He used that one glove for what seemed like forever. It's in the Hall of Fame now. I think he had the leather changed in the pocket a few times. A lot of players have favorite gloves or bats and they protect them. Not him. He'd come in and throw it in the locker. If it's there, fine. If it's not, he'll find another one.

He would take part in practical jokes, but he never hurt anyone. He was so popular, I think people took great advantage of him, but I don't think he cared. He would autograph for hours. I've seen the team bus ready to leave and everybody yelling, "Let's go," and he'd stand there signing until the very last kid left. He'd say, "Line up like gentlemen, and I'll take care of all of you. Make sure you say 'please' and 'thank you'."

There's a great painting by Norman Rockwell that shows Brooks autographing left-handed. Everybody knows Brooks is a third baseman, so he couldn't be left-handed. Rockwell told Brooks he got more critical mail about that apparent goof than anything else he ever painted. But Brooks does everything left-handed except play baseball. (Rick Dempsey's the same way.)

Brooks looked forward to All-Star Games, the World Series, big events like that, and he excelled in them, but he didn't push himself any more than he did every day. He just did what he

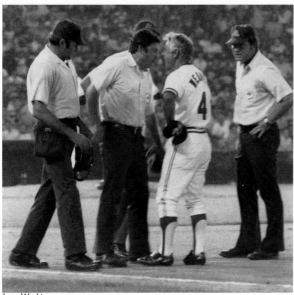

The only thing Earl Weaver liked better than arguing with one umpire was taking on four of them.

Johnny Oates began the '94 season with high hopes.

Earl and Billy Martin respected each other and enjoyed matching wits.

Paul Blair on a routine day at the office. Merv Rettenmund watching.

Eddie Murray about to pull the trigger.

Boog Powell and George Staller try a little friendly persuasion on Emmett Ashford.

Bobby Grich—the best second baseman the Orioles ever had.

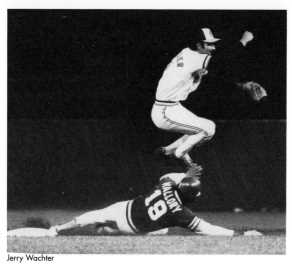

Mark Belanger goes for two.

Jerry Wachter

Doug DeCinces— almost as good as Brooks. If a ball got by him, everybody yelled, "Brooks would've had it!"

Jerry Wachter

I told Brooks that Billy Cox would have gotten this one without diving for it.

This infield—Brooks, Belanger, Davey Johnson, and Boog—made Orioles pitchers look good.

Junior is as efficient a shortstop as the game has ever seen.

Coaching at third base, Cal Senior never stopped teaching Junior—or any other Oriole.

Jerry Wachter

Rick Dempsey

Rick Dempsey's Invisible Orioles Magic Band in 1986 featured, from left, Mike Boddicker, guitar; Eddie Murray, drums; Dempsey; Rich Bordi, bass guitar, and Ralphie Salvon, keyboard and saxophone.

Is Rick Dempsey mad at Earl about something? Does the sun come up every morning?

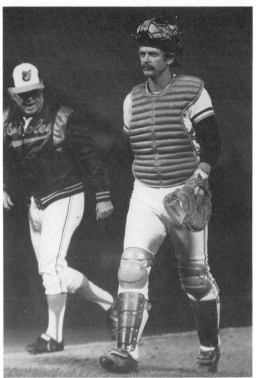

Jerry Wachter

Jerry Wachter

Lenn Sakata takes a curtain call after the biggest home run of his life.

Jay Spencer

Mike Cuellar was everything the word "pitcher" really means.

Jay Spencer

Moe Drabowsky was not joking when he was teaching the finer points of pitching.

Bob Miller

Me: "Palmer just thinks *he threw harder than I did." Palmer: "Why should I listen to this guy?"*

Jerry Wachter

A batter's-eye-view of number 22, pitching perfection in motion.

could.

I think he was beaned five times. The worst was when Phil Niekro hit him (when Niekro could still throw pretty hard). It happened in West Palm Beach, and the lights weren't so good, and Brooks just lost sight of the ball. He designed a special helmet, with a very narrow bill and an earflap, and said the narrow bill helped him see the ball better.

In his last year, 1977, he was a player-coach, and pinch hit eight times. One of them was a three-run home run that won a game in the ninth inning. I thought the place was going to go absolutely berserk. Couldn't happen to a nicer guy. There are a lot of cliches about people, but, boy, he lived up to all the good ones.

They gave him a day at the end of the season. There was rain in the air the day before. Somebody said, "I hope the weather clears up for Brooks."

"God takes care of him," I said. "It'll be a bright, beautiful day." And it turned out that way. What do I know? I don't know any more than anybody else. But I just thought, "A guy like this, how could God (or whoever that supreme being is) let him down?"

That rainy day was a Saturday. We're playing Milwaukee. In the ninth inning, George Scott is the hitter. All of a sudden the fans start chanting, "We want Brooks! We want Brooks!" Out of nowhere it started. No Brooks.

Scott goes up to the plate, but the fans keep yelling for Brooks. Scott backs away from the plate. Still no Brooks. I found out later he was in the clubhouse, sound asleep on the trainer's table. They had to put him together, get him dressed. Finally, here he comes out of the dugout, waving to the crowd.

Nothing bothered him. Nothing impressed him. Nothing changed him.

The next day—his day—as he rode around the field, there wasn't a dry eye in that ballpark, including mine. I just couldn't take it. Wait a minute. One dry pair of eyes—Brooks Robinson. He can handle anything. I've never known a guy like him. About as perfect a human being as you can find.

After Doug DeCinces, the Orioles had a string of guys who were going to make the world forget Brooks. I remember when

Weaver brought up Glenn Gulliver from Rochester. I went down to get the lineup and there's his name on it. I'm walking across the field and Glenn's out there, taking grounders. I said, "You better slow down. You're playing today."

He didn't believe me. "You don't just come up here and play the next day."

"You do with this guy," I said.

He did a decent job, but never lit up the sky. Very selective hitter; couldn't run.

Leo Hernandez...Wayne Gross (hit home runs on Sundays and holidays)...Ray Knight. Strange about Ray Knight. MVP of the 1986 World Series with the Mets, but he never got it back after that. The Mets wouldn't give him what he wanted, and the Orioles took him. He had been a good ballplayer, good hitter, pretty good fielder, not a good runner, but on his way down. One of the few modern players who was interested in the oldtimers, the guys who had preceded him in the game.

Jackie Gutierrez...Rick Schu...Craig Worthington...Leo Gomez...I'll talk about Leo when we get to the 1994 team.

7

The Iron Man

This may surprise some people, and I may get some callers who disagree, but on my all-time Orioles defensive team, Mark Belanger is the shortstop, over Aparicio and Cal. No hesitation. That is defense only. Belanger couldn't hit; he could bunt with the best, and run with the best, but you can't make a living on that. Of his 18 years in the major leagues, he had two, maybe three decent years at the plate. Charlie Lau, the batting coach, got through to him temporarily.

But in the field there was none better. Great arm. Tremendous range. Brooks, Palmer, Frank Robinson—guys who played with him a long time—would tell you that on all those great teams we had, all that offense and pitching, Belanger was as much the MVP on those clubs as anybody.

Mark's another one who gives Cal Senior as much credit as anyone for his development. During batting practice, Belanger would stand on the edge of the infield grass at short. Cal stood on the third base side of home plate, very close to Mark, and hit fungos as hard as he could, to the right and left and straight at Mark. Twenty-five, 30, one after the other. People would stop what they were doing to watch. I've never seen Pee Wee Reese or anybody else do that. Then he'd go back to his regular position and take infield practice with everybody else.

Jim Palmer was the traffic director. One day he was on the mound and he motioned Belanger to move a few steps one way or another. Belanger didn't budge. Palmer took a few steps toward him and waved his glove again. Belanger stood like a statue. Palmer threw up his hands and stalked back to the mound. He threw and the batter hit it straight to Belanger. Mark and Palmer ran off the field together, laughing.

Mark never got along with Earl Weaver. Earl had him in Rochester and there was some rhubarb about something to do with Mark not having what it took to be an everyday player. From then on, they just didn't like each other.

But Mark was well-accepted by the other players. They called him "The Blade" because of his build: six foot one, 170 pounds. I called him "The Scale Tester"; he weighed the same all the time. They could set the scales by him.

Mark was elected the player rep. He was a strong union guy; got it from his mother, who was active in a factory union in Massachusetts. Now he works for the Players Association, going to team meetings in spring training, keeping the players informed on what's happening. He kept the Orioles better informed than most player reps.

The young Cal Ripken Junior was an intense observer of Mark Belanger. Cal came up as a third baseman but he knew a good model to study when he saw one. Those lessons proved invaluable when Weaver moved Cal to shortstop over everybody's objections in 1982. A dozen years later, Cal is still there.

Every year, half the media are ready to move him to third. I say if he ever changes position he's going to go to first base. I'd move him there in a minute, if we didn't have a Rafael Palmeiro there, and if I had somebody who could play shortstop as well as Junior does. But not third base. (Manny Alexander has been the shortstop of the future—but when?)

Junior was born with baseball sense. His father taught him a lot, but he learned plenty on his own. I saw him grow up from a little kid hanging around the ballpark. Players used to kick him in the fanny when he got in their way.

He pitched a no-hitter in high school in Aberdeen, and when the Orioles signed him, they weren't sure if he was going to be a pitcher or an infielder. They really left it up to him, and he preferred to play every day. That's become obvious. But that great arm tells you he probably could have made it as a pitcher.

He moved up through the system, and maintained that playing in Bluefield was the most fun he's had in baseball, "because we're all the same at that level. As you go up and up, it gets to be more of a job."

Junior was the Player of the Year two years in a row in the Puerto Rico winter league. Ray Miller was his manager there. He told us then, "This kid can play."

From time to time Junior goes into a batting slump. A few years ago he was having a really rough time, so he went back to Little League basics. He came out early with Senior and hit off the Tee: move it in, out, up, down. He worked on his own, and he's the only guy I've ever seen who could stand flatfooted and hit the ball in the seats. You know how strong you have to be to do that? I mean consistently. I'd be sitting up in the broadcast booth preparing to go to work, and I'd hear WHACK! and knew where it was going.

That's Junior. Work, work, work. He said he got that from his idol, Brooks, watching him and Belanger take all those extra ground balls.

All the success and money has not affected Junior. Sure, he lives better than he did in Aberdeen. Has his own full basketball court, his own gym and exercise room. Some players used to work out in the winter at Hopkins or Towson State. Now they work out at his house.

I'd say Junior has no superstitions. On the field and in the clubhouse, he's one of the players. Never does anything different from everybody else. If you have to be in uniform at five, he may show up five minutes before, but he's in that uniform on time.

He's become a team leader. Guys will go to him, especially the new ones, for help on all sorts of things. Most of them call him Junior.

Cal will do interviews, but he has reached such a high level of visibility in the game, with so many people after him all the time, you get to the point in this business where you don't want to ask him. I don't think any of the modern players will ever be like Brooks or Nolan Ryan, who would stand there autographing for kids in the heat after losing a game. Maybe Cal will do that, too, when he gets older, just out of appreciation for the fans. I tell these younger guys, "You'll miss it, when they stop hanging on you."

I saw a change in Cal after the All-Star Game in 1993. He had been a little down, pouty maybe, because of his father being gone, but when he made the All-Star team, it told him, "You're still an All-Star; you're still Cal," and he picked up and had a good year. His attitude seemed to change, and he showed me a lot in the last half.

Cal's very big in local charities, especially reading. On the road, he reads a lot himself. I don't think he'll become a manager when he's through playing. But he likes the game so much, he could wind up as a broadcaster. He's articulate and bright. He might want to stay in the game, even with a giant cut in salary.

Luis Aparicio was here when I arrived. I saw him with the White Sox and Boston. Definitely Hall of Fame, no question about it. He could do it all. A little guy with a good arm, always popular in the clubhouse. He was the butt of most of Moe Drabowsky's practical jokes for a while, putting snakes in his glove and his locker. When he saw one, he would run for eight miles to get away.

Kiko Garcia was another one of those guys I fell in love with. Hit .400 in the '79 World Series, 4 for 4 in one game with 4 RBI. He was some kind of player, good fielder and everything, but he had chronic back problems and just kind of fell by the wayside. He didn't play that much, but he caught on with the fans and the players.

The only thing I remember about Frank Baker is that he and Larry Brown were roommates, and one night at the Sheraton-Cadillac Hotel in Detroit, they looked out the window and saw fire engines with lights blazing and lots of commotion. They tore out of the room and down the stairs to the street where they found a movie being made.

Rene Gonzales—another six foot three infielder. The Orioles seemed to sign nothing but six-footers for a while. He wanted number 8, but when he saw it on Junior he knew he wouldn't get it, so he took the next best thing—88.

As a youngster, Gonzo had a job taking tickets at the bleachers in Los Angeles. Whenever Fernando Valenzuela pitched, he'd let all the Mexicans into the park for a buck each. "I made more money when Fernando pitched than he did," Gonzo told me.

He had magnificent hands, a good arm, but couldn't hit. When he filled in, the infield defense never suffered. Didn't play much, but he was never down. Gonzo became a fan favorite, and one of mine. Everybody was rooting for him to hit better. He played wherever he was asked, and warmed up the pitcher before an inning if the catcher wasn't ready.

My favorite Orioles over the years are the big guys, like everybody else, but I always loved Rene Gonzales, Richie Dauer, Lenn Sakata. Those guys just fascinated the hell out of me. They get pushed aside, but they are always there to do something to help you. Every club has to have them; if you don't, you're in trouble.

They deserve to be remembered.

8

The Men in the Iron Mask

Every organization seems to have one position where they just never develop their own talent. For the Orioles, it was catchers. Except for Andy Etchebarren and Elrod Hendricks, none of the guys who caught a substantial number of games for them came up through their minor league system.

I think the best all-around catcher the Orioles ever had was Gus Triandos—until Chris Hoiles. A lot of people say Hoyt Wilhelm ran him out of town with his knuckleball, but Gus caught Wilhelm's no-hitter, so he must have been doing something right.

Gus might have been the world's slowest runner. If he and Hall of Fame catcher Ernie Lombardi ran a 100-yard dash, they'd have to call it the 100-yard marathon. Pee Wee Reese's phrase, "He looks like a turtle running with arthritis" would fit Gus. But he once hit an inside-the-park home run, believe it or not.

Gus started with the Yankees as a first baseman-catcher, but he really knew catching. One of the few to catch a no-hitter in each league, he caught Jim Bunning's perfect game in Philadelphia.

I arrived in Baltimore with Andy Etchebarren and Elrod Hendricks. Etchebarren is the pure prototype of a catcher; that's the only position I could imagine him playing. Tough, hard-nosed, you'd have to get a truck to move him out of the way. People like

Frank Howard, Harmon Killebrew, big strong guys, tried to knock him over and it just didn't work. One of the biggest collisions he ever had was when he knocked Thurman Munson about four rows up in the seats.

Andy was a fair hitter, but he had good knowledge of his pitching staff. He caught the four 20-game winners.

Another guy who caught those four—and a lot of others—was Elrod. Just a delightful man, always laughing, always smiling, but a very tough guy. If Palmer lost his concentration during a game, Elrod would go out to the mound and tell him, "Come on, you big dumb son of a bitch, you do what I tell you or I'm going to smack you." He'd say that on the mound, and it would shake up Palmer.

Elrod was a very quick, clever, artistic catcher. From the Virgin Islands, he was playing in Mexico, sometimes three games a day, when Frank Lane discovered him and brought him here. Elrod was known as the Babe Ruth of Mexico because he hit a lot of home runs down there. A left-hand hitter, he was one of the best pull hitters you'll ever see. Didn't hit that much in Baltimore, but pulled everything.

A tremendous PR person, Elrod has always meant a lot to this team. I don't think he should be a manager. I saw him take over for Frank Robinson when Frank had some back problems a few years ago. Seemed like utter frustration. Of course, when you're taking over for someone else, you want to do what they want. I think Elrod is better suited to running the bullpen or being a pitching coach or a minor league coach; he can be a big help to young players, and he likes working with people.

In 1973 we needed catching help. Elrod and Andy had not been hitting. Weaver said, "Get me Earl Williams from Atlanta and we'll win the pennant." So we traded Pat Dobson, Johnny Oates, Davey Johnson and Roric Harrison for Williams and Taylor Duncan, won the division two years in a row, but lost both playoffs to Oakland.

Williams was not the answer. This guy didn't want to catch. This guy wanted to stand around. When you bring up Earl Williams to Weaver, he gets a little upset. Evidently Williams had a great reputation in the National League, but he was never accepted here. Showed up at the park later than everybody else. Never took any extra practice, but thought he was something special. Called himself, "Big Money." You know what the ballplayers called him? "Small Change."

After two years the Orioles sent him back to Atlanta, for Jimmy Freeman and $75,000.

Then, on June 15, 1976, here came The Dempster, in a big trade with the Yankees. Can you name everybody involved in that deal? In addition to Rick Dempsey, the Orioles got Rudy May, Tippy Martinez, Dave Pagan and Scott McGregor for Ken Holtzman, Doyle Alexander, Grant Jackson, Elrod Hendricks and the well-traveled Jimmy Freeman. If you want to debate who got the better of that deal, call me sometime.

What can I tell you about Rick Dempsey that any Orioles fan doesn't already know? Concentrating on throwing runners out and getting base hits may have overshadowed his ability to call a game. I mean, with Rick you got it all; there was nothing lacking. He was MVP of the 1983 World Series.

He was so intense, if you didn't do everything the way he thought you should do it, he was liable to punch you out. He threw Weaver down the steps in the dugout a few times, because Earl took him out of a game. He doesn't mean anything personal by it; that's just the way he does things. He'll keep you awake.

Dempsey thought he should catch every game in spring training, every inning of every day of everything in baseball. Nobody else should even be allowed to put on the glove, not with him around. But that's the type of guy you like to have on a team.

Even when he was not in the game or there was no game going on, he was the same way: sliding across the tarp during a rain delay, imitating Babe Ruth's called shot in the '32 World Series, or leading the cheers spelling out ORIOLES.

What else can I tell you about The Dempster? Well, maybe I can give you a little insight into the end of Rick's playing days with the Orioles.

It's spring training 1992, Johnny Oates's first spring as the manager. After spending the '91 season with Milwaukee, Rick had come off that emotional last day farewell at Memorial Stadium yearning to be part of the team in their first year at Camden

Yards. He was burning to be a manager, but wanted to play two more years, and was invited to camp as a non-roster player.

In Milwaukee in '91, when it was apparent that manager Tom Trebelhorn was on his way out, Rick had gone to Bud Selig, the club owner, and said, "I want to be your next manager."

Selig said, "You have no experience."

"I can manage this club," Rick said. "I know what they need."

But he never seriously thought he would get the job.

"I want to play until I drop," he told me, "but I want to be a major league manager."

Rick was 42. The best he could hope for was backup to Chris Hoiles, who was slated to be the everyday catcher. He had to beat out Jeff Tackett for that job. I thought Dempsey would get a good look in Florida, because Oates felt that Tackett would be better off catching every day at Rochester. Barring injury— and at 42 it takes longer to heal—I was confident that Dempsey was ticketed to be the backup catcher.

But it didn't turn out that way. Tackett won the job on the strength of how well he played. Although he would have benefitted by playing every day, he balked at going back to the minors. His attitude was that he had made the major league team and he wanted to stay there.

Generally in the spring the close decisions take care of them-selves. Somebody will make a few mistakes or get hurt and the decision results from that. This did not happen in 1992. So Johnny Oates had to make the choice. I would have kept Dempsey as the backup and sent Tackett down to play every day. But the decision wasn't mine to make.

On the last day to make the cuts, the Orioles released Dempsey as an active player, offering him a spot as a coach. (Tackett survived the last cut two years in a row.)

Major league ballplayers never think their careers will end. No matter how long they play or how old they get, they are never ready for the end when it comes. It can be a difficult thing to handle. A few, a very few, can take off the uniform and walk away without looking back. Brooks Robinson. Sandy Koufax. They're the exceptions.

"As soon as I get to the clubhouse, I'm home," has been players' attitude for a hundred years. It has nothing to do with their families and home life. But that's their world, where there is a feeling of security, of belonging. And that is what makes it so wrenching for them when it ends. They are not all as lucky as people like me who find a way to stay close to the game for 50 years.

Rick Dempsey was the picture of despondency as the '92 season opened at Camden Yards. I've known Rick since his first at bat with Minnesota in 1969. And I never expected to see him like that. On opening day I was there early. I walked into the expansive new clubhouse and found Rick sitting there alone.

"I want to talk to you," he said, and we went into one of the empty rooms. When we got in there and closed the door, he broke down and cried. He and his family had all taken his release hard.

"What should I do today?" he asked me. He knew there would be a full house, and every Oriole would be introduced. He did not know how to handle it, or even if he could handle it at all. "I've thought about not going out there."

"No, no, no," I said. "Go out there and take your bows. You'll get the biggest ovation of all." Which he did.

Then I said, "Sit around here for a week, and don't open your mouth. Whatever they tell you to do, say yes sir and go do it. Have a meeting with Roland Hemond and Larry Lucchino (club president) together."

Later he told me he had met with them. "They offered me a pretty good deal," he said, "but I still want to play. I had an offer from the Dodgers to be a roving minor league coach. My home is in California, but I love it in Baltimore and want to stay here."

"If they make you a coach, they can pay you peanuts," I said.

"Well, they owe me $100,000 of deferred payment, so that would help," he said.

I sat there thinking, "To be a coach in Baltimore will eat him up alive, catching in the bullpen, throwing BP." I didn't know if he could handle that. I also thought that hanging around for a year would be a waste of time. Why not get started looking for a minor league managing job? But it's tough to part from being an active player, and he hoped he might get a call from some major league club needing help. The call never came.

Rick did return to the active list for a few weeks in mid-season. His first appearance at the plate, on July 6, was an emotional event for him and the thousands of fans lucky enough to be there. It was his first time at bat with the Orioles since 1986. It came in the tenth inning, and he beat out a perfectly-placed bunt.

In 1993 Rick joined the Dodgers organization and began his climb toward his goal of managing in the big leagues. He led the Class A Bakersfield club; although they had a terrible year, he must have done something right. The Dodgers promoted him all the way to AAA Albuquerque in '94.

Rick believes he knows how to get to players and handle them. I had my doubts at first. I told him he'd probably beat them up like the oldtime managers did if he lost his patience with them. But he knows that doesn't go anymore.

I don't think there's a single person in Baltimore who doesn't wish him all the luck and success in the world.

A few other catchers come to mind. Bob Melvin, a quiet, unassuming, excellent receiver. Called a game as well as anyone. Some pitchers preferred to throw to him instead of Tettleton. They had confidence in him. Not a big home run hitter, but he seemed to get base hits at key times.

Mickey Tettleton is the silent, John Wayne type of man. Very strong, not much to say. I'd get the lineup and he'd ask me, "Am I in there?" If I said no, he'd say, "Okay." Didn't like it, but accepted it. Tettleton is the calmest batter in baseball. Takes his stance, arcs the bat slowly back into position and waits like a statue. Not a wasted motion. Ever.

One day in a game against Detroit, Tettleton was catching for them and Harold Baines, another man of few words, was at the plate. There was a delay in the game; I looked down at the two of them standing at home plate and just knew there was not much conversation going on there.

I didn't think Mickey caught a real good game, from what I saw, but I was sorry to see him go to another team. I would have put him in the outfield or at first base.

He's the last guy I remember tearing up a clubhouse. He could erupt like a volcano and throw stuff around—mad at himself for striking out or losing a game. A switch-hitter with power, he had one miserable year here where he just kept striking out. I couldn't understand it. I mean, he wasn't even coming close. I began to wonder if there was something else bothering him.

Always one of the first to show up in the clubhouse, as soon as he got there he would light up a cigarette. I figured maybe he wasn't allowed to smoke at home. Wore contact lenses on the field, glasses off the field.

Dave Duncan caught here for a little while. Good receiver, and pretty good home run hitter for a catcher. Another one of those guys you could see was going to be a coach or manager. He studied the game, always asking Weaver questions on the bench. Now he's regarded as one of the best pitching coaches in the business.

Terry Kennedy—they called him TK—son of Bob Kennedy, a White Sox third baseman in my time. When Terry broke in he was heralded as one of the greats to be. Slow, pretty good arm, never lived up to all the ballyhoo. TK would stuff all his fan mail into boxes atop his locker (which is really just an open stall, not an enclosed locker), and once in a while show up early and answer it all.

Speaking of fan mail, only a very few players will throw it away without reading it. Most will get around to answering it in time. These days a lot of stars' mail is picked up by their agents. But they don't answer it or sign the player's name. If a person encloses a stamped, self-addressed envelope with a letter, I'd say they will get a reply from the player 99 percent of the time.

If I was an autograph seeker today, I'd use the method the kids used in New York 50 years ago: hand the player a postcard already addressed and ask them to sign it when they have time and drop it in a mailbox. Or mail them the postcard.

Some autographed baseballs used to be fakes. In Brooklyn we had a batboy who answered most of Leo Durocher's fan mail; he could fill a ball with the whole team's signatures. Joe DiMaggio's sister answered most of his mail. I don't think those things happen today.

Where was I? Catchers I remember. Dan Graham—looked good, but ate himself out of the league.

Floyd Rayford, a catcher-third baseman, built like Roy Campanella, looked like Campanella, but couldn't play like Campanella. Came to spring training 25 pounds overweight and never hit his weight again. Very likable guy.

Joe Nolan, a serious clutch hitter, but he had so many knee operations he had to quit.

Dave Skaggs. About the only time he ever caught was when Dennis Martinez pitched. Superstition or not, he became Dennis's favorite catcher. Stayed in the organization as a roving catching instructor in the minor leagues.

Which brings us to Chris Hoiles. When the Orioles got Hoiles from Detroit in 1988 in a deal for Fred Lynn, Sparky Anderson told me that he really hated to part with Chris. We all know why now. Chris could always hit; his numbers improved every year through 1993.

Hoiles has had the benefit of working with four former catchers since '88: Cal Senior, Jerry Narron, Elrod and Johnny Oates. When Oates took over in '91, he sat Hoiles down for a few games while Bob Melvin did the catching. But where did he sit him down? Right next to him in the dugout, taking him through the whole game, asking Chris, "What would you do here? What pitch would you call?"

Some other managers would have had Hoiles down in the bullpen warming up pitchers. Afterwards, Chris said, "I never learned so much in three days."

Chris is rapidly becoming a star catcher, but he'll never feel like a "star" inside. He worked hard on his foot movement and has improved 100 percent. No wasted steps, quick movements—that is one area of a catcher's work that the pros look at in rating them. He built a building on his farm in Ohio with batting cages, and practices hitting and catching using a pitching machine all winter.

I expect Chris Hoiles to go down in the books as the best catcher the Orioles had in their first 50 years.

9

Bambi's Bombers

I always say that behind a great pitching staff, you'll find a great defense. Pitching and defense. I know my listeners get tired of hearing me preach that.

But sometimes, especially these days, behind a great pitching staff you'll find an outstanding pitching coach.

Never was that more true than in the case of the Orioles' four 20-game winners of 1971 and George Bamberger.

Bambi didn't take credit for anything, but ask those four pitchers—and a lot of others—and they'll tell you to give him the credit. But to outsiders, he appeared lackadaisical about his job. What he was was honest.

"The pitchers did it all," he'd say. "Maybe I suggested they ought to do this or that, but that's all."

He had 100 percent confidence in all his pitchers, and they idolized him. Jim Palmer, who always thought he was right, never argued with Bamberger. Bambi was one of the first to go one-on-one, when it was rarely done. He got close to each guy and got to know him. He knew how to talk to them and get through to them, but he didn't give in to them, and would rip them when they deserved it.

As a pitcher, Bambi's another example of how the best managers and coaches are often the guys with little or no big league playing experience or success. He came up with the Giants a couple times, got into 10 games with no decisions. But he owned the Pacific Coast League for seven years, and holds the league record of 68.2 consecutive innings pitched without a walk. He pitched a no-hitter in the International League and won a total of 213 games in the minors.

Bambi, who couldn't put a sentence together without some profanity in it, had the right personality to deal with Earl Weaver. He ran the pitching staff, made the moves, and told Earl when to take somebody out.

Earl would get in his cups and fire people. He fired coach Billy Hunter on just about every trip home from the west coast. But Hunter always ignored it and showed up the next day. Not Bambi. One night he and Earl got into an argument about something up in Boston and Earl fired him. Bambi packed his bags, went to the airport and flew back home. Next day Earl went looking for him. Couldn't find him. Called him.

"What are you doing back in Baltimore?"

"You fired me."

"Aw, George, you know I was just kidding."

"No, I don't."

That was Bambi; he knew, but he figured it was time somebody called Earl's bluff.

The four 20-game winners in '71—Mike Cuellar, Pat Dobson, Dave McNally and Jim Palmer—were one of only two such foursomes in the history of baseball. The Chicago White Sox of 1920 were the other, with Red Faber, Ed Cicotte, Dickie Kerr and Lefty Williams (and they didn't win the pennant).

Mike Cuellar was an artist, one of the last guys to throw a really great screwball. A left-hander, he gave right-hand hitters an absolute fit. He cheated a little bit here and there, but that screwball was his out pitch.

Mike came from Houston in a trade for Curt Blefary and a minor leaguer in what has got to be one of the team's greatest steals of the half-century. Harry Dalton gets credit for that one. All Mike did was pitch 250 to 300 innings, 17 to 20 complete games, for seven years. Hard to believe it was less than 25 years ago that pitchers did things like that.

Mike appreciated the defense he had behind him, and why not. Brooks and Belanger and Grich and Boog—nothing got by them. Nothing. And Blair in center field. But still, not every pitcher will admit how much the defense behind him contributes to a winning record.

"Everybody hit the ball, everybody catch the ball," he said in his Cuban accent. "Brooks Robinson, he'll be in the Hall of Fame and I should get half of it, because I threw up all those ground balls he catch."

Cuellar's nickname was "Crazy Horse" because sometimes he acted that way. If he didn't want to do an interview, he would tell guys, "I no speak English." But he was not that bad. You could understand him; you just had to have a little patience.

With the whole season on the line, a lot of guys would pick Cuellar to pitch the game.

Earl Weaver was the most superstitious Oriole, but among the players it was probably Cuellar. He always wore blue on plane trips. Always approached the mound from the second base side. Always had to pick up the ball off the ground. If an infielder threw it to him, he would let it fall, then pick it up.

One year he had a winning streak going and they went on the road and the first stop was Milwaukee. He was due to pitch the next day. He had worn the same cap in every win, but on arriving in Milwaukee, he discovered that he had left it behind. Frantic, he got hold of Phil Itzoe, the traveling secretary, and begged him to do something. Itzoe called United Airlines and they picked up the cap at Memorial Stadium and gave it to a pilot who was going to Chicago where a supervisor brought it— in a plain brown paper bag—to Air Wisconsin and handed it to a pilot going to Milwaukee. Itzoe picked it up at the airport and took a cab to the ballpark and got there about 5:30 and handed it to Mike, who put it on, warmed up and got knocked out early in the game. He took off the cap in front of the dugout and stomped it into the ground. But I guarantee you, if he got into another winning streak, he would act the same way.

When Cuellar's career was almost over, he criticized Weaver for not giving him enough chances to work. Earl's response: "I gave Mike Cuellar more chances than I gave my first wife."

Pat Dobson was with the Orioles for two years and they were the best two out of his 11-year career. I like the word contagious. I don't like momentum. But things can become contagious. In his case, he caught the attitude of the other guys on the staff. He didn't have great stuff, but it pumped him up being with Cuellar and Palmer and McNally.

We got Pat from San Diego for Tom Phoebus and three other guys, and he recognized the value of the gloves behind him, giving full credit to them and to Bamberger for his success here. One of the clubhouse comedians, he always had a lot of fun, and the guys who go to the fantasy camps enjoy him down there.

At different times in different places, I have heard catchers Andy Etchebarren and Rick Dempsey asked the question, "Who's the best pitcher you ever caught?" And they both answered the same, almost word for word.

"You and everybody else is expecting me to say Jim Palmer. And he should have been, with all his natural talent, and all the things he had going for him. But the best was Dave McNally."

McNally didn't have the greatest stuff. He just flatout knew how to pitch. He was what I call a complete pitcher.

What does that mean? To me, a complete pitcher is one who has great control, of the pitch and of himself. Control is the key word; whether or not you have great stuff, you still have to get it where you want it to go. On the major league level, if you don't you're a thrower, not a pitcher.

Frank Robinson summed him up, "You could be five or six runs behind, standing in the outfield, and if McNally was pitching, you thought you were still going to win."

He never gave in. Nobody ever intimidated him. And when he went out there, you knew you were going to get a well-pitched game. He could throw the ball where he wanted to, and where the hitter would hit it. He pitched inside, had a great curve ball, and a great move with men on base.

But one guy owned him—Frank Howard. "I could throw the resin bag up there and he'd get a hit off me," Dave said.

He's also the only pitcher to hit a bases-loaded home run in a World Series.

Dave came from Billings, Montana, where he still lives.

Makes you wonder how he ever became a pitcher, with the short summers out there.

He had a caustic sense of humor in the clubhouse, and teased Palmer a lot. But on the mound he was very intense, more so than he let people think. In Memorial Stadium there was a long runway from the dugout to the clubhouse, lined with light bulbs hanging from the ceiling every five or six feet. Earl took him out of a game one night, and Dave didn't like it. As he walked through that runway, he broke every one of those bulbs.

McNally and Etchebarren roomed together for years.

Dave won so many big games for the Orioles: his 1-0 4-hitter against the Dodgers in the last game of the 1966 Series...his 11-inning 1-0 win over Minnesota in the '69 AL playoffs...

His last year in Baltimore was tough for him. He had a sore arm and other aches and pains he had never experienced before.

To me, McNally was an unlikely guy to become the pioneer in the players' labor movement when he and Andy Messersmith overturned the century-old reserve clause and began the era of free agency. He was near the end of his career in 1974 when he played the season without signing a contract. Messersmith, a pitcher with the Dodgers, did the same. After the season, an arbitrator declared both of them free agents. Dave signed with Montreal, but he wasn't getting the job done and quit midway through the season. I think he turned back part of his salary. That's the way he was.

When I talked to him about the free agency business, he was kind of stunned that he would have been the guy selected. I don't think it was his idea. I think somebody came to him. Maybe an assistant to Marvin Miller in the Players' Association went to David's agent. It surprised a lot of fans that he would go that route. But he did it for the players. He thought he was doing the right thing and, as it turned out, every player since that time should get down on their knees and thank Miller and McNally and Messersmith.

I don't think there was any discussion about it among the Orioles. He may have been prodded to take the step, but, if he was, it was not by the players on his own team. McNally was a popular guy, quiet but with a sense of humor, often aimed at himself.

"I don't throw hard enough to get anybody out," he'd say, and, "I throw the longest home runs that have ever been thrown in this ballpark."

McNally was the furthest thing from being a clubhouse lawyer. I love that term. I didn't know what it meant when I broke in at 18, but I soon found out that many clubhouses have one. Curt Blefary fit that term in Baltimore. Reggie, definitely.

What does it mean? A clubhouse lawyer is a guy who is full of advice for everybody else when it comes to dealing with the manager or the front office, egging guys on when they complain, then talking behind their back; in short, a guy who tries to run the clubhouse and everybody in it.

That was not David McNally, a very classy man.

Jim Palmer was and is the perfectionist that everybody talks about. He knows as much about pitching as anybody, but he knows more about himself than anybody I've ever known. He knew exactly how far he could go, what he could do and what he couldn't do. I never knew another pitcher who knew his own limits so well.

Jim pushed himself to stay in magnificent condition. It was nothing for him in his prime (or even out of his prime) to play a couple sets of tennis, go to the ballpark early and run by himself, then run with the pitchers, then shag flies in the outfield. When he chased a fly ball—you watch the pitchers out there, how they trot—not him. He went all out. He did all those things. At Steve Carlton's suggestion, he began sticking his hand into a bucket filled with rice, down to the bottom, to strengthen it. Try it sometime.

We had a pitcher, Dave Ford, who joined the club about a month after the season started. I was sitting talking to Earl Weaver, and Ford came over and said, "Skip, what am I supposed to do? What's the routine?"

Earl said, "See that guy?" pointing to Palmer. "Follow him. Do everything he does."

I guarantee you'd die before you could do what he did.

Earl had great respect for Palmer. When somebody asked him how he handled Jim, he said, "Nothing to it. I handed him the ball every fourth day. If he kept it, I knew I was going to get a great job. If he handed it back to me, I knew I was going to have to get somebody else."

Yes, Jim did give Weaver a bad time. In the middle of a game, he'd ask Weaver about some strategy, "Why did you do that?" and it was as much an editorial as a quest for understanding. He would stand in front of Weaver in the dugout and Earl would have to move him out of the way.

On a day he was pitching he would check the lineup posted in the clubhouse, and he might say, "Oh my God, I can't win with that," then tell Earl, "Can't we get so-and-so? Why isn't this guy playing?" Gave him a hard time whenever he could, but he was also looking for an edge, for the best chance to win.

Jim is a very intelligent student of the whole game: pitching, hitters, infielders, why players move for each pitch. He would move the infielders and outfielders. Once he waved Reggie Jackson to move. Jackson moved. Jim waved him to take another step. Reggie took another step. Jim went back and threw and the batter drove the pitch right where Reggie was standing. Reggie took off his cap and bowed to Palmer.

Jim knew what he was doing out there, but I think some of that stuff was psychological, to show up Weaver. He'd do anything he could to agitate Earl.

One night Jim was pitching during one of Earl's suspensions. In those days the manager could sit up in the press box when he was out of the game. Weaver was up there and Palmer got into trouble late in the game. Weaver got on the phone and called down to the dugout.

"Get Palmer out of there."

Bamberger was managing. He went out and I could see Jim arguing with him, pointing up at Weaver. Bambi said, "Give me the ball."

Jim said, "I'm not coming out. Tell that no-good bastard I'm not moving out of here."

Bambi said, "Well, I'm leaving, and there's another pitcher heading this way, and somebody's going to have to leave."

Palmer trailed off after him.

He hated to come out of a game, and with good reason. Great

pitchers have the ability to turn it up a notch when they need it. Christy Mathewson called it pitching in a pinch. Palmer was that way. Ask any manager from his time, they will all tell you that if he was ahead by a run in the sixth, you might as well pack up the bats and go home. You weren't going to get anything more.

Palmer was tough. Billy Martin used to say, "Don't let those pretty looks deceive you. He looks so nice and he is a nice guy until he walks out there, then he's not so nice."

Jim was confident, but not arrogant. He pitched high and inside his whole career and got by with it. People said, "How can you do that?" He did it because he could throw so hard. But he didn't live there exclusively. He could do anything he wanted to do. He always had a good curve and changeup to go with it. Later, when he lost a little off his fastball, he went to more finesse.

He was a fly ball pitcher, but you never got enough of the ball. His theory was: "Get the first pitch over the plate. Get the first out. Then you can do things." He preached that.

Palmer never gave up a grand slam. The closest he came was in a game where he had men on second and third and Weaver ordered an intentional walk to John Lowenstein, then with Cleveland. That loaded the bases. Jim then balked in a run, and the next batter hit a home run.

Like most power pitchers, Jim was heavy-legged, but not as big in the butt and thighs as guys like Seaver, Clemens and Ryan.

Arm trouble early in his career cost Jim a chance to win 300 games. They sent him down to a rookie league where Bambi was coaching. One day Jim's pitching, and some Class X kids are racking him. He came back to the bench with tears in his eyes, pleading with Bambi to take him out.

"Don't embarrass me anymore."

Bambi told him, "No, you stay in there and get your ass knocked off. Be good for you."

Jim took such a shelling that even Bamberger was close to tears for him. But he was not going to baby him.

In the end they never found anything wrong with his arm. It turned out he had one leg shorter than the other, and they built him a special shoe and the rest is history.

There are stories that Palmer would reject a ball the umpire threw out to him, and the ump would try later to put the same ball back into action and Jim would recognize it and throw it out again. I think those tales are exaggerated. Sure, sometimes he'd throw one out, even if he had just struck out a hitter with it. Maybe the seams felt right for one kind of pitch, but not for another that he intended to throw. He knew that same ball would reappear from the ump's pocket. That was okay. Once in a while there was really something wrong with the ball. But he never made that big a deal about it.

Like most pitchers, Jim has a great memory. That's part of being a successful pitcher. It's no big thing. To this day I can recall what I threw that DiMaggio or Musial or Kiner or anybody hit a mile off me, and what I got them out with 45 years ago. Pitchers like Palmer could be great hitting coaches, just as guys like Ted Williams would make great pitching coaches, because they studied so intently the opponents of what they were trying to do.

Jim was very popular with the players. They would laugh at some of his stuff, and he could take a joke, although he was not much of a joker himself. Sometimes the other guys egged him on, especially when it came to needling Weaver.

He would read some medical journal and bring it in and show the doctors something he'd read. They'd look at it, say, "Yeah, okay," and pay no attention to it.

When he was young and started to win regularly, he said he ate pancakes before every game. So they gave him the nickname, "Cakes."

Those four 20-game winners were close. I don't want to over-use that word, camaraderie, but it was different in those days. They all lived near each other, and they would carpool to the ballpark and do things together. They fit, despite different personalities.

Palmer seemed to know a little bit more about hitters and pitching, but they all shared their knowledge. McNally might go up to Cuellar and tell him so-and-so was getting to him, maybe he ought to try pitching him differently. Dobson would go to Palmer and say, "Jim, what do I do with this batter?" and Jim would tell him.

Dobson said of Palmer, "He made me."

You wouldn't find much of that today. But those four guys had a great understanding. If there had been one renegade among them, you wonder how far they would have gone. But there was none. They all depended on each other.

When Palmer pitched those great games, he'd give credit to everybody. Elrod Hendricks caught the no-hitter he pitched against Oakland; Palmer lauded Elrod for calling such a great game. And when they retired his number 22 and he made a speech, he said, "Everybody, including me, has to give thanks to the Brooks Robinsons and the Mark Belangers and the Paul Blairs and all those guys. But I want to pay special attention to a few others: Lenn Sakata, Rich Dauer, Terry Crowley, John Lowenstein."

He recognized what the big stars did for him, but he recognized the other guys, too. He always would go out of his way to do that. That's not put on. That's genuine.

The two roommates that I knew he had were Dave Leonard, a pitcher who worked very little, and Tom Shopay, an outfielder. Guys who were not big players at all.

Jim is a very giving guy. A lot of people don't agree. He came across to some as conceited. But he'd do anything for a teammate, especially the younger players. He was right there to help them out with anything they needed, from finding a place to stay to adjusting to life in the big leagues, whatever.

He autographs all the time and does a lot of charity work, and has always been that way.

If I were managing in the seventh game of a World Series, and they were all equally rested, I'd start Palmer. McNally would be close. Cuellar was tough, too. Palmer had more stuff, no question about it. He could make a mistake and get by with it, because he threw so hard.

Mr. Rickey used to say a lot of great stars get out of the game because they are afraid of failure. Dick Williams, a Rickey disciple, said that players give 100 percent out of personal pride, because they hate failure. I believe that. Jim Palmer was one. He got out a little ahead of when he had to; he was such a perfectionist, when he couldn't be perfect any longer, he got out.

Jim's a nervous, antsy guy. Can't sit still more than two or three minutes. Always moving. Always talking, with big gestures. He's too impatient to be a manager or pitching coach. He would be like the superstars who do not make good managers, wanting everybody's pitching to be like his. You can't do that.

Some years back, Edward Bennett Williams talked Jim into volunteering to help with the pitchers in spring training. I was there in Miami a few days after he started, and we're watching some big tall kid, built like Jim, throwing hard. Our conversation went something like this:

"Have you helped him?"

"I've talked to him."

"And?"

"Well, I talk to him, then Elrod talks to him, then Al Jackson talks to him, then Mike Boddicker talks to him, and he takes whatever he wants from it all."

"Can't they tell him that you're the guy they want him to listen to?"

"Yeah, but they don't. Boddicker is liable to tell him something I don't agree with at all. I can't take that. I'm not going to last. Besides, you can't teach these guys. They've all got so much money, they look at me and think, 'Who are you?'"

So he quit after a few days. "This is not for me. Goodbye."

One night in the winter of 1988 my phone rang. It was Jim Palmer. "What's up, pal?" I asked.

"I want you to meet me tomorrow morning at Cross Keys at seven."

"Okay. What have you got?"

"I'll tell you when I get there."

It was cold the next morning when I met him.

"What is it?"

"I want to make a comeback."

I just looked at him. Didn't say a word.

"I don't see any reaction," he said.

"My reaction is this. If you're really serious, you better go ahead with it. If you do it and fail, that's okay. You've done what you wanted to do. But I don't think you can do it."

He was 43.

"Why not?"

"Oh, I think you can do it, but if you get hurt in any way, you will not be back."

"Rex, you know I stay in such great shape, and I've been on the sidelines watching now for five years, and the kind of pitching I've seen, I know I can pitch better than some of these guys."

"Then you better do it. My only theory is, if you get hurt, you're going to have problems."

"I'm going to go through with it."

"Go ahead."

Frank Robinson was the manager and he was not keen on the idea. Palmer went to spring training on his own. He was pitching well, and he got to work in an exhibition game against the Pirates in Bradenton, and he pulled a groin muscle. It hurt him so bad he couldn't throw. When I got down there he was limping worse than I was.

"You were right," he told me.

That's not the end of the story. While he was down there, there were three guys in Baltimore who kept saying, "The only reason Palmer's coming back is he needs the money." One radio call-in show and two newspaper writers. They went on and on about that, and Jim became livid.

He called me from Florida. "Do I hear right what they are saying?"

"That's what I hear."

"What are you saying?"

"I'm saying that you are not doing it for that reason."

This went on for about two weeks. I asked him to come on my program for an hour. He agreed.

I said, "I'm not going to ask you about all this stuff that's being said about you." But I just knew some caller would bring it up.

Second caller, right out of the box: "Jim, there's a lot of media guys in Baltimore who say you're coming back because you need the money. What about it?"

I sat back, said nothing, but to myself: "Here it comes."

Jim said, "Yeah, I heard that. There are three guys saying that (and he named them). I'll tell you something. None of them know anything about baseball. That's first. The guy you're talking to now—Rex—knows me backwards and forwards, and he knows a lot about the game of baseball. What does he tell you?"

"He says you're not doing it for that reason."

Jim said, "I'm not. And I want to tell you something else. If any of those three had any guts, they would call me and ask me, but they don't do that. They can't face me. Rex calls me. Other people call me. We talk all the time. Why can't they call me and ask me for a clarification?"

That blew those guys right out of the water. They came to me and said, "You should protect us."

"Protect you. For what? Did you or did you not say that?"

"Yeah, that's what we thought."

"You thought it. Why didn't you call him and ask him?"

So that blew over. Later, when Jim broke down physically and had to give up the idea, he asked to come back on my show and explain what happened.

Why did he do it? First of all, he needed the money like God needs money. He did it because he was watching these guys out there on the mound while he was doing TV broadcasts of the games and he just knew he could do better than what he was seeing in major league pitchers. And I'm not so sure he couldn't, if he didn't get hurt.

I wouldn't say Jim is the happiest man in the world, but he believes he's on the right road now and has got his life together. The worst part for him is, as articulate and pretty (and you've got to use that word) as he is, and with all the things he does that seem to go counter to the atmosphere of baseball, he misses the clubhouse and the camaraderie that he was always right in the middle of.

It's tough for him to sit still through the game broadcasts, but, like the rest of us, it keeps him in the game. And, like me and some other oldtimers, that's life.

10

Martinezes, McGregor, and Moe

Dennis and Tippy Martinez both joined the Orioles in 1976, and you couldn't find two more different guys with the same last name. Dennis, from Nicaragua, didn't know any English. Tippy, from Colorado, didn't know any Spanish. Writers who assumed that all Martinezes were automatically Latins tried to speak Spanish to Tippy and he didn't know what they were talking about.

Tippy came to us from the Yankees in that big trade that brought Rick Dempsey with him. He wanted to be a starter—he had started two games for the Yankees in 1975—but he was already 26 and Earl told him he was going to be strictly a reliever.

He was born for that job. Not a big guy, five foot ten, he could throw a little harder than hitters thought he was capable of, and he mesmerized them. He had an unbelievable curve that would start out over your head and end up on your shoe tops. He had good control, but he needed a catcher who could block those curves, because he bounced a lot of them. Maybe that's why Dempsey came with him in that deal; he could catch Tippy like nobody else.

Tippy did a super job for the Orioles for 10 years. He holds the team record for appearances—76 in 1982. A delightful guy, he gave us that unforgettable inning against Toronto when he picked off three straight baserunners at first base.

Dennis Martinez was a pain in the ass when he came up. Knew everything. Wouldn't take any instructions. Palmer, who would and could help any pitcher, said, "I can't help him. He knows more than all of us."

I remember one winter when some of the pitchers worked underneath the stands at Memorial Stadium. Dennis was throwing. Scott McGregor was standing on the side, watching. He said, "Can you imagine how good he'd be if he had a brain?"

Dennis had a million dollar arm and a nickel head. He had tremendous velocity, but no control. And an iron man? It meant nothing to him to throw 140 pitches a game. But he was so slow throwing them. In those days our Friday night games began at 8:00 o'clock. And every Friday Dennis would pitch. That meant we were sure to be there past midnight.

Once in Milwaukee he threw close to George Scott and Scott charged the mound. Dennis turned and ran out to center field. Later they asked Scott if he knew who had been pitching. He said, "No, all those Latin pitchers look alike to me."

Dennis had four or five good years, hurt his shoulder in 1980, then went right downhill. Alcohol contributed to his problems. I'm not saying this to defend him, but I came to understand him, and to admire him for how he straightened out his life.

Dennis was the first major leaguer to come out of Nicaragua. He came from nothing. No shoes, no clothes, lived in a grass hut with a dirt floor. Learned to throw by pitching rocks. Then all this money came to him and he just couldn't handle it. He started hanging around in hotel bars, wearing dark glasses. He remained popular with the fans, who didn't really know what was going on with him.

The Orioles sent him down to Rochester in '86, then traded him to Montreal for Rene Gonzales. At the end of the season Montreal released him. He worked out here and wanted to sign with the Orioles, but the best they would offer him was a minor league contract. They suggested he see if he could do better somewhere else. He contacted the Expos, but all they offered him was a spot with Miami, an independent team in the Class A Florida State League. That was his home, so he took it. On his own, he straightened himself out and worked his way back up. He goes all over the country now, speaking for Alcoholics Anonymous.

At that point he could have signed with anybody. Montreal took him back, and he wound up winning 100 games for them after he'd won 100 for the Orioles. He became one of the top 10 pitchers in the National League.

In 1994 he signed with Cleveland at the same time as Eddie Murray. When the Indians came to Baltimore in May and he beat us, I could see how much he had learned about pitching since he left Baltimore. If he still had that great stuff, he'd have blown hitters away. Now he had become a pitcher. But he's still a slow worker.

When I introduced him as the Indians' starting pitcher, the Baltimore fans gave him a standing ovation. The next day I said to him, "It looked to me like you were shedding a bit of a tear when you went out to the mound and got that big ovation."

"I was," he said. "That's why I backed off the mound. I had no idea it would be anything like that. I was more worried about Eddie than myself."

I'm glad for Dennis. I admire him tremendously, because he overcame so much.

Scott McGregor was also part of that 1976 trade with the Yankees. According to George Brett, who knew him growing up, McGregor was "the wildest kid in all of El Segundo, California." By his own admission, Scott did cocaine, marijuana, alcohol, the works as a young kid. But in high school he became the best pitcher and hitter in the area. Outhit Brett every year.

His all-time favorite player was Eddie Mathews. Scott's father said, "Whenever the Braves were in town, he'd make me take him to Los Angeles. He would sit there and stare at Mathews for nine innings, and nothing else."

Scott was a fine pitcher, not overpowering. He could hit you between the eyes and not hurt you. Like Preacher Roe, you could tell when he was wild, but not by walks. If he didn't have perfect control, they would hit the ball. He could baffle sluggers like Reggie Jackson. He shut out California to win the 1979 ALCS, and blanked the Phillies in the last game of the '83 World Series.

In that '79 game Pat Kelly hit a home run with two on. Today both Kelly and McGregor are ordained ministers.

Moe Drabowsky was the preeminent practical joker of the Orioles. But for all his clowning around, Moe knows pitching.

I first saw Moe back in the 1950s when the Cubs brought him up. Could he throw! He still holds a World Series record: struck out 11 Dodgers in 6.2 innings of relief in Game 1 of the 1966 Series. (That was the Series where Palmer beat Koufax, 6-0, in Game 2; Wally Bunker beat Claude Osteen, 1-0, in Game 3; and McNally beat Drysdale, 1-0, in Game 4. That's pitching.)

Drabowsky has always been dedicated to the game and an intense student of it. But he was also dedicated to having a good time. He was in the bullpen in the old ballpark in Kansas City and somehow he got the phone number for the KC pen. He called them.

"Get so-and-so up."

The guy got up and started throwing. Pretty soon the Royals' manager was on the phone. "What's he doing up?"

"You just called and told him to start throwing."

Moe pulled that one several times and got away with it.

Once after a game they found the glass water cooler filled with goldfish. You couldn't help but know exactly who did it.

Luis Aparicio and a few other guys were deathly afraid of snakes. Moe would bring one of those little, harmless garden snakes in and put it in a cap or glove or locker. To Aparicio, it looked like a boa.

One of the few European-born players—from Poland—Moe did not have a brilliant career. He was 88-105, but he toiled on the mound for 17 years. He studied and learned and stayed in the game as a pitching coach with the White Sox and Seattle and, in 1994, with the Cubs. The Orioles had him in Hagerstown in 1993.

I asked him once, "Why are you staying in the game?"

He said, "Same as you. I could make more money at some other things. I tried to get away from it, but I just can't do it."

Not quite the same as me. I never tried to get away from it.

11

Cy Clone

Storm Davis, without a doubt, was born knowing how to pitch. And he had the stuff. He idolized and copied Jim Palmer, and should have been what Mike Flanagan called him: Cy Clone—a clone of Cy Young winner Palmer.

But Storm had nothing inside.

Palmer worked with him, did everything he could to make him a true clone. The best game he ever pitched was in the last series of the 1982 season. The Orioles had to sweep the closing four games against Milwaukee to win the division. Milwaukee needed only one win to clinch it.

On the plane coming back from Detroit for that series, Chuck Thompson and I were sitting together, and Storm was across the aisle from us. The plane had no more got off the ground when here came Mr. Palmer to sit beside Storm.

Chuck and I couldn't help overhearing their conversation (to be honest, we didn't try very hard not to). Storm was scheduled to pitch the second game of the Friday doubleheader. Jim took him through the Milwaukee lineup, hitter by hitter, over and over, Storm taking notes the whole time. I remember Jim saying things like, "I used to be able to do this; can't anymore. But as hard as you throw, and with your control, you can do it. Just keep telling yourself you can do it."

During the game Storm sat beside Jim after every turn on the mound. You could see them talking in the dugout. Palmer pitched that game right along with him. He won it, 7-1.

Magnificent. We all thought, from then on, here he comes.

But he never had the confidence or, for want of a better word, the guts.

Storm's major league debut in '82 was typical Earl Weaver. Weaver brought him in against Oakland with the bases loaded and nobody out in the ninth, handed him the ball and said, "Don't let 'em score." Maybe that shook up the kid so much he never recovered.

Storm's pitching one day and I'm doing the TV and it's the fifth inning and he has a 1-0 lead and I see him on the mound rubbing his shoulder, then his leg. The pitching coach, Ray Miller, goes out to the mound and Storm says, "My arm's getting stiff and my leg hurts. You better get somebody up in the bullpen."

He's got the game, 1-0, end of fifth. Can't lose if he comes out. Rick Dempsey's catching. Comes the start of the sixth and Mr. Dempsey goes out to the mound and, in his own crude way, gets right in Storm's face.

"You gutless son of a bitch. The way you're throwing, show some guts."

He's hollering and cussing away, and I could see the blood drain right out of Storm's face. I thought Dempsey was going to kill the kid.

Storm stayed out there, went the distance, shut them out. Didn't talk to Dempsey for about three weeks. But Dempsey got it out of him. That's what Storm needed, instead of all that babying that became the modern game.

I saw where Mets manager Dallas Green, another guy from the old school, was complaining about pitchers who go five or six innings, then either fold or look to the bullpen to finish their job for them. But it's not the pitchers' fault. It's the managers who are to blame. I have sat in on meetings where the manager would tell his starters, "Just give me five or six quality innings and we'll bring in somebody else."

They say that. Green knew it. That's why he said the managers should look in the mirror to find the cause.

Never mind going all the way back to my day. Can you imagine a manager saying something like that to Palmer, McNally, Cuellar, Flanagan? They'd get mad if somebody started to warm up. Or a guy like Don Drysdale? He'd probably punch you out just for suggesting it.

One day Drysdale was pitching. Walter Alston was the manager. Drysdale was getting hit pretty hard. Alston said to Preston Gomez, a coach, "Go get him."

"I'm not going to get him," Gomez said. "You're the manager. You go out there."

Alston said, "That's right. I'm the manager. You're the coach. I'm telling you to go get him."

Gomez went to the mound.

"I'm not coming out," Drysdale said.

"Give me the ball."

"No. Tell that gutless Alston to come out and get it himself."

"Let's not have a scene," Gomez said. "There's a guy coming in from the bullpen. Give me the ball."

Drysdale said, "I'll take it and stick it in Alston's ass."

"If you do," Gomez said, "that's the only place you'll put it today where they don't hit it."

And this business of counting the pitches. I know; I'm an old guy, but my God. I think back to that day I pitched 13 innings. Probably threw 300 pitches. But every time I came into the dugout, Durocher would say, "You all right, kid?"

"Yes sir."

It never did me any harm.

It has been written that Billy Martin ruined all those young arms on the 1980 A's because he made them pitch 94 complete games. That was the beginning of the fadeout of the complete game and the advent of the six-inning pitchers. Martin did not have much of a bullpen that year and he knew it. So he had to go with the best he had. They had five pitchers who worked more than 200 innings, and they made a big deal out of it. I think Billy got a bad rap.

Greg Swindell worked 440 innings in his three years at the University of Texas, and people said he was overworked. Some of the local experts said the same of Ben McDonald at LSU.

What a laugh. A big, strong 19, 20-year-old averaging under 150 innings a year is overworked? I don't understand that. I don't know what that means.

Everybody in the world says the athletes today are bigger and better and stronger. But they pitch less. How do you answer that? Robin Roberts went 12, 13 years pitching over 200 innings every year. Palmer, too. Never mind going back to ancient times and guys like Eppa Rixey's IP: 301...313...309...237...291. Look at Gibson and Koufax; it's scary. And nobody thought anything about it. Every four days, a complete game. Yet today the athletes are bigger and stronger and can't do that. You figure it out. I can't.

Not all pitchers are five or six and "Get me out of there." But a lot of them are. I talk to Jim Palmer about it. He said, "Rex, you have to understand..."

I tell him, "I understand but I don't understand."

I know that sounds like Yogi, but I just don't. I say to Palmer, "When you pitched, if a guy got up in the bullpen, you got mad. I know I did. Now, they almost look for it. 'Better get somebody ready.' How many times did you hear that on the bench toward the tailend of your career?"

"Well," he said, "one guy who did it all the time was Storm Davis. As good a pitcher as you'll ever see for five or six."

When Storm went to Oakland, Dave Duncan, their pitching coach, asked me about him. I said, "He'll give you five or six good innings, then he'll want out of there."

Duncan said, "I think I can correct that."

He didn't. Two years, 64 starts, two complete games.

Storm's real name is George. But he warned me never to use it when I announced him. It seems when his mother was in the hospital waiting to give birth to him, she was reading a book about a doctor named Storm, and she just fell in love with this doctor and this book, and nicknamed her son Storm.

Storm's father took Glenn Davis into their family when Glenn was young and raised him. The two young ballplayers were closer than natural brothers. I thought when Storm came back to the Orioles and Glenn was here, we would see a new Storm.

But we didn't.

12

Pitching for the Orioles...

When I think about pitchers or anything else connected with this game of baseball, my thoughts are filtered through my eyes and my experience. That's the only way I can see. I can't look through anybody else's eyes. When I try to recall the parade of pitchers I've observed in Orioles uniforms over the past 25 years, I may overlook somebody who was one of your favorites. And my comparisons and perspective will reflect my era in the game.

For example, I am against pitchers or any other players playing golf during the season, especially pitchers on the day they are starting. In my time you didn't even lift a tee, much less a golf club, for six months. I see nothing wrong with that. But today they bring the clubs to spring training and on road trips, and I have to believe it takes something out of you. I don't understand all that. In spring training, we were always so tired we didn't have the energy. Now I go to spring training and listen to the talk; it's not baseball, it's golf and auto racing and stuff like that.

I saw where Tommy Lasorda banned golf during the '94 season. When he found out that Orel Hershiser played, he fined Orel $250. But that was like an extra greens fee to the player, and he kept right on doing it.

Lifting weights and all that bulking-up exercise was also a

strict no-no. Does all that have anything to do with all these arm injuries today? I don't know. It's a world I never made, and don't understand.

But I think I know a little bit about pitching and pitchers, and here are some impressions that come to mind when I hear some names from the distant and recent past.

Tommy Phoebus was a Baltimore boy. Little round fat guy. One of the worst pitchers in the world to watch. Even I said, "With Phoebus pitching, I don't know if I want to go to the game." You know it was serious if *I* said that. I mean slow; walked everybody, and then would strike out the side. 3 and 2 on every hitter. When the players were ready to run out on the field at the start of the game and Tommy was pitching, Frank Robinson would say, "Let's wait until he's 3 and 2 on the first hitter and then go out."

Phoebus hated flying. He always carried the same book on the plane, "Rise and Fall of the Third Reich." Never read it. Just stared at it and never turned the page.

Tommy was the only Orioles pitcher I can recall who would take what they call a "walking step." That's when a pitcher goes into his windup and steps in front of the rubber with his back foot instead of maintaining contact with it. It gives him a little extra momentum. It's against the rules. I know all about that. I did it once myself.

Harry Brecheen was pitching for the Cardinals against me in Brooklyn. He was a crafty left-hander, but he was also a cheating left-hander. Did everything in the book, and I don't mean the rule book. He was planting his left foot about 12 inches in front of the rubber when he threw, and Leo Durocher was getting mad.

"I want you to start doing the same thing," he ordered me.

In those days we did what we were told, so I started doing it. Here comes Cards manager Eddie Dyer hollering to the umpire about me. I think it was Beans Reardon. Reardon comes out to the mound to tell me to cut it out and Durocher is right behind him.

"He's going to keep on doing it as long as the other guy does it," Leo barks. "When he stops, we'll stop."

That put an end to some of Mr. Brecheen's tricks for the day. Come to think of it, Harry Brecheen was later the Orioles pitching coach. Maybe that explains Tommy Phoebus doing it.

The most recent guy I saw doing it was Bob Ojeda in Baltimore in 1993. He scratched around with his foot, covered the rubber with dirt, then stepped a foot in front of it when he threw.

Nolan Ryan was accused of doing it during one of his no-hitters.

Other pitchers, of course, have done a little cheating now and then. Gaylord Perry did a lot of it, but he sometimes just went through the motions, playing mental games with the hitter. Lew Burdette was a master at that.

Elston Howard would rub a little mud in the seams for Whitey Ford's benefit.

Cookie Lavagetto helped out the Brooklyn pitchers with tobacco juice. When the umpire handed our catcher a new ball, Leo's orders were to throw it to Cookie at third base. When he caught the ball, it would go Splat! in his glove and come out half-black. He didn't throw it to the pitcher; he walked over and handed it to him. It was good for one pitch, but that one pitch could be devastating.

Don Sutton, Jim Bunning, Drysdale did things to the ball late in their careers.

In Baltimore we had Dave Schmidt. One day Wade Boggs said to me before a game, "Dave Schmidt pitching? He cheats."

"What do you mean?" I asked.

"You didn't know that? A little dampness on two fingers."

When it's hot, a pitcher sweats and is wet all over. It's easy to get a little on the fingertips. Al Lopez told me a lot of times a pitcher will throw a spitter and not even know it. They're out there sweating so much they pick it up unknowingly. The catcher knows it, when that fastball moves a little differently.

Mike Torrez is another member of the George Bamberger fan club. Bambi had him in his only year here, 1975, the only year he ever won 20. Torrez would come inside and was a good pitcher. Then he hurt his arm and was not the same. Popular, handsome, married at one time to a Miss Canada or a Miss something, one of the most beautiful girls I'd ever seen.

One particular scene comes to mind when I think of Torrez. He's pitching against the Yankees in Baltimore. Thurman Munson hits a home run off him the first time up. Next time up, he hits a double. Torrez has a big lead when Thurman comes up late in the game. Knowing Mike, I'm thinking, "Munson might go down on this pitch." Torrez whistles one right behind Munson's ear. Down he goes. Munson being Munson, he gets up and I can hear him calling Torrez everything but a person.

Next pitch, Munson hits a little comebacker to the mound. All the way down to first, he's screaming every profanity he can think of at Torrez, who lobs the ball to first. The umpire is following Munson down the baseline because it looks like all hell is going to break loose. Torrez is a big, strong guy. Munson wasn't that tall, but he was powerful and enjoyed a fight.

Torrez stands on the mound and throws him a kiss and says, "Sweetheart. I love you, too."

My God. That tore Thurman right out of his shoes. He headed for the mound but nothing happened. One of the greatest comebacks I ever heard.

Torrez won his 20, became a free agent and went where the money was.

Steve Stone was a little guy (with the Orioles, anybody under six feet tall was a little guy) who threw overhand. Strictly a curve ball pitcher, if he threw a hundred pitches, 85 would be curves. One night we counted 45 curves in a row. From 45 different angles. You just knew he wasn't going to last pitching like that. The only guy I've ever known who could pitch that way for a long time was Johnny Sain.

Stone was released by the Cubs in 1976 and was working that winter in the Pump Room restaurant in Chicago as a maitre d' or something, in a tuxedo. Roland Hemond was with the White Sox at the time. He had seen Stone pitch a few times late in the season and he thought Steve was worth a chance. So Bill Veeck dispatched him to have lunch at the elegant dining room and talk to Stone.

The White Sox signed him; he had a decent year in '77 and signed again with the Sox out of gratitude for the chance they gave him. But the next year his asking price was more than the

White Sox could afford and he came to Baltimore, where he became the Orioles' winningest pitcher ever, 25 and 7, in 1980 and won the Cy Young Award.

That was the only year he ever had like that. In '81 he was 4 and 7 and out of the game.

Dick Hall. Take a look at his walks and strikeouts; it'll scare you. He never walked anybody, and if he did, it was intentional. He was a six-foot-six overhand pitcher. Then he hurt his arm and came up with a sidearm, herky-jerky motion. It looked like anybody in the world could hit him, but he knew where to throw the ball. Location, location.

Dick studied to be a CPA while he was pitching. A brilliant guy, and one of Brooks's close friends. He'd sit in the bullpen, watching raindrops dribbling off the roof, and say, "You know, the way those raindrops are falling in the next five minutes there will be 37 of them. That means over so many days, we could have water so deep..." calculating that stuff in his head.

Doyle Alexander was traded by the Dodgers to Baltimore for Frank Robinson. One of the most sought-after young pitchers in the game, he was a tall guy who could throw hard, sidearm, with good control. He won some pennants for people, finishing strong in the last month. But he was selfish about everything he did. A loner with little personality, and not very friendly, he never mixed with the other players here.

Grant Jackson, a left-hander who threw pretty hard. Used in relief, very popular with the players, but just didn't have a great deal of talent. Later a coach in Pittsburgh, he shows up often at Dream Week.

Ross Grimsley, left-hander, threw so soft he couldn't hurt you if he hit you. But he'd throw inside, and throw a spitter. I remember Thurman Munson hitting against him, yelling, "Jesus Christ, throw the ball hard enough for somebody to hit."

He and Mike Flanagan are close friends.

Eddie Watt and Pete Richert were the righty-lefty bullpen for the Orioles during the pennant-winning years. Very good relief pitchers, but Eddie is remembered in this town for one thing—the home run he gave up to Lee May in the 1970 World Series, in the only game they lost to the Reds. From that day on, every time Watt made a move, he was booed. He didn't deserve that. But it did not get to him; he came back and was just as effective the next few years.

Strange what people remember. They don't remember all the good things he did. When he showed up for oldtimers games, they still booed him, up until a few years ago.

I pitched to catcher Mickey Owen, who was booed for years after he missed a strikeout pitch that led to a loss for the Dodgers in the 1941 World Series. Then, a few years ago, at a Dodgers reunion in Los Angeles, he got one of the biggest ovations of all, as if the fans were finally saying, "We recognize what a great player you really were." And he was.

As a former player, I've never booed anybody. I can't do that. That guy suffers as much as anybody. Put yourself in his place. Would you boo yourself?

Pete Richert came from the Dodgers organization. A bull-dog type of guy with a good curve and a sense of humor, he and Watt teased each other and did a good job for the Orioles.

Sammy Stewart: now there's a tragedy. Hard thrower, good control, great slider. But all screwed up in his head. Just his own worst enemy. The Orioles worked with him for eight years before giving up. You never thought you were getting 100 percent out of him. He thought he should have been a starter, but he didn't do the job and was used in relief. He went to Boston, and lasted a year there.

From North Carolina, he used that southern accent to try to be humorous. He might have been funny to some fans, but not to the players.

Sammy should have been a very good pitcher for a lot of years. It's too bad, because he had great talent. Could throw as hard as anybody, but just didn't use it. He's had more problems since he left baseball. I hope he's all right. I worry about guys like that.

Don Stanhouse. Stan the Man Unusual, Three-pack Stanhouse—the forerunner of Mitch Williams. Relief pitcher extraordinaire.

His philosophy was, "No hitter, even if I have to walk him, is going to hit his pitch. They're going to hit my pitch or they're not going to hit at all."

He drove the whole club crazy. Took his time, 3 and 2...3 and 2...Earl called him Three-pack because Earl would smoke three packs of cigarettes in the runway behind the dugout every time Stanhouse came in.

Don would come in with runners on first and second and promptly walk the next guy. Then he'd go 3 and 2 and get a popup or something and work his way out of it.

If he had a bad outing, he was one who could shake it off and bounce back. He did a good job for a couple years.

In the 1979 World Series, Weaver kept using Stanhouse and Don kept getting pounded. Earl said, "He got us here, and I'm going to go with the guy who got us here."

The last guy who followed that old maxim was Jim Fregosi with his closer, Mitch Williams in the '93 Series, and look where it got him.

I don't buy it. Stanhouse was wearing out at the end of the year, he was used so much down the stretch and in the playoffs. If you've got somebody better on the day you need him, you go with that guy, even if he didn't get you there. I think you have to adjust when guys stop doing the job they have been doing. But that's another one of those baseball arguments that will go on until the end of the world.

The Dodgers paid Stanhouse big money in 1980 but he was at the end of the line.

Mike Boddicker was a genius at throwing all kinds of junk, then throwing an 80-mph fastball that looked like 110. Never a hard thrower, he threw 20 different pitches 20 different ways, and they all did something different. More important, he could control them all.

A bulldog, he came up twice before he finally stayed. First guy in the clubhouse, he'd be in uniform at 3 o'clock for a night game. A nervous wreck even when he wasn't pitching.

The guy who probably did more for him than anybody was Ray Miller, the pitching coach. He helped Mike make the most of all that garbage and junk he threw, using it to set up his less-than-overpowering fastball. The way it looked, you'd want to grab a bat and run out on the field and start hitting.

Mike was inquisitive and intelligent, and learned from guys like Palmer and Flanagan. A tough little battler. He came from Iowa, and worked in the grain elevators during the winter.

When Don Aase broke in with the Red Sox, he threw very hard, and would knock you down in a wink. Then he went to California and hurt his arm. He had an operation and the Orioles took a chance on him. He gave them a few good years. A very popular guy, with a lot of heart, he'd battle you to the very end and give you everything he had. He and Boddicker became good friends.

Ken Dixon came up from AA Charlotte to the big leagues with a great curve, fantastic 90-plus fastball. However, hitters on other teams would tell me, "He throws as hard as anybody, but the fastball doesn't do anything. The ball doesn't move. If you wait two or three innings, you'll get to him."

He came up in '84; his first two starts he pitched okay, but lost one. He lasted three years.

One night on the air somebody asked me, "Why does Dixon give up so many home runs?"

I said, "Mr. Rickey taught us that if the fastball doesn't do much when you throw hard, it's because you grip the ball too tight."

The next day Dixon came to me and complained about what I had said. I asked him to show me how he held his fastball; it was like a vise. I couldn't pry it out of his hand.

I said, "Ken, that's my point. You might not agree with me, but with every fastball pitcher I've ever known, the ball is held very lightly. You get more rotation and more movement that way. The farther back and the tighter you hold it, the ball's not going to do very much. You might be able to throw it hard, but it won't move."

He didn't buy it.

To this day, I know that's the problem. I see it with other guys, but they learn to loosen the grip.

We used to ask Mr. Rickey, "Why does Koufax's fastball do so much?"

He said, "Take a look at his hands. Koufax should have been a surgeon. He's got very long, thin fingers. And the way he holds the ball gives it more rotation, and more movement."

All that makes sense to me, but you get a headstrong kid who gets away with a lot in AA, then comes up to the majors and thinks he's got it made. I like Dixon, but he just seemed to do himself in.

Not that these kids are uncoachable; they just don't want to be coached. A lot of guys get to the big leagues, and they might have a good year or two, then they think, "That's it. I'm a major league player."

Well, that's not it. It gets harder as you go on. Harder and harder and harder.

Talking about how hard pitchers throw—or think they throw—reminds me of an incident that happened in spring training with the Dodgers. We were in the Dominican Republic and had a pitcher named Ed Chandler who thought he could really fire it. One day he said to Arky Vaughan, "I bet I'm too fast for you to get around on me."

Vaughn, in his last year as a player, picked up a bat and stood at the plate. When Chandler threw, Arky dropped the bat, turned and caught the pitch barehanded. That ended the discussion.

Tim Stoddard was the six-foot-seven center on a North Carolina State NCAA championship basketball team that included David Thompson.

As the right-handed relief pitcher when Tippy was the lefty in the bullpen, Tim was a workhorse. He'd pitch every day if you asked him. He made 64 appearances in 1980. Threw very hard, and not afraid to come inside.

Steve Bedrosian said, "This is a game of peaks and valleys. A reliever's job is outhouse or penthouse. You have to be mentally tough. If you're not, this game is going to get to you...You just have to have the faith and the confidence that you'll bounce back."

Tippy was good at bouncing back; Tim was not.

Tim and Tippy hung out together, and they were a funny sight. Tim was nine inches taller and 50 pounds heavier. Occasionally, during early practice, they would swap uniforms and come out on the field. Honest to God, you'd just cry laughing.

That was a relaxed, fun-loving club in the late '70s, early

'80s. They don't come like that these days.

Jose Bautista was one of those guys who come in with a world of stuff. You watch him and you think, "How can he miss?" But I don't think he knew how to pitch when he was here. He's with the Cubs now; maybe he's learned. He was a thrower with the Orioles, not a pitcher. His fastball didn't move much, and his curve came in regularly above the waist. If you do that in the big leagues, you're in trouble.

His attitude was, "I'm a major leaguer, and I'll do what I can do, and if they don't like it, so be it."

They didn't like it, at least not in Baltimore.

You watch Jose Mesa and you have to say, "Don't give up on him," but the Orioles finally did. I like his arm and he'll battle you, but he didn't seem to get the job done, here or so far in Cleveland. Great stuff, but doesn't know how to pitch. He gets down on himself. If he gives up a home run, he thinks he doesn't have anything and can't win. Jose shows signs of brilliant pitching, and if he ever gets over that attitude and learns to pitch, he could be a good one.

Bob Milacki was a tough guy who could give you 300 innings if he was pitching back in the old days when pitches weren't counted. He was a hard-luck guy with the Orioles, and rarely got any run support. But he never complained, or ran off at the mouth about a guy who made a bad play or an error behind him.

Milacki was Big Bird in the clubhouse because he walked like the Orioles mascot. He went to arbitration one year when everybody, including me, predicted that he would back off and sign before going through with it. We all said he would cave in first. He told me, "I did it because I wanted to find out what it was all about, and I really thought I deserved more than they were offering."

He went, and he won.

I was high on him, but I was disappointed. He knew how to pitch and had great stuff and a good changeup. Maybe there is a pitching coach out there who can make a difference, but so far none has.

I like Pete Harnisch, another bulldog type of kid, who just won't quit. He'd pitch every day if you let him. A tough New

York street kid, he would pitch inside without hesitating, knock you down without a second thought. But he had wild streaks. His motion was kind of screwed up, and when they tried to change it, he didn't do very well and they traded him in the Glenn Davis deal. I didn't like to see him go, and hoped they would get him back in '94.

Dave Johnson's one of those guys who, if you're older and you've ever played the game of baseball, you fall in love with. Seven or eight years in the minor leagues, and he finally gets a shot with his hometown team. When we got him from the Houston organization, I asked Yogi Berra, then an Astros coach, about him. Yogi said, "He's a control pitcher. Doesn't have overpowering stuff, but he has the guts of a burglar."

The first time Johnson was in Memorial Stadium as a player, I had to show him where the clubhouse was.

He is one of the most delightful, appreciative guys I've known. Worked on garbage trucks and fuel trucks, pumped gas, did everything in the off-season to make a living as a ballplayer. That's all he ever wanted to be.

He told me, "There were times I thought I wasn't going to do it, but I'll make it now."

In his first game, he pitched pretty good in Boston, but lost. Then he came back to Baltimore and tossed back-to-back complete games. The fans went crazy.

During his couple years here, he made more money in one month on the banquet and clinic circuit than he used to do in six months in the wintertime.

Justifiably or not, Dave criticized the club a few times because he thought he should have pitched more often. I can understand that. No manager minds that. They'd rather have somebody with that attitude than a guy begging off working.

With all he's been through, Dave will wind up on his feet. While he was pitching in an Orioles uniform, it was, as he said, "the most unbelievable thing that ever happened to me."

The Orioles acquired Curt Schilling from the Red Sox with Brady Anderson for Mike Boddicker on July 30, 1988. His first spring training with us was 1989 in Miami.

Chuck Thompson and I used to go to a place on Key

Biscayne for breakfast. One morning about 7:00 we were sitting there, and in came Schilling, smelling like a brewery, with two of the worst-looking females I've ever seen. Lipstick all over him, a big earring in his ear, his hair in a ponytail.

I said to Chuck, "I'm going to ask Mr. Schilling to step into the men's room with me. If I don't come out in five minutes, you better come and get me."

I took him in there and said, "Curt, do you really want to be a major league pitcher?"

"That's all I want to be."

"Well, you're never going to be."

"Why not?"

I said, "Two of the reasons are sitting out there waiting for you. Another reason is you and that earring and that ponytail. Take that thing out of your ear and you know what you can do with it. Get a haircut and be a man. You have a lot of talent."

He said, "You really mean that?"

I said, "Yeah, I'm just trying to help you. You got a chance."

He was 21. He had great equipment, but the people in Boston thought he'd never get straightened out. At that time he could throw better than Ben McDonald. One day in Ft. Lauderdale, he and Ben were going to pitch. I sat in the bullpen and watched them warm up. They both looked good. Ben went first and shut them out for three innings. Then Schilling went out and left it in the bullpen. He tightened up and didn't have it.

Schilling went back and forth to Rochester a few times, and did not show much the few chances he got to pitch in Baltimore. He was still a wild kid off the field, and I guess the Orioles thought he would not straighten out. He got fed up and did not want to go down again, and the Orioles sent him to Houston in the Glenn Davis deal.

Then he got married and had a child. His father, whom he was very close to, died. And he grew up. That's when the Phillies took a chance with him. Johnny Podres, their pitching coach, had a lot to do with his success in '93. He could relate to this kid; he'd had some similar experiences. I always knew Curt had it physically. It was just a matter of getting his head on straight.

After his great 1993 season, Baltimore officials got crucified for letting him go. But timing is all-important in the development and success of some people. It reminded me of my old Brooklyn idol, Whitlow Wyatt, who failed with several teams and did not succeed until he was in his 30s.

Jeff Ballard came to Baltimore from Stanford with a great reputation as a bright, left-handed finesse pitcher. He grew up in Billings, Montana and played high school ball with Dave McNally's son. McNally recommended him.

Ballard's priorities got screwed up when they made him the player rep. I liked Jeff, but I never thought he was going to be a good pitcher. I just didn't like some of the things I saw. I'd get into arguments with Roland Hemond and some of the media guys about it. All I could say was, "It's a personal thing. I don't think he's a pitcher." I saw something; I don't know that I could tell you what it was.

Then he had a big year: 18-8 in 1989. Got a big raise. Had an operation after the season for chips in his elbow. Everybody said it was nothing serious. He was throwing pretty good in spring training the next year, but by the end of the year he was practically throwing underhand. Won 2 and lost 11. And got another big raise.

I can't handle that, and nobody has ever been able to give me an answer to justify that big raise after a 2-11 season. It bothered some other pitchers on the club who did better and did not get that kind of raise. Maybe I'm a throwback to the days when you were lucky to wring a few thousand extra out of a club after you had a big year. But that's the way I see it.

Ballard tried to make a comeback but he hasn't got it back yet.

Fernando Valenzuela in 1993? A miracle.

California and the Dodgers said he couldn't throw, had no fastball at all. He went to Mexico and pitched against minor leaguers. In spring training I didn't think he had a chance to make the club. It seemed like every time somebody got on base, he picked them off or they hit into a double play to get him out of trouble. He went into rehab and got himself into shape and came back throwing harder.

Fernando knew how to pitch, and he owned any inexperienced hitter who came up against him.

When I saw switch-hitters like Roberto Alomar bat left-handed against him, I thought of Arky Vaughan who told me that when Carl Hubbell, the greatest lefty screwball pitcher ever, pitched against them, they would play more left-handed hitters than righties, because the ball broke down and in toward them.

Fernando stayed pretty much to himself while he was in Baltimore. In his prime he was a good hitter, too, but he said he had all he could do to concentrate on pitching in the American League and was just as happy not to have to hit.

You hear me talk a lot about Michael Flanagan's sense of humor, and that sometimes overshadows his ability as a pitcher. But it shouldn't.

Michael was one tough left-hander out there. Great curve to go with a good fastball, control, confidence and plenty of heart.

He also had a good pickoff move to first base, and holds the Orioles record with 61 pickoffs.

Following his 1979 23-9 Cy Young Award year, he had some injuries that set him back for a few years and would have finished off a lot of other guys. Then, in 1983, after he got off to a 6-0 start, he tore the ligaments in his left knee in a game on May 17 and was out for almost 12 weeks. He missed the first half of the '85 season because he hurt his Achilles tendon playing basketball in January. His doctor told me, "There's only one guy I know who can come back from this injury, and that's Flanagan."

He drove himself in rehabilitation, tears rolling down his face, but he was determined to come back. And he did.

Mike had come up in the Orioles organization, which he felt was built on pitchers going nine innings. Then he was traded to Toronto in 1987. In one of the first games he pitched there, he was working on a one-hitter, leading 2-0. When he came off the mound after the sixth inning, manager Jimy Williams came up to him and said, "Mike, thank you for a good job."

Mike said, "Wait a minute. I've got a one-hitter going here."

"That's okay. You've done plenty," Williams said. "That's all we need from you."

Mike said from then on, he got into that frame of mind,

contrary to the way he'd been brought up in baseball. He didn't like it.

In '91 he pitched to the last two batters in Memorial Stadium and that was fitting and proper. He had come back after a few years in Toronto, went to spring training as a non-roster player, and wound up relieving in 64 games.

What a guy to have on a ball club. Always laughing, always with a wisecrack. They kidded him, too, but he seemed to have the last line. His sense of humor came from his mother, who wrote an Erma Bombeck kind of column for a New England newspaper. Flanny was part of the Irish Mafia on the Orioles. One of his favorite stories involves the first time he pitched in Yankee Stadium. They used golf carts to bring the pitchers in from the bullpen. The first time he got in one to go to the mound, the driver said, "You better lock the door."

Flanny was puzzled. "Lock the door? What kind of trouble can I get into from here to the mound?"

The driver said, "You'll see."

He was right. On the way the fans were throwing things that thumped against the cart. Flanny says, "That's when I knew I was in New York and Yankee Stadium."

We were on a team bus after flying into a city and it's about three o'clock in the morning and the players are half asleep and it's all quiet and Flanny yells out, "What a life! Big league ball! What a life!"

If somebody in a restaurant was being obnoxious, he'd say, "What a guy," sarcastically.

We were in Oakland one day, sitting on the rolled-up tarp alongside the dugout. It's early, and out comes Dennis Martinez.

"Come on, Flanny. Let's play catch."

"Okay, Ameager," he says.

I started laughing. "Why do you call him that?"

He said, "Everybody calls him Amigo, and he's got meager talent, so I call him Ameager. He doesn't know what I'm saying, anyhow."

He called Storm Davis Cy Clone, because he wanted to be a clone of Jim Palmer, who became Cy Old after Flanny won the Award, and when he was released he became Cy-onara.

Gregg Olson was improving every year until he hurt his arm. He had two things to work on. He had a problem holding men on base, and he had to come up with another pitch to go with his curve and fastball.

Guys who are great pitchers in college often come to the major leagues and have a terrible move to first base, and nobody understands that. The answer is simple: they rarely had anybody reach first against them. They just reared back and threw hard, with no concerns about pitching to spots. Kids swung at anything. But you get up to the big leagues and the hitters don't do you any favors.

Gregg had to work on his footwork and on speeding up his delivery. He was always a slow worker, walking off and circling the mound after every pitch. But it was his release of the ball that had to be quickened.

Gregg worked on developing a changeup, but it did not come easy to him. When he could not get his curve—which is outstanding—over for strikes, hitters sat on his fastball. Like a hitter, he would get into a slump a few times a year. Hitters detected it. When his curve was not working, they would go up to the plate thinking: "Curve, no. Curve, no. Fastball—yes!"

Olson was working on throwing his fastball more when he went down with arm trouble. He knew he could no longer rely as much on the curve. A crossword puzzle addict, he also takes his Nintendo on the road with him. He's into heavy metal music, and the Ninja turtles. He used to put some of those figures in the bullpen to jinx the other team. He was part of the regular game of Hearts that included Rick Sutcliffe, Bob Milacke and Joe Orsulak.

Olson had some great years with the Orioles, but he is yet to become the pitcher I believe he can be, if he recovers from his arm problems.

At one point there was some talk of making him a starter, but I'd keep him in the bullpen. That takes a different mindset, and I think he can handle it. Sitting in the bullpen, you've got to study everything that's going on in the game. When you come walking in there, you better get your head on: what's the situation, who's on base, who's at bat or likely to pinch hit.

Olson is a hard worker. I hope he can come back, but the jury is still out on that. After the Orioles released him in the fall of 1993, they made Gregg a pretty good offer to remain, although three doctors said he needed an operation. During the winter Elrod caught him under the stands and said, "It's almost like he's afraid to throw."

California and the Yankees looked him over and turned him down. Then his agent sent him to two doctors in Atlanta who said he did not need an operation, and the Braves signed him and took a gamble on his future.

But it got me when some guys in the media got on the club for letting Olson go. I don't understand guys who have been on the job for three or four years and know more about the game than guys who have been in it all their lives. I know what they say: "Just because you old guys have been in it all your lives, you think you know it all."

I've never known anybody yet who's been in baseball all his life and thinks he knows it all.

One day on my 4:15 show in the spring of 1994 I ripped the Orioles pitching staff. The next day they pitched a 1-0 shutout. I got back on the air and said, "Now you know why I say nobody knows baseball."

Rick Sutcliffe was more than just a pitcher while he was with the Orioles. He was more than an unofficial pitching coach, too. Rick helped everybody. Hitters would ask him about certain pitchers they hadn't seen before. He taught Chris Hoiles some things about calling a game. He told the young pitchers what he thought, and worked with them.

As a National League pitcher, Rick lived on the inside. Pitching inside has always been part of the game, but for some reason it was accepted more in the National than the American League, despite the fact that pitchers have to hit in the NL. I don't know why that is. When you start out in the Dodgers organization, as Rick did, you come up pitching inside.

So when Rick came to the Orioles I was a little concerned that he might lose some of his effectiveness if he did not get the calls on inside pitches or, worse, if he got into trouble with hitters complaining and umpires warning him. But he was not about to change his style, even if some hitters squawked.

There have always been some pitchers who are afraid of hitting a batter and will not brush them back. I recall a meeting at the Polo Grounds in 1950, when Charlie Dressen was the Brooklyn manager. Carl Erskine was pitching that day. Dressen said, "Carl, there are certain hitters on the Giants I want you to knock down."

Carl said, "I can't do that. If that's what you want, get somebody else."

Some pitchers do not want to risk starting a brawl. Others couldn't care less. Sutcliffe was one of the latter. Even though he had to go up to the plate as a batter in the National League, it didn't bother him.

Nolan Ryan got away with murder, because the umpires shied away from warning Mr. Ryan. In 1991 when he beat Jose Mesa, 1-0, in Baltimore, he flipped Ripken, Milligan and a few others quick. Everybody said, well, he's just a little wild. Baloney. I knew what he was doing and the hitters did, too. He was taking away that outside corner.

Much as I liked Sutcliffe, I think the Orioles did the right thing when they let him go after the '93 season. They needed a more consistent pitcher in that spot in the rotation, and they had the young arms to put in there. There comes a time when the older guys have to move on and give the younger kids an opportunity.

13

Now Pitching for the Visitors...

One of my pet peeves about baseball these days is this closer business. If a guy is going good after eight innings, why take him out? I can't buy that. In a close game, let him go into the ninth. If he gives up a hit or a walk, then maybe take him out. But not this automatic stuff where your closer pitches the ninth—if there is a save in it for him.

I'd like to see them take the save stat out altogether. I think it's a joke, a nonsense stat. But every agent would go berserk, because their guy has to close and get every save and build up his stats for arbitration or contract time and that's baloney. The agents and the front office put pressure on the managers. They run the game today.

The so-called set-up guy or middle reliever, who may pitch four or five shutout innings to get to the ninth for the "closer," gets nothing out of it in the won-lost-save stats. What's fair about that?

I'd go one step further. Bob Feller advocated this: there should not be a winning pitcher and a losing pitcher. It should be, "Bob Feller pitched and the team won...Sandy Koufax pitched when the team won...Joe Black when they lost...Rex Barney when they won—sometimes." The pitcher is just part of the team, except in the American League where you have to have some dumb

DH.

But I don't expect my saying these things is going to change anything, so let's talk about some closers I have watched over the past 25 years.

Relief pitchers are a different breed. They have to think differently. They sit out there and watch the game, and if you are a Rollie Fingers or a Gregg Olson, you know exactly where you are coming from. Middle relievers never know from day to day, but those closers know exactly when their time has come to work.

Whenever Fingers came in, it seemed as if the tempo increased on both sides. His team felt, "We've got our guy in there; we're going to win," and the other team felt, "It's going to be tough, but we have to get to this guy." They both turned it up a little.

Fingers was all business out there. He kidded around in the clubhouse. Players would tease him about that big mustache, try to pull it straight, and he went along with it.

When a reliever gets up to throw, you could set off a bomb under the bullpen and they wouldn't hear it. They are concentrating so hard. The worst thing for them is when they warm up and are ready and then they have to stand there for another hitter or something. And some of them can be ready after five pitches. Tom Henke was one who was ready almost immediately. Bobby Thigpen, too.

Dave Righetti is another one of my favorite people. Yogi Berra talked him into being a reliever. I'd bring him in against any hitter, didn't matter how he batted. Always one of the first in the clubhouse, he and Ron Guidry would play cards before every game.

Dave would do an interview any time with anybody. He doesn't have a mean bone in his body except when he walks out on the mound.

One day I was in the dugout waiting for the end of the game to do an interview. Righetti was pitching. Yogi had been thrown out of the game, so he was standing in the runway in back of the dugout where I was waiting. Jeff Torborg was running the club.

A situation came up with a man on second and first base open. Torborg said to Yogi, "Shall we pitch to him or put him on?"

Yogi turned to me and said, "Okay, Rex, you think you're so smart. What do you want to do here?"

I said, "Oh, he can take this guy. Pitch to him."

The game wasn't that close, so there was no harm done, and Rags got the guy. But that's not the only reason I like him so much.

Sparky Lyle had a great sense of humor; he could take it as well as give it. He loved to tease Yogi about everything.

Dan Quisenberry was another guy who could take teasing. His own players would say things like, "That stuff you throw, my little girl could hit," and Quis would reply, "That's why I throw it; your little girl could hit it, but you can't."

His control and unorthodox underhand delivery made him successful. Batters don't see many pitchers coming from that angle.

Dennis Eckersley was a dour, serious guy as a starter. I never thought he would be the great reliever he became. A hard-working guy, he'd run five or six miles early in the day. He's become looser and more talkative. Nothing shakes him up. I've seen him signing for kids after a tough game, the other players waiting for him on the bus.

Goose Gossage liked to come off as mean, but he wasn't. He was a great kidder, and loved to fish. He could not work two days in a row. I think he relied on his sidearm throwing too much. I remember two guys who could hit him: Kiki Garcia and Mark Belanger.

Most pitchers say their best pitch is the fastball. At the same time, every hitter looks for the fastball to hit? How can that be? Pitchers' best pitch is the same as what hitters like to hit. It has always been that way. Maybe for pitchers, it's because they can control the fastball better. And hitters don't like to swing at junk. Another one of baseball's eternal mysteries.

There has not been a new pitch in baseball in the past 100 years. There are just new names. The slider has been around a long time; they called it a nickel curve. (Burt Shotton, who managed the Dodgers in the late '40s, called it a horseshit curve.) A lot of managers did not like it.

In Game 1 of the 1949 World Series, Tommy Henrich hit a home run off Don Newcombe in the last of the ninth to win it, 1-0. The next day Henrich said to me, "That Newcombe has some kind of slider." What he didn't know was that Newcombe never threw a slider. He never had a curve that amounted to anything, either. That pitch had been as good a curve as he could throw.

The split-finger fastball used to be called a forkball. But there is a difference between them. The forkball was pushed far back between the fingers before it was thrown. It was used as a changeup, and was very difficult to control. The split-finger is not pushed back as far. Elroy Face was the best at controlling the forkball.

Hitters do not have to face the spitter as much as they once did, nor the emery ball and slippery elm ball, and hitting the same ball for half the game, as they did in the first 20 years or so of this century.

But there are a lot of tough major league starting pitchers out there. One reason minor league hitting champions often cannot follow through in the majors is that in the minors they may see one very good pitcher a week; in the majors it's almost every day.

Here are some snapshot memories of a few of them.

Bill Lee, the Spaceman, a delightful, fun-loving guy. Pitchers love to go out to the outfield during batting practice and fool around. Lee would turn his cap backwards and catch fly balls behind his back. People who came out early would applaud and he'd entertain them and take his bows.

Bert Blyleven was born in Holland. Highly competitive, very outspoken, he would knock you down in a second. A great curveball pitcher.

In the winter of 1977 I was riding to Cumberland to do a banquet with Chuck Thompson, Jim Frey and Al Bumbry. Somebody mentioned that Blyleven had been traded from Texas to the Pittsburgh Pirates. Bumbry let out a whoop. "That's the best news I've ever heard. I never could hit that S.O.B. He has the greatest curve God ever put on earth. I'm a left-hand batter and he's a right-hand pitcher, but that curve was deadly."

When school was out, Blyleven always had a couple of his

sons with him at the ballpark.

Roger Clemens is another big star who is very gracious when it comes to an interview. One night in Baltimore he was taken out of a tough close game in the ninth. I knew he hated to come out of a situation like that. I was waiting in the runway to do an interview and I had selected him as the star of the game. When he came in, he said, "What are you doing here?"

"I was going to do a postgame interview with you, but you're losing, so I guess you won't want to do it."

He said, "No, I'll be back to do it."

He went into the clubhouse and got a big icepack on his shoulder, and when the game ended he came back out and did the interview.

I once asked Clemens, "What do you want to accomplish?"

He said, "I just want to be known as one of the best pitchers ever, and I'll work hard to get there."

Dave Stewart, that mean-looking, glowering intimidator out there on the mound? Looks like he's ready to walk up to you and pinch your head off? A bright, giving, sweetheart of a man. And he has a squeaky, high-pitched voice that belies everything you see.

The Orioles might have signed him in 1986 when he was released by the Phillies. The Dodgers and Texas had given up on him before that. Elrod Hendricks invited him to come down and talk to Hank Peters. Peters told him, "The only thing we can offer you is a AA contract, and if you can work your way back, fine."

Oakland was his home town. He decided to go back there and try to get a better deal. Oakland offered him a AAA contract and a little more money, and he took it.

People say the Orioles flubbed it, but they didn't. Stewart was no great prize at the time. He was 0-6 in 1985. He had started with the Dodgers, got out of shape, then discovered the martial arts and worked on that. He became a different person, but remained a gentleman.

Jim Kaat belongs in the Hall of Fame. A great fielder and good hitter. I first saw him when he was a rookie with the Washington Senators and they were playing the Dodgers at Vero Beach in the spring of 1959. I was visiting with Cookie Lavagetto, the Washington manager, and I asked him if he had any prospects worth watching.

"Yeah," he said, "the kid starting today, Kaat. He may not make it, but he is very teachable, throws hard and has a great attitude."

As a broadcaster today, he is still asked for advice by players, and is as well-prepared as a broadcaster as he was as a pitcher.

Denny McLain was not friendly, but aloof and very cocky. His most memorable game to me was a ten-inning 1-0 loss to Mike Cuellar in freezing weather in Baltimore the year they shared the Cy Young Award.

Gaylord Perry was another unfriendly guy, not popular. He played the cornpone image to the hilt. Cheated and everybody knew it, but he talked about it more than most.

Mickey Lolich was very outgoing, and kidded himself about being fat. But he did the job. A better pitcher than McLain, he was also a motorcycle rider.

Luis Tiant was loved in Baltimore because he threw the pitch that Frank Robinson hit out of Memorial Stadium. Much liked by other players, he was the butt of many jokes, but he kidded himself about his popularity in Baltimore.

Tommy John, the Philosopher, the modern Preacher Roe. Always talking. The kind of guy you say hello and a half hour later you might get away. And of course he was a good interview; all you had to do was ask him one question and he was good for ten minutes. It seems inevitable that he would wind up in broadcasting.

There is not a negative bone in Tommy John's body; he is all positive. Very popular in the clubhouse and respected by every manager he played for. They'd kid him about being an old man, but he took it and gave it back. Whenever the Yankees were in Baltimore, he'd have a few of his sons with him. They'd be out in the outfield with him in their little uniforms.

I first met Tom Seaver in the 1969 World Series. Gil Hodges introduced me to him and I interviewed him. Hodges told me, "We have two hard throwers on this club, Seaver and Nolan Ryan. Seaver will be the better pitcher of the two."

Confident is the word for Seaver. I thought he would make a great pitching coach, but like so many stars he probably would not have the patience. He was a broadcaster with the Yankees. I saw him when they came to Baltimore, and he said, "Imagine how tough you'd have been if you had my control."

I said to him, "Imagine how tough you would have been if you could throw as hard as I could."

They all tease me about that, but you gotta get back at them. You can't let them roost on you.

When Chuck Finley is going to pitch for California, I can't wait for the game to start. Well, I can't wait for any game to start. But I get a little more keyed up when Finley is pitching. Like Greg Swindell, he's pitched with bad ball clubs. You never know how a pitcher will do going to a winning team. They don't always make the adjustment easily. Baseball is a mind game, and there's a world of difference between pitching for a last-place team and one fighting for the pennant.

I feel the same way about Jim Abbott. Nobody notices his missing hand anymore. He's become a real pitcher in a hurry. Never changes his demeanor.

Nolan Ryan was just a down home farmer. Always great with the fans, he would wave and greet people on his way to the bullpen to warm up. One night in Baltimore he gave up three home runs and lost. As I left the park later, the Texas team bus was waiting outside the stadium. When a visiting team loses, they walk to the bus, heads down, talk to nobody, and nobody stops to sign autographs.

Here comes Ryan, wet with perspiration, the losing pitcher that night, and he sees people waiting for him. He stops and says, "Okay. Line up, let's go." And he starts signing. The players on the bus are yelling for him to get in, and he says, "You guys go ahead. I'll take a cab." And that's what he did.

The only other people I ever saw do that after a loss were Tony La Russa and Dennis Eckersley.

Why was Nolan Ryan a .500 pitcher? Sometimes lack of control. Not just walking people, although he averaged about five per nine innings and is first in walks as well as strikeouts, but not getting pitches right where he wanted them. And check how few runs his teams scored behind him. Not a lot.

Ron Guidry was a silent little guy who spoke with a slow Louisiana accent. One of those players who didn't think the fans wanted to hear them. But the fans do. They want to hear the players firsthand, not what somebody else has to say about them. Guidry was mean on the mound, threw hard, had a great slider. An avid card player, he lasted through all the Yankee turmoil because he had a steady attitude and did not let any of that stuff bother him.

I liked Mark Fidrych a great deal. A non-roster pitcher in spring training in 1976, he pitched a great game one day and Ralph Houk, the Detroit manager, told him he had made the club. He was 21. Mark tore up the clubhouse whooping and hollering with joy. Later he confided to some of the other players that the most exciting thing of all happened that night. He found some cute girl in Lakeland and they celebrated together and sneaked into the ballpark and made love on the pitcher's mound where he had made the team.

He had that one good year, 19-9, and then hurt his arm. He could flatout pitch. For all his antics on the mound, he was very intense out there. He lost a close game in Baltimore one day, and when Houk took him out he stomped off the mound and fired his glove into the dugout. Of course, that turned on the boo birds, but he was just mad at himself.

I feel bad about guys like that, who wind up with such a short career because of an injury.

Jack Morris is a serious, grumpy, moody, dedicated, big game pitcher.

Frank Tanana threw as hard as anybody when he started out. He was a wild, Hollywood-type guy off the field, but when he was traded to Detroit, he turned his life around, and became an artist as a pitcher, a dart thrower with different-speed curve balls.

Dave Stieb was highly competitive, a little like Jack Morris, battling you every second. He was part of a Toronto staff that included Jim Clancy and Jimmy Key, another pair of old school, pitch-inside hurlers. Like a lot of players, Key is an avid fisherman. He and Flanagan would talk more fishing than baseball whenever they got together.

Moose Haas, from Baltimore, a bulldog type who gave you everything, but was hurt a lot.

Don Sutton is one of my favorite people. One day when he was with Milwaukee I was interviewing him and I said, "Don, you have more than 200 wins now. I imagine your goal is to win 300."

He said, "No, I'll never win 300."

When we were off the air, he said, "Do you really think I can win 300?"

I said, "Yes, I do. Just go out there and do it. You'll have some more good years."

The he went to California and did it. Wound up with 324. He had started with the Dodgers in Los Angeles and he finished up with them.

One day I asked him, "Don, who taught you the spitter?

"Drysdale," he said, "but he never threw it until he was almost finished. He didn't have to. I asked him about throwing it, and he told me I didn't need it, then gave me this advice: 'There is always one guy on every team who is a real motormouth, always flapping. Go to him when you're running in the outfield and just mention that you've been working on a spitter and can throw a great one now. He'll tell everybody else on his team, and that'll put it in their minds that you throw a spitter. That's all you have to do.'

"I did that," Sutton told me, "and it worked. I never threw a spitter for several years after that, but guys would accuse me of throwing it all the time."

Whenever anybody asked Drysdale about it, his pat answer was, "No, I never threw a spitter. My mother told me never to put my fingers in my mouth."

They all have an answer. Bob Gibson used to say, "I just practice it on the sidelines, so if they ever legalize it, I'll be ready."

Charlie Hough is a good old country boy. He'll mix a slider in with his knuckler. He's a great interview. One day Phil Niekro got kicked out of a game when umpire Steve Palermo looked inside his cap and found an emery board. Hough told me, "God, I laughed when I heard that. Come over here."

He showed me his cap in the locker room and there was an emery board stuck in the sweatband. "I've been doing that for years," he said. "I use it between innings for my nails."

Yeah, sure.

Hough rides the stationary bike in the clubhouse every day. Skinny as a rail.

It's tough for me to watch those guys who just push the ball up to the plate. I don't think there has ever been a pennant winner that depended on a knuckleball pitcher. I know I wouldn't have one on my club. I just think in a tough situation, it draws the whole ball club up tight, especially the catcher. I don't think there is such a thing as a good knuckleball catcher, one who is able to catch the ball in the air before it hits the ground. Sure, they may be able to block it in the dirt, but is that a good knuckleball catcher? Not in my book.

Bruce Hurst is a friendly, talkative guy who never uses profanity. Popular with the players, his teammates like to play behind him, because they know they will get a well-pitched game.

Oil Can Boyd was a skinny, outgoing guy who knew how to pitch and could really throw hard before he hurt his arm. Players kidded him a lot; he always wore dark glasses, and it took him 20 minutes to get the jewelry off.

Bob Welch is one of the most profane people I know, but he straightened out his life after he had an alcohol problem early in his career. Very, very intent on the mound, he is a typical Dodger-trained pitcher: he lives inside, and if the batter gets too close to the plate, he is going to be more inside, and as soon as he establishes that, he's pitching out on the corner. That's a Dodger pitcher. Look at his record; double digit wins just about every year.

Mike Moore beaned Cal Ripken in 1982. Split the helmet. It upset Moore more than it did Cal. A quality pitcher, very serious, not very forthcoming in an interview.

When Bobby Witt broke in with Texas, manager Bobby Valentine said, "This guy will drive me into an early grave." Witt would go five or six innings and look like nobody was ever going to get a hit off him, then suddenly come apart, walk a bunch of guys. One time he'll look like the world's greatest pitcher, and the next time out he'll break your heart.

I can relate to that. One day the hitters don't have a chance, and the next time the pitchers don't have a chance. I learned this when I was in the major leagues at 18. There are days when you go out there and feel like you've got the greatest stuff, and you don't get past the first inning. Another time I retired 19 in a row at Ebbets Field and had nothing. I had Snider and Furillo climbing the walls all afternoon hauling in drives. That happens.

When I pitched my no-hitter, I knew I had something extra that night. I never threw better. But it doesn't always work out that way.

They must have one fine pitching coach at Stanford; they turn out a lot of good pitchers, including Jack McDowell. He came up to the majors, but had to go down again before he got it together. Has his own rock band; he might be too involved in his off-the-field interests. I'm an old guy; I kind of look down on that kind of distraction. We couldn't do anything but eat and talk and live baseball. Physically, when he's sound, he's as good as anybody.

Teddy Higuera could pitch from the day he came out of Mexico. As good as anybody from the start, he was hampered by arm problems and other injuries. But when we'd go into Milwaukee and guys would hear that Higuera was pitching, they shuddered.

Wilson Alvarez came up from the minors with great stuff but couldn't get it over. One day he started against the Orioles at Memorial Stadium, and Jeff Torborg told me, "If he gets the ball over the plate, we have a chance, but I doubt if he can do it."

He did it, and pitched a no-hitter. But he had to go back down until he could gain better control. When he gets it over the plate, he's tough.

I like the way the youngster, Jason Bere, conducts himself. Reminds me of Catfish Hunter. If he gives up a home run or gets in a jam, he pitches like he's still 10 runs ahead. Hunter was the greatest at that. No matter what the score was or the situation, he always looked as if he was going to win.

I saw Alex Fernandez pitch once for the University of Miami against the Orioles in spring training. Then he transferred to

Dade Junior College so he could get more pitching experience. He had it. He did not have to develop it.

Why is any left-hander who is any good called crafty? Have you ever heard of a crafty right-hander? They're all hard-throwing. When Frank Viola made his major league debut for Minnesota, you could see he was—crafty. A likeable kid with a thick New York accent, he didn't do too well in that game; Benny Ayala hit two home runs off him. But you just knew he would be a crafty left-hander, and he has been that.

Ron Darling came out of Yale. A real gentleman who knows how to pitch. That's the key word; pitcher, not thrower.

The greatest mental concentration goes on between the pitcher and hitter. I'd like to be able to listen to what's going on in their minds when a great pitcher is pitching to a great hitter.

14

The Hitters

Pitchers are not the only guys I watch on the field. Like any pitcher, I study hitters, too, and they are no longer the enemy. Here is a random, incomplete tour of some memorable non-pitchers through the years.

Bobby Bonds, Barry's father, got the unfair kind of treatment that I don't like to see any young player get: being compared to some great from the past. When he came up, he was ballyhooed as the next Willie Mays. I don't buy that stuff. Like when Sparky Anderson called Kirk Gibson another Mickey Mantle. That's not fair to the player. Bobby Bonds put up some great numbers. Will his son, Barry, do even better?

Dwight Evans was as popular all around the league as he was in Boston during all those years with the Red Sox. An elder statesman type, he had time for everybody. Always out on the field early, he had strict working habits. I don't think he liked the nickname Dewey; I never used it.

Kirk Gibson was very surly, no humor, little personality. He'd push a photographer aside if the guy was in his way going to the dugout. I was doing television one night and he was the choice as star of the game. I'm back of the dugout and Sparky Anderson says to me, "Who do you want?"

"I want Gibson, but I don't know if he'll do it."

"I'll take care of it."

Game's over. Gibson comes in and Sparky grabs him by the arm.

"You know Rex?"

"Yeah."

"Go on the air with him. You're the star of the game."

"All right, if you say so."

From then on, I had no problem with Gibson, but he'd always let me know, "Sparky would make me do it anyway."

I tell you, friends help in this business.

I always hated to do that star of the game show between games of a doubleheader. Players are in a hurry to change clothes and grab something to eat. I would ask a coach or a manager.

Kent Hrbek hung around with pro wrestlers, and expressed an interest in getting into that when he retired as a player.

Kirby Puckett is one of the best and nicest players in the game. Early in the clubhouse, smiles all the time, talks to everybody—stars, clubhouse boys, batboys, cleaning people—and knows them all by name. I've introduced him to TV cameramen before an interview, and a few years later he's, "Hey Joe, how are you." Remembers them all. Full of enthusiasm, he stands 10 feet tall in that way.

Kirby credits Tony Oliva with showing him how to sit back and wait on the ball. Loves to shoot pool. He puts on a pool tournament in Minnesota for charity.

Bob Boone got more strikes for his pitchers that were out of the strike zone than any other catcher. He would catch an outside or inside pitch and bring the glove in toward himself as he did it, so it looked like he had caught it in the strike zone. George Brett told me Boone could catch half the ball. On an inside pitch he would go farther inside with the glove and catch just the inside part of the ball, so the white part closest to the strike zone was the only part showing, and the opposite on outside pitches. On every low pitch, he swept the glove up as he caught it; on high ones, he brought it down. He expected to get every call and he let the umpire know it. And he was always talking with his pitchers, on the field and in the dugout. He made any pitcher better.

Boone will be a manager in the major leagues.

Bob's father, Ray, was a good third baseman. A lot of guys whose fathers played in my time ask me to tell them about their dads, what kind of players they were. That happens more and more these days.

Dick Allen knew more about the history of baseball than a lot of people realized. A nicer guy than he's been portrayed, Dick got some bad press about his coming to the ballpark late and not getting along with people.

When our Tops in Sports gave him a trophy as the top home run hitter in the American League one year, he turned around and handed it to the widow of Jack Ogden, the scout who had signed him.

He loved the horses and is now a licensed trainer.

I remember Dick used to play tic tac toe on the field with the other first baseman. He would draw the squares in the dirt behind the base and put an X or O in one. When they changed sides, the other guy would put a mark in it, then it would be Allen's turn.

Carlton Fisk suffered a severe groin injury in Boston in 1974 and some people were afraid it might end his career. But he worked and worked and lasted almost 20 years more. Again that word "attitude" comes into it. He worked out before and after a game.

When he was 20 and when he was 40 he was so quick down the line to back up first base on every play there. Of course he also walked back to home plate slower than any individual in the history of the game. And he walked out to the mound and back slower than anybody since Connie Mack was catching. And he took his own time walking up to the plate to hit.

Graig Nettles was a fun-loving guy who picked on everybody and took it in return. He created the line, "When I was a kid I had two ambitions, running away from home to join the circus and playing in the major leagues. I did them both playing for the Yankees." I'd love to see a clubhouse with Nettles and Mike Flanagan as teammates. They'd have more needles flying than a quilting bee.

By today's lower standards, Tony Oliva belongs in the Hall

of Fame. A popular player and great hitter, he was hampered by knee injuries. Tony was one of those Latin players whose accent seems to get thicker as the years go by.

Rod Carew was appreciated by other players as a technician with the bat, but he was not a popular guy. He was one of the first to advertise the sale of autographed bats and things, and players looked down on that at the time. As a coach, Rod has mellowed.

Bobby Murcer was another guy who was cursed by all the ballyhoo about being the next Mickey Mantle. A little guy, he was very popular.

Dave Winfield is so articulate and bright, he has always been a favorite guy to interview. A museum visitor and photographer, he has had shows in this country and Europe. He signed for 10 years with the Yankees for some enormous sum, and a few years into the contract I asked him about renegotiation. He said, "I hate that word. You'll never see me change my playing habits. I'll play harder in that tenth year than I did in the first. All the years you've seen me, have I ever let down?"

I had to answer, "No." I love to watch him play.

You can single out the guys who played that hard every day, every year. You'll have a vast list of those who don't.

Winfield is one of those guys who will see kids hanging out waiting for him and will go outside the confines of where they are staying to sign autographs. Clemens, Boggs, Mattingly are some other stars who come to mind who will do the same.

Thurman Munson was a surly, unfriendly guy. In his last few years, if the Yankees played a day game in New York, then played in Baltimore the next night, he'd fly his own plane back to his home in Ohio, then fly to Baltimore the next day. I never understood why the Yankees let that happen. He got killed practicing landing one day.

Billy Martin always got on his catchers more than his pitchers; he figured they were more responsible for any mistakes that were made. But he respected Munson and did not get on him. Rick Dempsey said he learned a lot from Munson while he was with the Yankees.

Frank Howard and I go back to his early days with the Dodgers at Vero Beach. Hondo is one of the best-loved guys in the game, a real "Yes sir—no sir" person. Can outwork 50 people. "You want to hit early? I'll be out here, young man, and we'll work as hard as you want." He'll pitch BP a half hour, go down to the batting cage under the stands for an hour, then go out on the field and watch the hitters.

Off the field he'll have a big black cigar in his mouth. He's so huge and so nice, a very special person.

Bill Buckner carried a bad rap about being interested only in his own stats. If that was true, he would have taken himself out of that '86 World Series game with the Mets. But he wouldn't take himself out of a game, ever.

I'll tell you something about Bill Buckner. He had such bad ankles, you would see him in the clubhouse every day with two buckets filled with ice and a little water, and he would sit there with both feet soaking in that ice water over his ankles in order to play. I did an interview with him one day, with him sitting with his feet in those buckets. How many guys would do that every day.

I like him; he's such a dedicated guy. I never heard him say he couldn't play. Maybe that hurt him, playing when he was hurting. Look up his records. But whatever they show, Billy Bucks will be remembered for the one play in the '86 World Series. It drove him out of his New England home.

Mark McGwire is a big, blond, frecklefaced, schoolteacher-looking guy who wears glasses off the field and is soft-spoken and popular with writers and players. I feel bad for young guys like that who start off so well, then get hit with injuries and have a hard time doing the job.

Jose Canseco was one of two new players I saw who had their own press conferences on the first trip to a new town in their rookie years. Wally Joyner was the other. Canseco got a little big for his britches as he got more established. I don't care for some of the things he does, but he can do it all on the field. A power hitter having enough speed to hit 40 home runs and steal 40 bases in one season—wow. Great arm, too.

Willie Randolph was very serious, but he took a lot of kidding. They called him Junior on the Yankees, and I don't think he really appreciated it.

Chris Chambliss was a student of the game and had the respect of the other players. You could see he would be a coach or manager, and he should be a major league manager.

George Brett was friendly with everybody, the rawest rookie to the top star. In the Kansas City clubhouse, he was the guy the players went to for everything. A tough guy, he played hurt, wearing a bulky knee brace every day for years. His idol was Charlie Lau, who helped him with his hitting.

Lou Whitaker just goes about his business, a very religious guy but not much frivolity there. He and Alan Trammell are very close and have been together in the middle of the Detroit infield for years.

Carney Lansford was a money player, a sound contact hitter. I never understood why any team would trade him.

Butch Hobson, now the Red Sox manager, was a hardnosed player who was hurt a lot. With the Yankees he was the designated commuter one year; every time New York needed a space on the roster, they sent him down to Columbus. He didn't mind; they paid him a bonus every time he went.

Freddie Patek was a tiny, outgoing guy who kidded himself about being a midget; he was five foot five. A good contact hitter. One of the great things about the game is that you don't have to be six foot nine or weigh 300 pounds to play the game. Every club has some small guys. Except a few years ago; I used to walk into the Oakland A's clubhouse and thought I was in with the Raiders. What giants they were.

Dave Henderson is a perfect gentleman, very outgoing, smiling all the time.

Rickey Henderson is just the opposite. When the real Rickey Henderson shows up, he is one of the best in baseball. There is nothing he cannot do. The best leadoff hitter we've seen in a long time. But some days or some years, the real Rickey does not always come to the ballpark.

When he is up to bat, I sit on the edge of the chair. He played the left field corner in Memorial Stadium better than any outfielder in the last 25 years and I saw them all. Usually, a hit down the third base line was an automatic double. But with him out there, Orioles hitters stopped at first base unless the ball got away from him.

Dave Stewart tried to settle him down when they were both in Oakland, but Rickey is basically an unfriendly loner. He could have been a great running back.

Jerry Remy and Rick Burleson of the Red Sox went about their business on the field, but that clubhouse was alive when those guys were in there. They reeked of confidence and ability.

I liked Jim Rice. In Boston, he was the guy most likely to go over to the player who made an error that cost the game, or a pitcher who grooved one, or the guy who was 0 for 5 and say, "Hang in there, kid," or "We'll get 'em tomorrow."

Other guys in other clubhouses who would do that without a second thought: Eddie Murray, George Brett, Brooks Robinson, Joe Carter, Grich, Baylor, Don Mattingly, Dave Henderson.

One day Jim Rice was in the on deck circle at Memorial Stadium and a line drive foul went by him and hit a teenager in the box seats. Rice dropped his bat and ran over and picked up the kid, lifted him over the wall and carried him into the clubhouse. It was an instant reaction, and I thought it was a great thing to do.

Watch a batter after he hits a line drive foul into the stands. They are very concerned when that happens. They'll step out and try to see if anyone was hurt. After the game they'll ask if anything happened.

In Los Angeles Rick Monday saw some kids trying to burn a flag in center field. He ran out there and grabbed it and carried it to the dugout. That's the kind of act that fans appreciate.

I like Wade Boggs. We hit it off right away because he was born in Omaha, too. He is a big fan of Nebraska football. The clubhouse is home to him. He's there by two o'clock or 2:30 for a night game. He has his routines, timed down to the minute, and is always working on his hitting. He could be hitting .365, but if he didn't like the way he swung the bat the night before, he'd be in that batting cage early.

Don Mattingly was so intent on trying to beat out Boggs for the batting championship one year, he'd come out early and work in the batting cage toward the end of the season. Both of them are fiercely competitive. I like Don. He's a down to earth, gracious, humble guy. One year I was at the New York writers' dinner, a big formal affair, everybody in tuxedos. We're getting ready to parade in from the VIP room to the head table and I look down and Don's got tennis shoes on with his tux.

I said, "Don, what is this?"

He said, "I was home and I packed and thought I had everything, but I didn't bring any shoes. I walked around town but it's Sunday and I couldn't find a shoe store, so I said the hell with it, and wore what I had on my feet."

It didn't bother him. He was comfortable with it. I like that kind of guy.

Wally Joyner lit up the world when he first came around. He had it all: attitude, talent, nice guy. The first time I met him, I had never seen such a baby face. I asked him, "Do you shave?"

He said, "Oh, sure, at least once a week."

I first met Ken Griffey, Jr. when his father was with the Yankees and Junior was about 16, but he looked like a man then. He can do everything on the field, meaning the five things Branch Rickey looked for: hit, run, throw, catch and hit for power. I hope he can keep the intensity and attitude; I would like to see him on a contending team.

Julio Franco, a leader among the Latin players, got a lot of negative publicity in Cleveland. I respect that he moved from shortstop to second base without moaning and complaining. Not everybody would do that.

Danny Tartabull deserves his reputation as tough to get along with and handle. He is self-centered, a fair fielder.

Bo Jackson was a great athlete who thought he could walk right in and play major league baseball. He wouldn't take any direction, and I think he got Billy Gardner fired as a manager at Kansas City. Doctors told me he did not hurt his hip playing football; he aggravated a chronic condition he had from birth. But he is still playing.

Ozzie Guillen is another delightful guy. When Roland Hemond was with the White Sox, he was scouting in the Dominican winter league, and he saw a skinny little kid in cutoff jeans fooling around on the field.

"Who's that?" he asked his Dominican scout.

"That's one of yours."

"What? He can't play."

Ozzie was maybe 16 at the time, but it did not take long for Hemond to realize that this skinny little kid could play.

He won the Gold Glove at shortstop in 1990 over Ripken. The first time Chicago played in Baltimore the following year, Ozzie said, "Hey, I bet they boo me today."

He was right. When I introduced the players before the game and got to, "Shortstop, Ozzie Guillen," the fans went crazy. He just stood out there and tipped his hat and smiled, and really turned them around.

I rate him a better shortstop today than Ozzie Smith. Very intense on the field, he gets mad at himself when he fails to get a hit. But he is the life of the clubhouse, and gets a little better with "the Henglish" every year. He wears his uniform pants up around the knees the old-fashioned way. I wish they all did.

I saw Jesse Barfield make an unbelievable throw early in his career and knew he was something special. One night at a banquet he took me aside and said, "Somebody told me that you said on the air that my arm was almost as good as Carl Furillo's. Who's Carl Furillo?"

I told him about my old Dodger teammate, who had the greatest arm I've ever seen, to this day.

"How could his arm be better than mine?" he asked.

"He was more accurate," I said. "He could not only throw the ball through a brick wall, he could hit any spot on the wall, from any angle."

Barfield was a special person in another way: he was very obliging to interviewers, filling in at the last minute when somebody like the truculent George Bell refused.

George Bell is a good hitter, but a little nasty and selfish. I did not like it when he gave Toronto manager Jimy Williams a hard time because Williams wanted him to DH. The manager is generally the guy who gets fired, when they can't stand up to that.

Chili Davis has a perfect swing, and always has had one. If I had a kid who wanted to be a hitter, I'd tell him to study Chili.

I'll tell you a story about Cecil Fielder. It's the winter of

1990. The Tigers need a first baseman. General manager Bill Lefebvre calls Sparky Anderson and says, "We're going to try to sign Kent Hrbek. He's a free agent and he's flying in to see us."

"Fine," Sparky says. "I've always liked him. I'll be there."

They talk, and when it's over, Hrbek says, "You've offered me more money than I can make in Minnesota, and I may be wrong for turning it down, but staying with the Twins and playing in my home town means a lot to me."

Sparky says he was such a gentleman they hated to lose him.

Lefebvre says, "What do we do now?"

Sparky says, "Let's try for Pete O'Brien," who at one time was considered the best first baseman in the league. But while they were talking about it, O'Brien signs with Seattle. It turned out that O'Brien never became the player everybody thought he was.

So Sparky goes home. One day he gets a call from the GM.

"I have only one other idea. You know that kid, Cecil Fielder, played a little with Toronto?"

"Yeah, the big guy."

"Well, he had a couple good years in Japan. I think we ought to look into him."

"Well, you're the general manager. If that's what you want, let's see what we can do."

They sign him. Now Sparky goes to spring training. He's sitting in the dugout in Lakeland next to coach Alex Grammas, and he sees this fat guy come waddling across the field in a Detroit uniform. He says to Alex, "That guy's got a Tiger uniform on."

Alex says, "Don't you know who that is?"

"No."

"That's Cecil Fielder."

Sparky says, "We've been screwed again. If I had Lefebvre here right now, I'd kill him."

All through spring training Sparky knew they'd been had, and the first few weeks of the season made him surer. Then, as a last straw, he let Fielder play against Toronto one night and Cecil hit two home runs. You know the rest of the story.

Fielder is a mild-mannered guy, a good team player, not a good first baseman, but he gives it all he's got.

Steve Sax is one of those guys people overlook, but check his figures every year. He does the job wherever he plays, and is very hard on himself.

Joe Carter is one of my favorites. All he does is hit 30 home runs and drive in 100 runs year after year. He's a leader in the clubhouse. I would have him on my team in a second. He's a big Oklahoma football fan.

Robin Yount, MVP shortstop. When Harvey Kuenn asked him to move to center field, he said, "Whatever you want," and won another MVP in the outfield. How many guys would do that today? A class act through and through. Showed up, did the job, and when he retired, got on his motorcycle and rode into the sunset.

Paul Molitor is another guy who played third, short, first, outfield, DH, whatever, and never uttered a word of complaint.

Why do the Younts and Molitors and Winfields last so long? They didn't need the money. Look at the caliber of people we're talking about. You never saw any controversy about them. They just went out and did the job. They exemplified dedication and preparation.

15

Coaches

How did major league teams get along so well for so many years with just two coaches and a manager? How did the hitters hit without hitting coaches, the pitchers pitch without pitching coaches, the managers manage without bench coaches?

I think that one reason is, the players learned their trade in the minor leagues, usually from guys with years of big league experience: Pepper Martin, Donie Bush, Joe Hauser, Lefty O'Doul, even Hall of Famers like Home Run Baker.

You didn't get to the majors until you knew the game, after three, four, five years pitching hundreds of innings, getting thousands of ABs. (I didn't do that, and I've always believed that was a big factor in my lack of success. But that's another story, one I've already told.)

So why do we have a dozen coaches at the major league level, instead of in the minor leagues where they are needed? I think there should be dozens of well-paid Cal Ripken Seniors—if you could find them—throughout the minor leagues, teaching the prospects how to play the game.

Why are the minor league managers who are supposed to be doing the most important job of all—teaching the younger players how to play the game—the lowest paid people in the game?

Why are players learning the game at the major league level?

Players used to learn the game in the minors, but your education didn't stop there. Despite the small number of coaches, we continued to learn from older guys on the club. Every team had a veteran pitcher or catcher who ran the bullpen. With the Dodgers it was Bobby Bragan. And you paid attention. In those days the bullpens were right out on the field, either outside the foul lines or, in the case of the Polo Grounds, in the outfield. You sat there in full view of everybody. There was not much fooling around. A guy might spit tobacco juice on your shoes or put chewing gum where you were going to sit. But that's about it. You couldn't sit there eating a hot dog. You were so close to the action, when you warmed up, you had to have somebody stand in front of you to protect you from line drives. A ball hit into the bullpen was in play. You scattered in a hurry if your guys were chasing after it, but you made it hard for the other team to retrieve the ball. In Wrigley Field there was hardly room for two pitchers to throw at the same time.

We also talked a lot of baseball on the long train rides, in the hotel lobbies and with our roommates. Not every second, of course. We knew what the city streets looked like at night. But all that has changed. Not only changed, it's practically nonexistent.

The manager ran everything. A coach might sit next to him on the bench when the team was on the field, and they'd talk: Durocher to Dressen, "Charlie, don't you think Barney's losing it? Run out there and see what's going on." It was all very informal.

Today pitching coaches usually know more about pitching than the managers, unless a manager is a former pitcher or catcher. Over a period of many years, the Orioles had just three pitching coaches—Harry Brecheen, George Bamberger and Ray Miller. I've talked about Brecheen and Bambi already.

Ray Miller was a hands-on coach. He got in their faces constantly, trying to run their whole lives, while Bambi's attitude was, "You pitch, you pitch."

I remember one time Mike Boddicker pitched a hell of a

game. He was in the trainer's room, icing down his arm. Miller came in and said, "Goddamn, Mike, let's go. You've got to get out here and give these interviews. These are the guy who are going to make you."

Boddicker said, "Well, they're going to have to wait."

Ray kept on top of everything. When he turned in a report on something, it was a whole report, not just a few sentences. He could tell you how long a pitcher threw every time he got up in the bullpen. Bambi wouldn't keep track of all that stuff. He would go to a reliever and say, "You pitched last night. Can you give us an inning tonight?"

Ray might tell them; Bambi would ask. Both good coaches, just different personalities. Ray is very enthusiastic and likes to talk. He always wanted to be a manager—had two years at Minnesota—but he talked his way out of the job. He thinks he knows the game, and probably does, but he couldn't get it across to people.

Ray liked the slider; he worked with Joe Altobelli and Joe kind of let him run the pitching staff. Now he's at Pittsburgh and has done an outstanding job there.

Coaches today have videotapes of every game. They can isolate just the pitchers and put together a tape of nothing but one guy throwing over and over. They study those things, even on the planes where they take little portable VCRs. They can see if a pitcher is not staying on top with his fastball, or he's dropping his arm down a little, or he's doing something different when he starts losing.

A pitching coach has to suggest more than teach. When a pitcher's in the major leagues, he knows pretty much what to do. At least he should.

One thing pitching coaches might do for their pitchers is try to get some uniformity among bullpen mounds. That's a big complaint among pitchers. They warm up in the bullpen, then they go on the field to pitch and find an altogether different mound. Some are higher, some are lower.

Mark Williamson told me, "It's atrocious in some parks. You've really got great stuff warming up, throwing well, and then you go into the game and it's completely different."

Dick Bosman was a pitching coach for Oates in Rochester. He knew all the young pitchers who came through there, and they think highly of him. He has a lot of input, works hard and I don't think he'll ever let down.

Elrod Hendricks runs the bullpen. Nowadays everything is done by phone. If two right-handers are warming up, Oates or Bosman might call and ask Elrod who looks better to him. Of course, if the manager wants a certain matchup, or it's a case of bringing in a lefty to face a lefty batter, that's often automatic. In those situations, the team at bat has the advantage. They can take a hitter out for another hitter whenever they want to, but a pitcher, once announced, has to pitch to at least one batter, unless he is injured. (Bobby Bragan once made five pinch-hitting changes in a row without a pitch being thrown, but he did that mainly to agitate the umpire.)

I never knew what a hitting coach was when I broke in; we had no such thing. George Sisler worked for the Dodgers, and he would help the hitters, and everybody else, in spring training. But that was it. Sisler made Duke Snider, who was a wild swinger when he was a kid. Get two strikes on him, and Snider would swing at anything in the western hemisphere. Mr. Rickey sent Snider to Vero Beach from the Dominican Republic to work with Sisler, who would sit in the hot sun for hours and work with him.

Why are most hitting coaches unknown as players? For the same reason most managers were unknowns as players. Hitting coaches don't have to have great careers to be students and teachers. Look at the great musicians and singers; they had teachers nobody ever heard of outside the music world. A Ted Williams can overpower a young kid with his knowledge and his theories and his demonstrations of how he did things. It can leave the kid reeling, and with no better chance of hitting like Williams did than I have.

The key word is patience. Superstars have little patience with lesser mortals swinging bats. Like Frank Robinson. I think Frank felt that everybody should do what he did, just by his telling them to do it. Crowd the plate like he did, swing the bat like he did. If that was all it took, why wouldn't everybody do it?

Not all hitting instructors agree. Charlie Lau, who was with the Orioles in 1969, went to Kansas City where he made George Brett into a great hitter. Lau belongs to the school that advocates chopping down on the ball. He helped Mark Belanger and Brooks Robinson while he was here.

Casey Stengel, when he was with the Mets—the Yankees didn't need any help—would stand behind the batting cage during BP, hollering, "Butcher boy! Butcher boy!" That was his way of saying, "Chop down on the ball."

Rogers Hornsby held the same theory.

On the other hand, Ted Williams, who would talk hitting with any player on any team at any time, maintained that the natural swing is upward, and why change it? Swinging down was awkward for him. Who am I to argue with Williams? Or any hitting coach?

There are other aspects to hitting, a thousand of them. Tony Oliva, a Hall of Fame hitter although he has not yet been recognized as such, made Kirby Puckett into a home run hitter. How?

"He made me wait on the ball," Puckett said.

How do you wait on a 90 mph fastball?

"You do. Keep your head down, watch it closely, and have a quick bat." Oliva taught him that.

The Orioles have had a lot of hitting coaches over the years. Jim Frey, Jim Dwyer, Terry Crowley, Ralph Rowe come to mind. Guys had confidence in them. They could stand behind the batting cage and help guys accidentally.

I remember Ralph Rowe standing there for hours, watching guys swing, making suggestions about footwork, stance, timing, head and hands and wrists. "Let's try it," he would say, never insisting, always suggesting.

Give Greg Biagini credit for turning Brady Anderson around. Brady opened the 1988 season with the Red Sox. He could run like the wind and idolized Ted Williams—still wears his number 9—but couldn't get the job done. Went 3 for 36 and went down to the minors. The Orioles got him in a trade in mid-season. He struggled in '89 and went to Rochester. Struggled in '90 and spent time in the minors. Struggled in '91 and went to Rochester for a short time, where Biagini was the manager. Biagini got him to swing down on the ball, not uppercut it.

In 1992 Brady had one of the most productive seasons ever for a leadoff man.

During the game, the third base coach is the most important man on the field. Some of my friends ask me, "What does he do?" Well, put yourself out there some time. It's easy to sit in the stands and say, "That runner could have scored," or "He never had a chance." But put yourself out on the line, open to ridicule and criticism. It's a no-win position. If he sends a guy home and he scores, that's what he should have done. But if the guy doesn't score, or he holds a runner at third and the fans think he should have scored, the coach gets booed.

Cal Senior did the job for years, and Billy Hunter and Jimmy Williams. In 1993 the Orioles had Mike Ferraro, and the following winter they put Jerry Narron in that spot. Narron, one of the quietest, nicest guys around, had volunteered to take it in '93; as a minor league manager he had coached third, and knew the job and the Orioles who had played for him in the minors. He does a good job.

The first base coach has maybe the best job in major league baseball. The best definition of the job was one I heard when I was in the hospital after I had my stroke. Somebody was filling in for me on my postgame interview show from Memorial Stadium. One day Jimmy Williams, then the first base coach, went on the show. The announcer asked him, "What does a first base coach do?"

Jimmy said, "He stands there and puts in time so he'll get more money on his pension. And we pick up the baseballs during batting practice." I thought that was a great answer.

They are all knowledgeable baseball men, but they don't have a lot to do as a first base coach. They may have other duties: Davey Lopes works with infielders and outfielders, and on baserunning with guys.

Jimmy Williams neglected to mention one other role he had when he was the first base coach: keeper of the coffee cakes.

In 1970 there was a newspaper strike in Baltimore. In order to fill the fans' hunger for baseball news during spring training, I did two radio shows a day from Florida. I noticed that, in Miami, somebody brought in a coffee cake every Sunday morning. So when the season opened, I decided to do the same, and from then on I did it every Sunday.

One Sunday morning I was all hung over and I jumped into the pool at Cross Keys and while I'm in the water I get a phone call. It's Jim Palmer. "Where are you? Where's the coffee cake? We can't play without it."

I hustled over there, and I have never missed since.

When I had a stroke, I arranged with someone at the bakery to deliver three coffee cakes on Sunday mornings. Once they were a little late. I'm lying in the hospital bed and the phone rings. Jimmy Williams says, "You okay, partner?"

"Yeah, I'm doing pretty good."

"So where the hell's the coffee cake?"

Ralph Rowe was always on a diet and wouldn't eat it, but Jimmy helped him out and ate his share.

Paul Blair came up to me one Sunday when I was eating a piece of the cake. Dead serious, he said to me, "Rex, that's for the players only."

I thought he was putting me on, but he was dead serious.

I said, "Paul, do you know who brings these coffee cakes in?"

He said, "No, but they are for the players."

I said, "I am the guy who brings them in."

Bambi liked cheese-filled, and Johnny Oates anything with apples. I had to keep all that straight. I don't know why I did it, or still do after 24 years. But they enjoy it and it gives me a way to show my appreciation for their cooperation.

16

Unsung Heroes

I want to talk about some unsung heroes behind the scenes in baseball, beginning with the traveling secretary.

Phil Itzoe has been the Orioles road shepherd for almost 30 years now, the longest tenure with one club in the business. If there is ever a place in the Hall of Fame for traveling secretaries, he should be the first one inducted.

For the team and for individual players, he makes all the travel arrangements. When the team travels, he arranges the charter flight, the food on the plane, departure time, the shipment of the equipment, the bus to and from the airport, and the hotel rooms. The team bus goes right out on the tarmac; they don't go through the airport. On the plane the food is served on china set on table cloths. Beer and wine are still available, but liquor is out.

If a player has a birthday, Phil will arrange for a cake.

Itzoe also arranges everything in spring training: schedules, rooms, buses, rooms for press and broadcasters. He never gets ruffled.

"Buses give me more problems than anything," he says. "Will they be at the airport when we land? Once in a city, will they leave for the ballpark on time?"

Sometimes the bus is not there waiting when they land, and

he gets on the phone and burns some people while the players tease him.

Meal money is distributed to the players at the start of each road trip. Right now it is $59 a day; for a ten-day road trip he will pass out little brown envelopes containing $590 in cash. He likes to get as many $50 and $100 bills as he can, so there's less to handle.

Many players carry laptop computers and Nintendo games on the road. There are more headsets than cards in evidence. Some of them use the time to answer fan mail. The manager and coaches may use little portable VCRs to watch videos of players or other teams.

The players get paid on the first and fifteenth of each month. They can arrange to have their checks deposited directly. If payday comes while they are on the road, they can get the checks on the day they are due, or on the way home at the end of the trip.

Sometimes weather or other problems force a change in plans. One night the Orioles flew out of an airport near Anaheim headed for Seattle. As usual, as soon as they boarded the plane, you heard, "Let's go...let's go." But they didn't move. Suddenly a bunch of policemen appeared on the plane and ordered everybody off. There was a bomb scare.

Everybody got off and sat around for an hour and a half while dogs sniffed everything, including everybody as they got back on the plane.

If the weather forces them to land someplace other than their destination, the traveling secretary has to arrange for a bus to meet them.

He takes care of ticket requests from players, but no longer has to check the turnstile count.

In the old days, when every player had a roommate, it was up to the traveling secretary to make sure roomies were compatible. Today maybe only a half dozen younger players will share a room; the rest have single rooms, for which they pay half the cost.

Over the years the job has changed, but the importance of it has not.

Every club has two trainers. The only complaints I ever hear from them is about insurance paperwork. They work hard, keeping up with everybody's aches and pains and routine maintenance. You see pitchers with big ice packs on their arms and shoulders. In the old days they preached heat. Sandy Koufax was the first to use ice, then everybody started using it. Gone are the days when a split finger was stuck in the dirt and sprayed with tobacco juice.

There is a training room, a weights room, and a doctor's room, whirlpools and rubbing tables. Players' names and times of treatment are written on a blackboard.

Ralph Salvon is a legend among trainers, but I do not think he was a very good trainer. He was more of the team psychiatrist. The players and he teased and kidded each other without letup.

Richie Bancells was his assistant, and he is now the head trainer. They have another trainer, James Reed, and a strength and conditioning coach, Tim Bishop.

The managers consult with the trainers every day, to get the latest reports on players with some kind of injury or problem: can they play today or not?

The trainers work hard, starting about 2:00. It gets quiet in their quarters during batting practice, when one of them is on the field. No media people are allowed in the trainers' rooms or the players' lounge, before or after a game.

You never know when a medical emergency may occur. I once saw a member of the grounds crew have a heart attack while rolling up a tarp. Some doctors came out of the stands and saved him.

Dr. Leonard Wallenstein, a premier person, was the team doctor. He got into the players, took them and their families to heart, and was like part of the team. They trusted him and knew they could talk to him. Dr. Sheldon Goldgeier was his young assistant in those days.

I could see in the clubhouse how the players idolized Dr. Leonard. Jim Palmer used to bring in some medical journals he'd read and show Dr. Leonard some stuff in them. He knew Palmer like the back of his hand, and knew Jim was looking for any edge he could find to help him win.

Dr. Leonard, Dr. Goldgeier, who succeded him in 1985, and Dr. Charles Silberstein, the orthopedic surgeon, were all as much friends to the players as physicians. Dr. Leonard had a few heart attacks and had to ease up in his practice, but he didn't think the players could get through spring training without him, and he died in Miami in February, 1985.

There was a closeness among these healers and athletes that I may not see again. Dr. Silberstein is semi-retired now, and the new owners of the Orioles have brought in new team doctors.

Ernie Tyler has been with the Orioles longer than I have, and very few people can make that claim. Ernie began as an usher at the 1958 All-Star Game, in Section 10 at Memorial Stadium. Two years later he had a two-week "tryout" working on the field providing the balls to the home plate umpire and retrieving foul balls behind the plate. Thirty-five years later he's still at it, but that's not all he does.

In the old days the umpires had a dressing room about as big as a closet across from the visitors' clubhouse. They had nothing, and nobody to provide whatever they needed. They asked Ernie to help them out and now he is the premier "umpire's valet" in the league. He does everything from cleaning their shoes and uniforms and making the coffee to rubbing up the game balls with that special mud every team uses. The umps depend on him as much as the players depend on the clubhouse men, who happen to be Ernie's sons. Jimmy Tyler is in charge of the Orioles' domain and Fred runs the visitors' clubhouse.

We used to kid Ernie, call him "Iron Hands" because, when pop fouls rolled off the screen behind home plate at Memorial Stadium, he never failed to drop them. Sometimes I'd announce, "Give Ernie Tyler an error," and the fans loved it. But I also gave him a contract when he made one good catch. He sits behind the plate by the field exit and I don't think he's ever been hit by a foul ball. Everybody who's ever been to an Orioles game has seen him, dashing out to hand the umpire a new supply of balls or chasing down a foul. But most fans have no idea who he is, or what else he does. A thoroughly delightful and loyal guy.

When Ernie retired after 32 years with the state Health and Mental Hygiene Department in 1988, he began working at the minor league spring training camp and the fantasy camps every year. In addition to Jimmy and Fred, the other three of Ernie's five boys have been batboys, and two of his six girls have worked in the ticket offices. Since they all grew up two blocks from Memorial Stadium, they didn't have far to go to work.

The clubhouse man has a tough job. Every day the team is home, he and the kids he supervises have to pick up the dirty stuff and wash it or get it cleaned. Shoes get shined every night. When a new player comes in, he should find a uniform with his name on it when he arrives.

There are soda dispensers, sometimes beer, fruit juice, snacks, cases of sunflower seeds, pregame snacks, and a post-game spread of food. In the old days nothing was free, and the clubhouse guy had to keep track of who owed what. No more. Now it's all free. But the players still pay clubhouse dues, and tipping is up to each one. Bubblegum is still big, but tobacco and snuff are gradually being eased out.

The term "clubhouse man" is taken lightly, but the players rely on him to have clean practice and game uniforms hanging in their lockers every day, and every kid's bedroom should be as neat as the clubhouses at Memorial Stadium or Camden Yards. Fred and Jimmy Tyler are very important people.

Scouts do more with less recognition than anybody in baseball. People think of them as men who do nothing but go to games and look at young players.

A lot of scouts feel underpaid and undervalued, and I think they are. I'm not talking just about scouts who beat the bushes to find the kids, many of whom are brought to their attention by bird dogs, local coaches and athletic directors who have ties to a major league scout. The real unsung scouts are the ones who watch other major league teams, either looking for players who might help their own team, or working as advance scouts to help prepare their teams for an upcoming opponent.

Let's say the Orioles are looking for a left-handed hitter. Their scouts will look at teams in both leagues, filing reports on who looks good, who is hurt, who might help and who might not. Often, the standard is: will this guy help us more than somebody we already have? Sometimes they have to look beyond the playing field. A few years ago Doug Melvin had scouts check out Joe Orsulak at Pittsburgh when he was hurt and not playing much.

They had to find out what kind of guy Joe was and whether he could help the Orioles, without seeing him swing a bat.

Sometimes they make mistakes. Keith Moreland had a reputation for willingness to play several positions and for being a cheerleader type of guy. He didn't produce and quit before the season was over.

The process begins in spring training and goes throughout the season. Everybody is watching everybody else's players. Most scouts are on the road a lot from February to October.

Advance scouts seldom see their own teams. They are always watching the other guys and filing reports on them for their own managers: who's hot and who is not; managers' strategy tendencies; how other pitchers are getting certain hitters out...

I enjoy talking to the advance scouts at Camden Yards. I learn a lot. Many of them never made it as players, but they love the game and can't untie themselves from it. Others are former major leaguers, some of whom played when I did: Frank Malzone, Sam Mele, Buddy Kerr, Timmy Thompson, Broadway Charlie Wagner.

You generally see them sitting together a few rows behind home plate, although some scouts prefer to be off by themselves.

Jim Russo was the Orioles' head scout—the "Super Scout"— in Earl Weaver's time. He turned in detailed reports, especially on playoff and World Series teams. Weaver used to kid him: "Russo's here, we'll win for sure now."

Scouting for young prospects has changed since the advent of the amateur draft. If your team drafts low—say, 20 or 25— there is not much point in concentrating on the top prospects everybody knows about. They are unlikely to be available by the time your turn comes. A scout can be more valuable to his team by coming up with gems who are bypassed by other teams and are still there to be selected after 50 or 100 selections have been made. Mike Piazza of the Dodgers, for example.

Gone are the days when scouts prowled the rural dirt roads searching for diamonds in the rough that nobody ever heard of, or tried to outwit other scouts in pursuit of the hot prospects whose fame had spread. They made mistakes in those days, too, but they had better stories to tell. A lot of them turned down the clumsy, uncoordinated Brooks Robinson. Ralph Branca was turned down by the Giants and Yankees and wound up in Brooklyn, although he hated the Dodgers at the time. Phil Rizzuto followed the same trail in reverse; the Dodgers shooed him out the door, and the Yankees took him in.

And sometimes scouts go looking for one thing and find another. George Mira drew the scouts; Boog Powell got the contract. A scout went to see a pitcher on a playground in Chicago and took a chance on a little fat kid who lit up the place with his enthusiasm—Kirby Puckett.

That goes on all the time. I find it fascinating to talk to these scouts, whose value and accomplishments go unsung.

The Orioles have had an outstanding succession of general managers and other front office people beginning with Paul Richards, who established a lot of the things that became the "Orioles way" throughout the organization.

Frank Lane was something of a nonconformist, but he was a baseball man through and through.

Lee MacPhail made the deal for Frank Robinson that changed the course of Orioles history.

Frank Cashen was an excellent administrator, didn't know much about baseball, but he hired people who did.

Harry Dalton and Jim McLaughlin really knew the game and the players. McLaughlin was with the Orioles for many years, as was Tom Giordano. Over the years the front office people worked together, never pulled apart.

Hank Peters was outstanding, well-respected throughout baseball; he built the last pennant winners, but then Edward Bennett Williams decided he knew more about the game than Hank.

Roland Hemond is a top-flight baseball man, well-liked and respected throughout the game. He relies on his scouts and minor league managers, as any successful GM will do. An example of that occurred on June 2, 1994, when they had to bring up a pitcher to replace Ben McDonald for one start. All the scouts, the minor league managers and pitching coaches were involved in the decision to bring up Scott Klingenbeck from Bowie (AA) to face Detroit instead of somebody from Rochester.

They knew that decision put them out on a limb with the media who were ready to crucify Roland and the rest if Scott failed. I know that. They all knew that. They could have brought up Arthur Rhodes or any AAA pitcher, and if he failed not get criticized. "We brought up the best we had," they could say.

But they picked the guy with the best temperament to fill that spot on that day. Did they know what they were doing? He won, 11-5.

Doug Melvin has worked hard as an assistant GM. He runs the farm system. He knows the players. He deserves much of the credit for the team's success and will make an excellent GM.

Of course, not every trade or deal these people have made worked out, but not every prediction made by the self-anointed experts who criticize them worked out, either.

The only time most people notice the groundskeeper is when it rains and they want the tarp rolled out in a hurry, or it stops raining and they want the tarp taken off in a hurry.

But keeping the playing field looking pretty and in perfect condition is a fulltime job for the Orioles' Paul Zwaska. The definition of "perfect condition" varies from one player to another. Some infielders like the grass cut short, or faster; others want it long for a slower infield. Some pitchers like one slope on the mound, some another. Outfielders complain about insufficient padding on the walls, or divots in the outfield grass.

If every pebble but one is screened out of the infield dirt, a ground ball will find that one for the other team at the wrong time and the infield will be condemned as a rockpile.

The Orioles have never been much for doctoring the field to suit the team. They were accused of making the mound higher for Jim Palmer, but Jim came out early and worked on it himself.

In Philadelphia they tilted the grass to keep bunts along the third base line from rolling foul to help Richie Ashburn.

Some teams will wet down the area around first base to slow down a visiting base stealer like Rickey Henderson.

But even without all that stuff, there is a lot more to the job than just mowing the lawn and dragging the infield.

When I came to Baltimore Joe Brown was the groundskeeper. He was not well, and Earl Weaver brought Pat

Sandirone in from Elmira, where Earl had managed. When Brown died, Sandirone took over. And he ran the show. His life was that ballpark. I really believe he thought people came to Memorial Stadium just to see his lawn.

Pat was friendly, but tough and serious when it came to his job. He would consult with the pitchers about the mound, and talk to the managers to find out what they wanted. He and Cal Senior had some run-ins. In the minor leagues Senior had done the groundskeeping and drove the bus and did everything else when he managed. So he had his ideas, too, and they didn't always agree with Pat's.

If somebody was hitting fungoes from the fungo circle near home plate and he put one foot outside that dirt onto the grass, Pat didn't care who it was. "Get that foot back on the dirt."

If a coach wandered outside the coaches box at first or third, Pat would let them know: "Stay inside the lines. That's what they are there for." He was serious.

One day in the 1970s I was sitting in the broadcast booth early with Chuck Thompson and we noticed some confusion in the seats behind the dugout. It was long before game time. It looked like a man was slumped down in the seats. I noticed Doc Medich, a pitcher for Texas, running in the outfield, so I got on the P.A. and announced, "Would Doc Medich please come to the Orioles dugout." He raced over and saw what had happened and worked hard on the man, who had had a heart attack. He said he almost lost him twice, but he saved him, and a year later that fan threw out the first pitch at a game. But that's not the end of the story. They got the guy onto a stretcher and an ambulance came through the outfield gates and around the warning track to the dugout, and they got the guy inside. The driver turned onto the grass to turn around and Sandirone had a fit. "Get that thing off the grass!" The driver had to back off the grass and go all the way around on the cinder track to the gates.

Earl Weaver's passion was gardening. He had a big vegetable patch back of his house. Sandirone was an avid gardener, too. They got into a big discussion about who could grow the biggest tomatoes. I mean, serious stuff. So they each planted some tomato vines down in the left field corner against the wall. They mixed their special feeding formulas, and accused each other of cheating—going out and buying big tomatoes and tying them on the vines. Billy Martin got into it sometimes. He'd buy some giant things and bring them out and claim he grew them.

The fans watched those vines growing up the wall and it became a big thing. Earl and Pat developed their own plant food and marketed it.

In his own field, Sandirone was as competitive as Earl. His biggest rival for top honors was always George Toma at Kansas City. Toma is hired to prepare the field for every Super Bowl. One year Notre Dame was having problems with their practice field, and when they went outside to hire somebody to solve the problem, Pat got the job. He also took care of the grass track at Pimlico.

Sandirone hired Paul Zwaska as his assistant. Paul's another guy who's dedicated to every blade of grass out there. He's also the best weather forecaster around.

There are a lot of other loyal, dedicated people working behind the scenes in any ball club's operation, who are never seen or known by the fans. For many years Bob Brown was the very able public relations man, putting together the media guide, dealing with the press—local, visiting and occasional drop-ins— and turning out voluminous notes and stats for every game. That's something that has grown over the years, thanks to computers and statsmania.

But there is always someone behind—or in front of—the PR guy. And for a long time that very special person was Helen Conklin. She's the one who dealt with requests for press credentials, handling many difficult people and situations in such a way that she never forfeited the respect of anyone. Many a time she worked long hours into the night in the cramped office space of Memorial Stadium and never complained. If there was anyone anywhere in the sports world that I wanted to contact, I went to Helen and she always came through.

17

The Owners

Jerry Hoffberger of National Brewery owned the Orioles when I came to Baltimore. Everything was family-owned and operated. They operated on a small budget, but in those days baseball was still a small business.

Hoffberger was a real fan who sat near the dugout and cheered the players on. He was a smart owner; he admitted that he didn't know anything about baseball, and left it to the front office to run things. But he wanted to be kept informed ahead of time. If there was a deal pending he wanted to know about it, checked with the rest of the family, then gave the okay. He never said no; he just wanted to know. Nothing wrong with that.

I think other business considerations forced him to sell. I know he never wanted to, and wishes he still owned the team.

Edward Bennett Williams bought the Orioles after the 1979 season. For Williams, it was an ego trip. He loved publicity. As much as he got as a high-profile lawyer, he got more attention as a club owner than from anything else. And he loved every minute of it.

The first few years he owned the team, I would see him in the elevator after a game and he was full of questions: "Why did he hit and run...why did he walk that guy...why did he change pitchers... why did he pinch hit..." and on and on. And I'd explain things to him.

By the time the Orioles were winning the pennant in 1983, things had changed. Now he was telling me. When he began to say things like, "Do you know why he walked that batter" or whatever, I thought, oh, oh. We've got a problem: an owner who's become an expert in three years.

Don't get me wrong; I liked the man immensely. And I don't care if his defense was that he wanted a winner; everybody does. He went about it the wrong way. I didn't like what he did to the organization. I didn't like it when he fired Cal Senior after an 0-6 start and gave Frank Robinson a longterm contract and a big raise while he was losing 15 more in a row.

Like a lot of owners, he was enamored of big names and stars.

He had a topflight general manager in Hank Peters. Many baseball people called him the best in the business, and I don't argue with that. But after they won the World Series in '83, Williams decided that made him more knowledgeable about the game than Hank Peters and everybody else.

He called Hank into his office. "What do we do now?"

Hank said, "Well, we have to make some trades and get rid of some people who are finished, and make some moves."

"What do you mean? Who?"

"Dan Ford and Jim Palmer are about through. They'll have to be released."

"Wait a minute," Williams said. "When you win something, you keep the people who helped you win it." Ford had done a good job, but was near the end of the line. Palmer had started only 11 games for a 5-4 record.

Hank pointed out the need to bring new blood onto the team, but Williams prevailed. From then on, whatever Hank offered a player, all the guy had to do was go around him to Williams to get a better deal.

When Fred Lynn, Lee Lacy and Don Aase became free agents and Peters offered them two-year contracts, they went to Williams and got four-year deals. None of them had four more good years left.

When Alan Wiggins was kicked off the San Diego team,

*Dave McNally was
one tough southpaw.*

*When Tippy came in, his curve
ball closed the door.*

Who ever dreamed that Dennis Martinez might one day be president of Nicaragua?

Michael Flanagan threw the last pitch at Memorial Stadium, and it couldn't happen to a nicer guy.

Storm Davis looked *like Palmer on the mound, but that's where the resemblance ended.*

Dennis Martinez douses Scott McGregor to celebrate Scotty's winning his 20th on the last day of the 1980 season.

*Cal Ripkin, Sr.,
headmaster of the
Orioles School of
Baseball.*

Jo Winstead

*Weaver perches on a trunk to see eye to eye with his coaches, from left, George
Bamberger, Billy Hunter, Jim Frey, George Staller.*

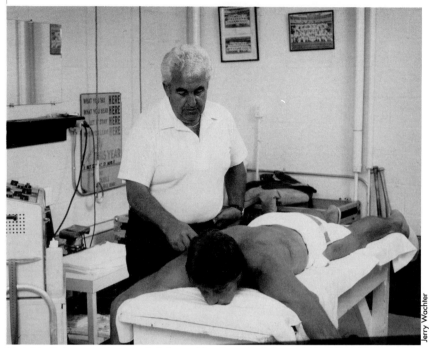

Ralphie Salvon, trainer and club psychiatrist, administers to Palmer's golden arm.

Players and umpires depend on these keepers of the clubhouses: Ernie Tyler (center) and sons Jimmy (left) and Fred.

Brady Anderson, the best all-around left fielder in Orioles' history.

Bob Miller

Bob Miller

Leo Gomez was the O's comeback player of the year in '94.

Ben McDonald takes time to chat with a youngster before a game.

A lot of great memories were born on 33rd Street.

I have to admit that Camden Yards is magnificent.

and nobody else would have him, Williams took him. That was a disaster.

I've already told you how he got on Eddie Murray when Williams became an expert on how to play first base.

Sometimes on Sundays Williams would go out on the field and stand behind the batting cage during BP. One day he asked hitting coach Terry Crowley, "What's wrong with the hitters? Can't you do something to get them hitting?"

Crowley didn't know what to say. There was really nothing to say. Just because he owned the club, Williams thought the batting coach was supposed to make everybody hit .300.

Williams and George Steinbrenner are the only two examples of meddling owners I can think of, and they won nothing as long as they meddled. In 1993, Steinbrenner was out of the game and Gene Michael and Buck Showalter, left alone, did a great job. If the Boss can keep his nose out of it in '94, they could go all the way.

Ted Turner leaves his baseball people alone in Atlanta, and Andy MacPhail enjoys the same freedom to do his job in Minnesota. The same is true of Pat Gillick in Toronto. And all those teams do is win. Does that maybe tell these owners something? Only if they're listening.

Long before he was fired in October 1987, Hank Peters told me he knew it was coming. "I'm going to be relieved to be relieved," he said.

I'm going to go against the public grain when I talk about Eli Jacobs, who bought the team from Edward Bennett Williams's heirs, because for years the media knocked him, called him cheap. I didn't find him cheap at all; I hate the word. I never knew any player who left the team over money problems. He inherited a bad team with a low payroll.

Jacobs never got involved in deals. He gave the front office a budget and told them if they wanted to go over it, they had to come to him first. I find nothing wrong with that. (Cal Junior's three-year contract was a budget-buster; Jacobs approved it.)

Anybody who went to arbitration and won got paid. I think he did everything he could. He paid a lot of money to Glenn Davis, who didn't work out, but that's not the owner's fault. Rick

Sutcliffe, Harold Reynolds, Harold Baines were added. They signed their top draft choices, Ben McDonald, Mike Mussina and Jeffrey Hammonds.

And in my opinion a lot of deals involving big money never got past club president Larry Lucchino, a holdover from Williams.

Mr. Jacobs cared nothing for personal publicity, just the opposite of Williams. That hurt him in the press; they knocked him because he did not give interviews. I found him to be a good guy, and not just because he was an old Brooklyn Dodger fan, which is why the right field corner in Camden Yards bears some resemblance to Ebbets Field.

When I had physical problems near the end of the 1991 season, he was one of the first to offer me whatever help I needed. He made sure I got to the annual Baseball Assistance Team dinner in New York, representing the Orioles, every year, including the one in 1993 after the team was sold.

Local ownership is a good thing. Peter Angelos grew up in the streets of Baltimore and did very well for himself. He is proud of being a self-made success, and I don't blame him. He did a magnificent thing in putting together a group of partners with great reputations in the area.

There's a lot of glamour in owning a team and having people like Tom Selleck and George Will on your board of directors. It's a real ego trip.

Angelos, like Williams, is a one-man law firm. That parallel is scary. His first year of ownership was barely under way when the New York papers began comparing him to Steinbrenner. I hope that never happens.

I get sick and tired of reading that Angelos makes the baseball decisions. He is not making them, and I hope he never does. Roland Hemond is the general manager. He makes the decisions. Certainly, Angelos can tell him no on something. Will Clark was highly rated to come here until Angelos found out some things about him and turned him down. I know he wanted to bring back Eddie Murray and Dennis Martinez, but he couldn't sign them. I was hoping they'd bring back Cal Senior and I thought Angelos would do it, but it didn't happen.

My only suggestion to Mr. Angelos would be to look at the teams that have been winning. Those owners have nothing to do with running the team. Nothing. They let the general manager and his staff do their job.

18

Watching the Game

Baseball can get too technical at times, with all the computerized matchups and pitch counts and charts. That stuff may make the game more scientific, but to me I'm more interested in the classic confrontations between a good pitcher and a good hitter: Clemens vs. Boggs, Mussina vs. Thomas, Viola vs. Mattingly. That's something to watch.

There is a lot the average fan can pay more attention to and get more out of the game. Most people pay no attention to the count, which means so much. It's a sin for a pitcher to give up a hit with a two-strike count on the hitter. And giving up a home run on an 0-2 pitch is a mortal sin. That doesn't mean the pitcher wants to "waste one." Every pitch should have a purpose. Usually the pitcher will throw one or two out of the strike zone, but not too far out, hoping the hitter will bite. The trick is not to make it too good.

Hitters have to protect the plate with a two-strike count, or at least they should. Some of them are still swinging from the heels, instead of edging a little closer to the plate and choking up a little on the bat to control it better and get a piece of the ball. There are a lot of called third strikes, too, because hitters don't swing even if the pitch looks a few inches off the plate. If the umpire is calling those pitches strikes, you have to be aware of that and swing at it.

Wade Boggs is probably the best two-strike hitter in the game today. Somehow he seems to hit better in that situation.

Most pitchers pitch from the middle of the rubber. Sometimes you see one working from one end or the other. And they might shift on certain hitters to have a better chance of pitching inside or outside, if that's what they want to do.

Watch the infielders and outfielders move for different hitters. Sometimes they will move again as the count changes. If you've got a good right-hand hitter up and they're pitching him inside, they're trying to make him pull the ball. If they're pitching him outside, they're trying to get him to hit to the opposite field. The fielders will position themselves accordingly.

Sometimes the hitter will get himself out trying to beat the way they are pitching him. A few years ago they were pitching outside a lot to Cal Ripken, and he kept trying to pull the ball. He should never have done that, because he's got enough power to drive the ball out of the park to the opposite field. Guys like Canseco, Baines, Thomas can hit outside pitches for home runs without trying to pull the ball, which usually results in a popup or a weak grounder to second.

Try to guess how the pitchers are going to pitch to the big hitters.

Watch the catcher set up—where he starts out with the glove and where he winds up waiting for the pitch. A tipoff to how good the pitcher's location is that day is how often he hits the catcher's mitt right where it's set up.

When a pitcher stands out there and shakes off the catcher, that doesn't always mean he disagrees with the sign. He knows that shaking off the sign bothers some hitters, especially guess hitters. If you see the pitcher shake his head and the batter backs out, I can tell you what's going through the hitter's mind: "Oh oh. I'm thinking fastball; now what am I getting?"

If a hard thrower like Ben McDonald throws five changeups a game, he becomes a more effective pitcher. Hitters can pretty well gauge a fastball and pick up a curve. But if a guy comes up with another off-speed pitch, it not only throws off the guy at the plate, but the others on the bench. They'll sit up and say, "Wait a minute. What was that?" They talk among themselves.

When you get to the major leagues, it becomes a mental game. That's not true in the minors, where one strong kid throws hard and another strong kid tries to hit the ball hard. They don't have that finesse yet.

Every time a batter hits a fly ball to the outfield, you hear the big "oohs" and "aahs" from the fans. If you want to have some idea of how far that ball is going, don't watch the ball; watch the outfielders. You can tell by how fast they are running and the direction they are going whether it's going to be a routine can of corn or somebody's going to be climbing the fence. You won't ever see an outfielder take the first step if you're watching the pitch and the hitter. It can't be done. But once the ball is hit in the air, it may be easier to follow the fielder's movements than to pick up the ball in flight.

Notice how the infielders position themselves before the pitcher starts to throw, and what they do at the last second when he delivers. Players have different habits. Some, like Ripken, will be leaning in anticipation of where they expect the ball to be hit. He knows how the pitchers intend to pitch to each hitter. They go over all that stuff in meetings before the start of each series, and Cal knows the veteran hitters by now.

The first baseman often gives the sign to the pitcher to throw over with a man on base. Watch the third base coach giving signs and see if you can tell what's going on. The manager gives the signs for pitchouts and steals. Try to pick them up yourself, like the other team is trying to do.

19

The Old Ballpark

Memorial Stadium was comfortable as an old shoe, something you never wanted to throw away. I get misty just talking about the place. It was like home, very easy to move around in. Everything—and everybody—was closer. Camden Yards is a magnificent place. But if I had too good legs, I wouldn't like it. Everything is so far apart, so distant. No wonder they have all these kids, "baserunners," running around delivering things, and golf carts to take the players to the parking lot.

At Memorial Stadium, everybody knew everybody. You knew every usher, all the grounds crew by their first names. It took just a few seconds to go from one clubhouse to the other.

That old place was magical. Sure, they had a little tiny training room, crowded little clubhouses. But everything got done. And pennants were won. The general manager, the head of public relations, the traveling secretary, and two secretaries were all in a room about as big as my little apartment—*all* of them. But it worked. How did they do it?

I don't understand the new palatial layout. Well, I do understand it, and I know, I'm an old guy, but I think about things like that. It bothers me when somebody complains that they don't have enough room for whatever, whether it's a player with 18

pairs of shoes or the office people. Today's new young employ-
ees expect what they have at Camden Yards and the warehouse,
but a few of us old-timers know the difference. My "office" at
the old ballpark was a closet where people hung up their coats.

The original Orioles clubhouse was on the first base side,
but Paul Richards switched it to third, so now the home club-
house was smaller than the visitors'. When the Colts played there,
they used the visitors' clubhouse. They hung big canvas sheets,
the kind that painters use, all around the room to cover the base-
ball lockers when they played there in September. Nobody com-
plained.

Pat Sandirone would have to take down the pitchers mound
and the foul poles for the football games, and put it all back to-
gether after the game.

The press box was small and crowded, and the press dining
room shouldn't even be dignified by calling it a "dining room."
It was no bigger than most people's kitchens. But Helen Arena
and Hazel Bobbitt fed a lot of people in there. Now you wonder
how they did it, but they did.

Those old press box inhabitants were something else. Ev-
erybody was close in more ways than one. There was Bob Maisel,
as nice a guy as ever walked the earth. All those years he was the
beat writer and sports editor, I don't think his credibility was ever
challenged by anybody. There were no confrontations with man-
agers.

John Steadman was another standup guy. Jim Elliot, Lou
Hatter the same. Neal Eskridge was a serious, intense guy. Some
of them still showed up in a suit and tie every day. It could be
110 degrees. That's just the way they were. It was no rule, they
just did it. On the road the Orioles had a dress code: jacket and
tie. Earl Weaver ruled out jeans. A guy could be wearing a hun-
dred dollar pair of designer jeans, and he'd growl, "Whattaya got
on, your overalls?" The Orioles still have a jacket and collar rule,
tie optional.

A few old-timers in baseball still wear a suit and tie to work.
Sparky Anderson, for one. Some of the older coaches, too. But
not the younger guys. But I don't understand the mode of dress
in the press box these days. Do they have any self-respect? I

wonder if they have mirrors. Not all of them, certainly, but some. I know, times and styles change. I used to wear a shirt and tie when I was in broadcasting. I don't anymore.

Why did all that change? I ask myself dumb questions like that. Did all the money change it? I guess not. It's the whole society. You watch old World Series films from the 1930s and '40s. Everybody in the stands is wearing a suit and tie, and a felt hat. The women wear gloves and hats. That was not just the Series, it was every day. I guess it changed in the 1960s, when a lot of these guys were growing up.

In the old press box there was a lot of humorous agitating and teasing. The writers took turns as the official scorer. Yes, they got yelled at sometimes by players. No, they didn't back down. No, they didn't have any instant replay to look at.

Doug DeCinces was one of those players who would call the press box and complain about an error he was charged with. One night Lou Hatter was the official scorer. He gave DeCinces an error on a play. About three innings later Gordon Beard, who covered the games for Associated Press, called out, "Lou, phone call." It had come in on the phone near him.

Lou goes over and picks up the phone and listens and gets this stricken look on his face. All you hear out of him is, "But...but...but...." He hangs up.

I'm sitting in the middle of all these guys. I ask him, "What's that all about?"

Lou says, "You won't believe it. Mrs. DeCinces just called complaining about that error." He looked like he was going to have a heart attack. "Can you imagine, Mrs. DeCinces calling me?" It was like the world had come to an end. It was okay if some player called you, but the player's wife? That was too much.

We found out later that Gordon had called the newspaper office and gotten some woman working there to make the call and pretend she was Mrs. DeCinces. The place was in an uproar when we learned that.

That was the atmosphere of the place. One day during a game one of the vendors came by in the stands below the press box yelling, "Hot dog! Hot dog!"

I said to Gordon, "They're calling you."

A few games later he got back at me. We heard a vendor cry out, "Rex Barney's a hot dog!" Gordon had tipped the kid to do that.

Jim Elliot was the butt of a lot of jokes. A bunch of California writers would stand in the back of the coop and serenade him with, "I hate to see the Morning Sun come out."

Lou Hatter was a delightful guy. A game would be flowing along with the outcome apparent, and late in the game the guys would start typing their leads. All of a sudden the game changes and they have to pull out the copy paper and throw it away. When that happened, you could count on Lou to comment, "I've seen it happen many times." Never failed.

Loretta was the Western Union telegrapher who sent all the stories out over the ticker. You could hear that tickety-tick-tick and the clatter of typewriter keys after the game. I loved it all.

One day Jim Elliot was the official scorer and there was a close call, could go either way. Neal Eskridge said, "What is it, Elliot?"

"I'm not sure."

"Well, watch the goddamned game."

After that, whenever a close call came up, somebody would yell out, "Watch the game!"

They watched the game intently. Today I see a lot of walking around, fooling around, watching some damned basketball or hockey game or whatever on the TV monitors. We didn't have any TV in the early days, but even when we did, that would have been a no-no. One night there was a rain delay and Pat Sandirone came up to the press lounge, which he rarely did. There was a TV in there and some of the younger writers were watching a basketball game, Pat reached up and turned it off.

"What are you doing?" the writers complained.

"This is baseball," Pat barked. "What are you being paid to do?"

There are still a few of us old-timers around who don't miss a pitch: Chuck McGeehan, Gordon Beard, Bill Stetka, who is the full-time official scorer now and sits beside me. We have a TV monitor and he watches a replay occasionally before calling a play. But I've seem some scorers who won't make a decision until they look at the play a few times or go down and talk to the players involved. after the game. They would never have survived in the days when the call had to be made right now, without the benefits of high technology.

I can't stand it when some columnist or TV commentator shows up three or four times a year and knows everything that's going on and how to run the ball club.. One guy wrote that Johnny Oates talks to only one of his coaches, Jerry Narron. My God! Common sense tells you that can't be. But this expert sees Oates talking to Narron once on the field, doesn't stick around long enough to see him talking to anybody else, and goes back home and writes that Oates doesn't talk to the others.

As my pal Charley Eckman likes to say about the experts, "How many jock straps did they ever pull on?"

I've see thousands of games and I still don't know baseball. So it aggravates me when some writer says he sees 81 games a year, so he knows the game. Guys like Sparky Anderson have probably seen a million games and he'll tell you he still doesn't have baseball figured out.

Sure, I miss the old ballpark and the old press box and the old writers and the old good times, and if that makes me an old guy, sure, I'll admit to that, too.

20

Hall of Famers

Being around the game as long as I have been, I have had an opportunity to play against and to watch up close some of the all-time stars of the game who had no connection with the Orioles. I'd like to share some of my memories and impressions of them with you.

I have good and bad memories of Ralph Kiner. I like him tremendously as a person, but I don't think he deserves to be in the Hall of Fame. He was a one-dimensional player. All he could do was hit with power.

A decent man, gentleman, good guy. But when he came up to the plate, he would scare you. He was tough. I think one year he hit four home runs off me. But if he didn't hit the ball a long way, it was generally an out, often a double play. Some sluggers could hit the long ball and bat around .300, too. Not Ralph.

Sandy Koufax had the world's worst move to first base for a lefty. But his attitude was, "If I'm so dumb to let the guy get on base, I'll have to fan the next guys."

Koufax would not walk anybody intentionally. It got so Walter Alston quit asking him if he wanted to pitch around somebody. He knew the answer would be no. Koufax would just strike the guy out in a spot like that.

I am a great admirer of Mickey Mantle. He endured as much

pain as anybody I've ever seen. Before every game he had to wrap his left leg from the ankle up with an Ace bandage wrapped as tight as a mummy. After every game he would unwrap it, tears of pain on his face. Never say a word. I saw that. Every day. Fans never saw that, and could not appreciate how he could run as fast as he did despite it.

Mantle was named after Mickey Cochrane, his father's favorite player. His father drove Mickey to become a major league player. It beat riding a plow behind a mule.

Mickey is a very shy guy outside the clubhouse. I was in a hotel bar in Detroit one night with Mel Allen and some other broadcasters when the Yankees were in town. There were a few young ladies in there and they saw us. One of them said, "Mickey Mantle said hello to me at the game today."

Mel Allen said, "If he did, Billy Martin told him how to do it."

A lot of guys are like that; they change when they are in their element, at home in the clubhouse.

I saw Willie Mays briefly when he came up in 1951. An electrifying player. You knew he would be great just by his actions on the field. He had it all, and got better every year. I don't think there was anything he couldn't do.

The Giants brought him up from Minneapolis, and Durocher fell in love with him. But he got off to a slow start, 0 for something, and he begged Leo to send him back to the minors. But Leo kept him in the lineup.

He was the on deck hitter when Bobby Thomson hit the home run in the 1951 playoff. Nobody was more overjoyed than Mays, who was praying that Thomson would win it so he would not have to hit in that spot.

A magnificent ballplayer, Mays later became a surly, unfriendly, world-owes-me-a-living type of guy. I don't know what turned him off. He goes to card shows and signs things, but not graciously, and he gives show promoters a hard time. They are always after him, because he is a big drawing card, but they can never be sure if he'll agree to show up or not. I don't like that.

Roberto Clemente was a very nice man, smiled a lot off the field, but on the field he wasn't out to beat you, he wanted to bury you. Whoever wrote that he was playing against mere mortals had it right. Hitting with that ungainly, unorthodox style, and that great arm, he did everything with great flair.

Al Kaline was the closest looking hitter and fielder to Joe DiMaggio that I had ever seen when he broke in with Detroit in 1953. Same type of actions. A complete, smooth, class ballplayer. I have never had any reason to change that opinion.

A Baltimore boy, Kaline missed being an Oriole by a year. Baltimore was still in the International League in '53, and they thought they had him signed. But Al and his father did not think Baltimore would get a major league team, and they wanted to go with an established organization.

When Al was 15 or so, he was so good he would play three games a day for three different teams. He kept the uniforms in his car and changed while going from one section of the city to another for games at 10:00 in the morning, 1:00 and at 5:00. He was 20 when he won a batting title hitting .340 in 1955. The next year he "slumped" to .314. One day he had a chance to ask Ted Williams for some help. I thought it took a lot of nerve for a kid who won a batting title to go to the greatest hitter of them all and ask him for instructions. It says something about both of them.

Al had a foot operation and played in a lot of pain. A Hall of Fame person as well as player, he carried himself in such a way that he commanded respect. If a player wanted to know about an opposing pitcher or outfielder, Al was the one they asked.

Harmon Killebrew was popular with players and fans, so much so the Orioles brought him back for an appearance during their farewell year at Memorial Stadium. He was kidded a lot about his lack of speed and his baldness. His retort: "The Lord took my hair away so I could think better."

Carl Yastrzemski was a cold, calculating, surly guy. A team player, yes. He was probably a better all-around player than Williams, but he lived under the shadow of being another Williams, and that's a pretty heavy shadow. He played hurt a lot. Wouldn't go outside to sign autographs for kids. Would do one interview a year. It wasn't until his farewell game at Fenway Park that he bent a little and walked around the park waving to the fans and shaking hands. He never goes to oldtimers games.

Bill Dickey was one of those poor well-intentioned good guys who thought he could help me with my control. He was a good teacher—he taught Yogi Berra how to be a catcher—but I was too great a challenge for any man. Brooks Robinson was his newspaper carrier in Little Rock when Brooks was a kid.

Gabby Hartnett was the manager at Jersey City when I was at Montreal in 1943. A complete catcher, he was a big, jovial, apple-cheeked Santa Claus kind of guy.

Lefty Gomez was a delightful guy, full of stories and jokes. I once asked him if the stories he told on the banquet circuit were true, and he claimed they were. Well, maybe they were exaggerated a little. He said the only number he knew was 5 when he was pitching, because that was DiMaggio's number and he saw DiMaggio's back so often; Joe was always going after long fly balls in center field.

Gomez was the world's worst hitter. One time he was hitting against a wild young fastball pitcher—not me. The count got to 2 and 2 and the next pitch whistled by a foot over his head, but he ducked anyhow. The umpire called, "Ball three."

Gomez said, "Like hell, That was strike three. I'm getting out of here."

He said he did those things, and I believe him.

I knew Bob Gibson from his Omaha school days. Mean all his life. You never saw him smile. Just a mean, belligerent, very intense, woundup person. Worked fast on the mound.

One day Tim McCarver was catching him. Gibson had given up a few hits or something that prompted McCarver to go to the mound.

"Gibby, why don't you..." That's as far as he got. Gibson glared at him and said, "Go back behind the plate. The only thing you know about pitching is you can't hit it."

When Red Schoendienst was his manager, he said the worst part of the job was going out to take Gibson out of a game. Gibson told him once, "Don't come out to get me unless I tell you to."

Gibson once knocked down a hitter before the guy got up to the plate. He was warming up before an inning in St. Louis. Willie McCovey was the first batter up. He came out between the on deck circle and home plate to get a better look at Gibson's fastball and WHOOSH! down he went.

Gibson yelled at him, "Get up to the plate and I'll give you a better look."

When Gibson pitched against Koufax, nobody ever scored.

Many years later Gibson was visiting with Frank Robinson in Baltimore. Frank said Gibson hit him more times than he hit Gibson. That's a confrontation I wish I'd seen: Frank Robinson hitting against Bob Gibson. The intensity level must have gone off the charts.

You'd get the impression if you ever met Gibson that he likes nobody. But he has mellowed some. A few years ago he was in Baltimore and he asked to have a picture taken of himself with me and Gregg Olson; we were all from Omaha.

Whitey Ford came up late in the 1950 season and went 9-1. He was in the Eastern League and the Yankees needed pitching help. He wrote to them and told them to bring him up. A tough, brash kid, he was cocky, reeked of personal pride, and could do the job.

I saw him pitch one day that year in Yankee Stadium, when we had a day off. I was sitting there and an usher handed me a note from my friend, Bobby Brown, who was then with the Yankees: "Welcome to a major league park."

Ford pitched like Preacher Roe but could throw harder. In later years he cheated, no question. He'd have a damp place on the mound and stick a little mud in the seams of the ball. When you know what you're doing, that's all it takes. But even without that, he was a good pitcher and tough competitor.

Ford and Stengel were right for each other. They really clicked.

Steve Carlton was a magnificent pitcher. Look up his numbers for innings pitched and complete games. Nobody will ever attain those figures again. He was total concentration on the mound. A very astute, bright guy, he was high on martial arts. He would take a five-gallon bucket and fill it with raw rice and dig his finger down to the bottom. That hurts. He got Jim Palmer to do it, and Palmer seldom got to the bottom.

I met Luke Appling a few times in his later years. A delightful, southern gentleman. Guys like Chuck Dressen and Paul

Waner told me he was a genius at fouling off pitches until he got the one he wanted. He always complained about his aches and pains, then went out and killed you on the field.

In one of the first oldtimers games, he played one inning and hit a home run, then announced in the clubhouse, "Boys, I don't know about you, but I'll be glad when this season is over." He was probably close to 80.

Lou Boudreau hit a home run off me in an exhibition game in Cleveland. A tremendous guy, he had been the Indians' manager since he was 24 years old. He played the shallowest shortstop of anybody I'd ever seen. Pee Wee Reese told me why. "He can't throw, has a fair arm but not a shortstop arm."

Mel Ott was the playing-manager of the Giants when they invited me to try out in the spring of 1943. A very nice, accommodating man, he checked with me and my father to see that everything was all right when we got there. He astounded me when I first saw him; he was only five foot nine. But he had power. Although he played in the Polo Grounds with those short foul lines, he hit half his home runs on the road.

I pitched against him and he lifted that right leg high in the air before he swung. Some guys lift the front leg before they swing, but nobody as pronounced as Ott.

Ernie Banks is one of the most effervescent, easy-going, fun-loving people to be around, smiling all the time.

He is famous for saying, "It's a beautiful day in Chicago; let's play two," and "Welcome to magnificent Chicago and the friendly confines of Wrigley Field."

And he meant it. But he was also a much better hitter and player than a lot of people realize. He was a tall, skinny kid who hit the highest home runs I've ever seen. They seemed to go straight up in the air and then take off. I picked up his bat one time; it was like a toothpick. Nothing there. But he had quick hands. You could see the catcher go for the pitch and Banks would rip it right out of the glove and pull it.

What does it take to be on a terrible team and win the MVP back to back? He did that. When you think of all the other great players in the league at that time, you realize how great he must have been. He was one of those players I'd pay to watch. He was something special. Go to the ballpark, don't know anything about baseball, you'd say to yourself, "That guy there; he's a little better than everybody else."

He's still the same refreshing, delightful person. When they have an oldtimers game and he's going to be there, he's the one the other players can't wait to see.

Now I know I'm going to make some Brooks Robinson fans mad, but there were two guys who rivaled him as a third baseman: Eddie Mathews and Mike Schmidt.

The funny thing is, where Brooks's fielding took away from his hitting—and he was a great clutch player—the hitting of Mathews and Schmidt took away from their fielding. Look up their numbers. I admire both those guys; they'd get me on the edge of my seat to see what they would do.

If Schmidt doesn't walk into the Hall of Fame, there's something wrong.

21

All-Star Teams

Fans like to read about imaginary all-star teams; it's always a great source of controversy. They can call in and disagree with my choices, and I like that.

In addition to the usual lineups, I've tried to come up with some variations. Here goes:

Orioles 1969-1994

Catcher—Before the arrival of Chris Hoiles, I would have said Andy Etchebarren first, then Rick Dempsey. But given the way he has developed in the past few years, I would say Hoiles is the best we've had over the past quarter-century.

1B—I'd take Eddie Murray over Boog Powell and Jim Gentile for consistency, and all-around performance. He did the job year in and year out. He never won the MVP Award, but over a five-year span, Eddie had more MVP votes than any other player.

2B—Bobby Grich. No contest.

3B—Brooks Robinson is another no-contest. Doug DeCinces deserves a mention. He did an outstanding job, but his timing was bad; he followed Brooks.

SS—This is more difficult, even though the edge goes to Cal Ripken, Jr. Mark Belanger is right up there.

LF—The most difficult position. Fans might nominate 20 guys. My choice is Don Buford. An excellent leadoff man, Buford was not the outfielder that Brady Anderson is, but he was more consistent with the bat, had a higher on base percentage, averaging almost 100 walks a year for three years, and had good power. He scored 99 runs a year for three years.

CF—Paul Blair flatout. Among the excellent center fielders the Orioles have had, he stands out.

RF—Frank Robinson is automatic.

DH-PH—Terry Crowley against any kind of pitching

RHP—Jim Palmer.

LHP—Dave McNally, narrowly over Cuellar, Flanagan, McGregor.

If I am in the seventh game of a World Series, my starter would be McNally first, then Palmer. Tough question. I liked the way both of them worked. Both had guts.

If I have a one-run lead in the ninth inning of Game 7, who is my closer? Depending on the hitters, Tippy Martinez is my first choice. Dick Hall threw nothing but strikes, if I want a right-hander. Don Stanhouse would drive you crazy, but get the job done. Gregg Olson for a few years was as good as anybody. But Tippy was tough. Even with the bases loaded and a right-hand batter up there and a strikeout needed, I'd take Tippy Martinez. I'd also have Rick Dempsey in there to catch him, handling those curves that wound up in the dirt.

Orioles Defense

If I were a pitcher for the Orioles during the past 25 years, the eight other O's I would want on the field—strictly defense—would be:

> C —Bob Melvin
> 1B —Eddie Murray
> 2B —Bobby Grich
> 3B —Brooks Robinson
> SS —Cal Ripken, Jr.
> LF —Brady Anderson

CF—Paul Blair
RF —Frank Robinson

American League Opponents All-Stars 1969-1994

C—Bob Boone, with Carlton Fisk a close second.

1B—Carl Yastrzemski. Yaz was the best left fielder who ever played in Fenway Park, and there were a lot of good first basemen but I'll put Yaz here and find another left fielder. I have to have him somewhere in my lineup. Could I ever watch him play the game. Frank Thomas could force me to change this, but not yet.

2B—Roberto Alomar is as good as I've seen, but Bobby Richardson was excellent, as was Frank White.

3B—Craig Nettles. But how can I leave out George Brett, even though he was not a great defensive player? I know; I'll DH Brett.

SS—Alan Trammell is a complete player.

LF—Jim Rice was better than a lot of people think.

CF—Robin Yount. Ken Griffey, Jr. is as good as any; again, he may force me to make a change here in a few years.

RF—Al Kaline.

Amos Otis was a very good outfielder. Dave Winfield belongs very high. Winfield exemplifies to me how different the fans' opinions of players are from the truth. You will never, ever see him loaf on any play, any time, anywhere: running to and from his position, beating out a one-hopper to the pitcher. What a pleasure to watch him uncoil that big body when he takes a swing.

I'm leaving out Don Mattingly, a guy I would pay to watch. And Kirby Puckett, one of my all-time favorite players. Leaving out those guys is a baseball sin.

For pitchers, start with Roger Clemens. Frank Viola I enjoyed watching. Bret Saberhagen I could watch pitch every day. Catfish Hunter gave you a good game every time. He walked off the mound after giving up a home run the same as if he had struck out the side. I liked to watch Vida Blue.

My closer against the Orioles would be Rollie Fingers; didn't matter who or what the hitters were.

If I'm the manager and I need a clutch hit to win it all, I'd like to see Alan Trammell up there. A contact hitter, he'd put it in play where it would fall in or people would have to handle it. I'd never send a strikeout slugger up in a spot like that. Wade Boggs would be great, too, but he'd scare me to death before he did something. He's liable to take two down the middle before he swings. But he needs only one to hit. Rod Carew could do the job. His bat was a magic wand. No matter how the defense lined up, he'd poke it between them.

My big game pitcher would be Clemens, even though he seems not to win the big ones. When he gets in a jam, he turns it up and blows them away.

Of course, I'm going to leave somebody out and somebody will disagree with me, but that's okay. It's all my opinion, not revealed truth.

All-Popular Stars

It's difficult not to leave somebody out, but as best I can recall from being in clubhouses over the years, the best-liked guys— regardless of their stature as players—would include Rick Dempsey, Ruben Sierra, Boog Powell, Frank Howard, John Lowenstein, Frank Viola, Mike Flanagan, Harmon Killebrew, Carlton Fisk, Rick Burleson, Jerry Remy, George Brett, Pete O'Brien, Steve Beuchele, Alan Trammell, Dave Winfield, Kirby Puckett, Robin Yount, Paul Molitor.

These are guys who talk to everybody, do their share of kidding and can take it, too. Players can be brutal to each other. But let an outsider do it and they circle the wagons.

All-Tough, Battle-you-all-the-way Team

These are guys who played hard every day, every inning, every play as if the game, the season, their careers, their lives almost were on the line. Maybe it's easy to single out these great players, but that's why they were great: they never let up. About the time you think they've let up, you're dead.

C—In his day, Yogi Berra never let up on you, didn't know

what that meant. Bob Boone and Carlton Fisk were that way.

1B—Don Mattingly; no matter what the score, he battles you all the way.

2B—Bobby Richardson was always tough in his own quiet way, and Bobby Grich played every day like he was going to win everything.

3B—Frank Malzone acted like the game was on the line on every play, and Brooks never let down. If he was 0 for 4 he would be battling you to get a hit on that next at bat; if he was 4 for 4, same thing.

SS—Cal plays the game that way. Gene Michael was another tough, aggressive player.

OF—Frank Robinson of course. Dave Winfield never gave up. Reggie Jackson, Kirby Puckett. They came to play hard every day. Young pitchers have to learn that when you're facing guys like these, no matter what the score is, they are waiting for you to make a mistake and they'll hop on it.

For pitchers: Jack Morris, Dave Stewart, Palmer, Catfish Hunter, McNally, Fingers. Bret Saberhagen pitches like he's ahead 10-0 every game. If he gives up a home run, you don't see his head down. He just says, "Gimme the ball. Who's next?"

As a manager, Billy Martin would drive a team like this to the most extreme lengths they could go, and everybody else better stand aside.

All-Barrel of Laughs Team

If you had these guys in your clubhouse all together on the same team, you'd have a good time all season win or lose, and they wouldn't be that bad on the field, either.

Graig Nettles and Lou Piniella, always the center of the noise in the Yankee clubhouse.

Dick Allen, who said of Astroturf: "If a horse can't eat it, I don't want to play on it."

Joe Rudi and Ray Fosse, teasers and jokesters.

Ron Fairly kept things alive, teased himself a lot. Pete Vuckovich was loose. Butch Wynegar at Minnesota. Harold Reynolds kept things alive in the Seattle clubhouse as much as anybody could in that clubhouse when he was there.

Ozzie Guillen is always up.

Saberhagen is loose enough to kid himself.

Mike Flanagan had a lot of great one-liners, and Moe Drabowsky was a practical joker.

Palmer and Lowenstein were as funny as any vaudeville team.

Merv Rettenmund and Terry Crowley.

For a coach, George Staller, a hotfoot artist. He gave one to Commissioner Bowie Kuhn once.

The manager: Don Zimmer, who would let his hair down if he had any. "Come over here and look at my head," he'd say. "See what you can predict."

Players were always drawing pictures on it.

The trainer would be Ralph Salvon, a big fat guy with a great sense of humor. A master at doubletalk. Somebody would ask him, "How's Flanagan's arm?" and he'd say, "Well, let me tell you frabbleideemurfer...but outside of that, he'll be all right."

"What did he say?" the writer would ask.

"He just said his arm is okay."

One day in Kansas City Rettenmund was hurt in the outfield. Salvon came waddling out of the dugout to right field. It took him forever to get out there. After the game, Crowley said, "We found out one thing. Ralph is faster on Astroturf than he is on grass."

All-Nerve-wracking Team

In some ways baseball just fractures me. You can't wait for the game to get started, then on the first pitch you hear, "Hurry up, let's go" in the press box. As a player, when it was my turn to pitch I couldn't wait for the game to get started, and when it was under way I couldn't wait to finish it.

As much as I enjoy the game, there were some guys I hoped would not be in the lineup when I was watching.

Carlton Fisk was a great catcher, but walking back after backing up first base on a play, he took forever. When he went out to the mound he never trotted; walked out there slowly and walked back slower.

Ray Fosse was difficult to watch. He would catch the pitch, step out and pump three or four times before he threw the ball back to the pitcher.

Among pitchers, Diego Segui was the world's slowest, and Tommy Phoebus went 3 and 2 on every hitter. Gregg Olson circled the mound after every pitch. That bothered me. I wished he would just stand up there and take the throw and get ready to pitch again.

I kid modern players about all the electronic stuff and the batting gloves and the wristbands and all that stuff. They have the radar gun back of home plate that relays the pitch speed into the dugout: 94 mph, 88 mph. I ask them, "What good does that do anybody?" I don't get any answer.

And the batting gloves; does that make them better hitters? I think Ken Harrelson started that. He is a good golfer and he figured, if it helped with golf clubs, it might help with a bat. George Brett never used them, and could not tell me why anybody else did. Cal Ripken sometimes bats without them, or with just one. I see guys wearing two batting gloves, then they get on base and they take them off and put on two other gloves. Does that make them better players? If it does, then think how much better the old guys must have been who did all that super hitting without batting gloves, helmets, wrist bands, head bands, nothing. I don't understand it.

The Orioles had a guy one year—Carlos Lopez. Unbelievable. He wore shin guards, wrist bands, head band, and he had to adjust everything he had on before he was ready to step into the batters box.

Mike Hargrove was another one who went through a routine after every pitch: hand in this pocket, then that pocket, gloves, wristband, cap...same routine every time. Never varied. Chuck Thompson described it on the air one time with a rapid fire delivery in great detail: "His left hand goes to his cap, his right hand goes to the back pocket, he goes to his glasses he goes to his wristband, he goes to..."

Nerve-wracking manager? Weaver took a lot of time haranguing the umpires way beyond making his point. And Maury

Wills visited the mound over and over.

But not even those guys could dull my anticipation of the next game and my desire to be out at the old ballpark.

All-Quiet Orioles

I get a lot of callers who complain that the Orioles need a player or manager who will fire up the team, put some life into them. No matter how often I point out all the quiet, laid-back managers who win the world championships year after year, and the quiet players who win batting titles and go to the World Series, it doesn't change anything.

Well, here's a lineup of Orioles who would neither light fires nor need them lit under them, and would do a pretty good job for you on the field. A few of them I saw when I was broadcasting the Game of the Day, before I came to Baltimore.

C—Mickey Tettleton
1B—Eddie Murray
2B—Bobby Grich
3B—Woodie Held
SS—Cal Ripken, Jr.
LF—Larry Sheets or Don Baylor
CF—Larry Harlow
RF—Joe Orsulak
DH—Harold Baines
P—Digger O'Dell

22

1994

This chapter is a mixture of memories and current impressions, of progress and regress, of the pleasures of seeing young players develop and begin to fulfill their potential, and some reminders of what it took to get there, and of the pain of seeing careers decline.

The 1994 Orioles were the best club Johnny Oates has had since he's been here. He came into the season with an up attitude, expecting them to score a lot of runs. But in the early going, the pitching was better than expected, and the hitting was worse.

When the Orioles signed Rafael Palmeiro, Chris Sabo and Sid Fernandez during the winter, some idiots in the media immediately proclaimed, "We're a cinch to win it all now." And when the team didn't win every game up to June 1, they were yelling, "Oates has got to go."

Other managers in the league expressed their amazement to me at the Oates-bashing that took place all summer. "He's a terrific manager," they said. "I don't understand what all this fuss is about. What more do they want out of that team?"

You know when you read this how the year turned out, but at about June 15, the Orioles were just one game out of first place.

Now let's take a look at the '94 Orioles as of June 15.

On July 30, 1988 Baltimore traded Mike Boddicker to Boston for Brady Anderson and Curt Schilling. For the next three years, Brady, with all his talent, showed them nothing, and GM Roland Hemond got crucified for that deal.

The Orioles wanted Brady to use his speed by becoming a bunting, slap-hitting leadoff man. Brady resisted. He was in and out of the lineup, with a brief demotion to the minors. But the organization stayed with him.

When he first joined the team I introduced myself to him and wished him a lot of luck. I watched him closely for a few years; I like people who are struggling. I guess I have an affinity for them. I sure have an understanding of what they're going through.

Then one night in 1991 he got into a game in Texas and had a great game. So I called him and congratulated him on accomplishing what he was supposed to do and what was expected of him.

Johnny Oates took over the club during the 1991 season. The following winter Oates called Brady and told him, "You're my leadoff man, and my left fielder until you play your way out of the job. You can hit any way you want to, play the game any way you want to."

All the callers on my radio show, and all the local writers said, "What a mistake. He's been here three years, he can't play. . . we all know that…it was a bad deal…"

That spring the first person I interviewed was Brady. He was surprised. "No one ever interviews me," he said.

Off the air I told him, "Son, this is it. You better get your head together."

I have been rooting for him ever since, but sometimes he drives me crazy. Early in that '92 season in a game in Toronto, in the ninth inning of a close game with two men on and two out, he took a called third strike. I'd have made him walk from Toronto to Boston. To me, that is a worse sin than giving up a home run on an 0-2 pitch. I'm sure Oates went berserk inside. You can't have that. If it's close enough for the umpire to call a strike, it's close enough to swing at in that situation, even if it appears to be outside the strike zone.

But Brady got it together and went on to have one of the most productive years in history for a leadoff man. You can look it up.

I don't believe that year was an aberration. He's got a lot of talent and baseball sense. A natural center fielder, he can cover as much ground as anybody. He's a great kid, works hard, is a good guy to have on your ball club. I think the biggest problem with Brady is, he hits a home run and he's a home run hitter. I fear that trying to hit the ball out of the ballpark all the time is going to get him. It just doesn't work.

Like a lot of other people, I have kept after Brady to bunt more, drag more, the way he can run. I think bunting wins games. But he's stubborn. I try to point out guys like Stan Musial who bunted for base hits and added maybe 20 or 30 points to their BA.

"Yeah," he says, "but I can hit...a bunt's only a single...." It's been like talking to a wall.

Bunting, and the possibility of a batter bunting, draws the infield in a little, enhancing the chance of hitting a shot by the first or third baseman.

And then, in the first two months of 1994, I saw Brady taking more practice bunts in BP and putting down more bunts for base hits in games. They didn't always work, but he was getting better at it. He's got one of the best teachers of the art in Johnny Oates, whose bunting ability helped keep him in the major leagues for ten years. There was a time when a guy like Brady would be out early before anybody was in the place, practicing hundreds of bunts, dragging them and pushing them, until he could drop one on a dime. That's the kind of preparation that wins games. But that doesn't happen much these days.

What can a manager do about it? He can make the best of it. That's all.

I hope Brady keeps working at it.

We expected more out of Mike Devereaux in spring training. I think he has regressed since his big year in '92. I never believed the experiment of moving him to right field in the spring would work. But it wasn't a mistake; that's what spring training is for. Unfortunately, the first day he ran into a fence in Dunedin during a practice game. He was used to roaming the prairie out in center field and didn't realize the fences were so close. That ended the experiment.

Devereaux was hit in the face with a pitch early in the season. He came back and played the next day, but I buy some of that about his becoming plate-shy after that. It bothers certain guys. Paul Blair was beaned and never was the same again. But Brooks Robinson was beaned five times. Never bothered him. Cal Junior really got hacked by Mike Moore in 1982. He wanted to play right away, and it never bothered him.

Devereaux has a weak arm, but contrary to what some people say, the weakest arm belongs in center field. The cutoff man is the vital link in the defense. Veteran managers go berserk when outfielders—especially center fielders with weak arms—overthrow the cutoff man.

Mr. Rickey used to go insane about that. When he held sessions on the cutoff man, you'd hear more "Judas Priest" from him than you ever heard in your life. We'd be playing an intrasquad game, and he would be sitting there watching. Then: "Whoa! Stop! Run that play again," and we would do it over and over until we finally got the message.

They don't learn that way any more.

It's like that immortal play in the 1955 World Series. Everybody talks about the Sandy Amoros catch off Yogi Berra in left field. Amoros had no arm at all. The biggest part of that play was when he threw to Pee Wee Reese in short left field and Reese whirled and threw a one-hop shot to Gil Hodges at first base to double off Gil McDougald. That's the play.

With his arm, Devo should never try to throw somebody out. He's got the best cutoff man in baseball in Cal Ripken. If I'm an outfielder, I flip it underhand to Ripken and let him make the throw. He can throw guys out from anywhere.

Jeffrey Hammonds seems to have more talent than all the other outfielders put together, but at this point, is he going to be injury-prone? Time will tell.

Jack Voigt is a great fill-in outfielder; that's his best position, but he plays first base or third, and goes out and warms up the pitcher sometimes. He gives you everything he's got. Voigt knows the game and has such hustle and desire, he can be a good backup man for years. He doesn't ask any favors, never complains, just loves to play. He's one of those guys who can get up out of bed in the middle of the night and swing a good bat for you. He's a lively, mouthy presence in the clubhouse, and a good guy to have there.

Damon Buford has a chance to be a good player. He has the tools and the knowledge of the game that you often find in the sons of former players.

Damon created a quandary in spring training. He hit up a storm. But if he stayed with the Orioles, what would he do? Sit on the bench and pinch-run occasionally. If he went back to Rochester, at least he could play every day and still be in Baltimore on short notice if he was needed. Which was the right thing to do—keep him or send him back down? It's a tough question, especially when the player would rather be in the major leagues, even if he is gathering splinters. But doing that is not always in his best interest for the long term.

Mark Smith threw another positive monkey wrench into spring training; he looked so good, he had them talking to themselves.

I had gone to Frederick to see him play a few weeks after they signed him in 1991. A writer asked him, "What do you think of this Class A pitching?"

"It's nothing," he said. "It was tougher in college."

He was hitting about .210 at the time, finished at .250. Now he's grown up, got his head on straight.

Harold Baines just does his job, as well as anybody does it. It's sad he has those bad knees; he was a good outfielder. As a hitter, he doesn't care who's pitching, left or right. He reminds me of Arky Vaughan, who used to say, "The ball's got to be in the strike zone. I don't care where it's coming from, if he's right-handed, left-handed, cross-handed, or what angle it comes from. If it's in the strike zone, I'll hit it."

Harold is one of the quietest guys I've ever been around. An Eastern Shore waterman, he's a tough interview; you get a lot of short answers. But he's loosened up a little in later years.

I give Leo Gomez more credit than a lot of people do for what he has accomplished. I saw him when he was 20 in spring training in 1987. I remember asking Billy Hunter who he was.

"A kid from Puerto Rico. Can't speak any English."

The next time I saw him was one night in 1989 at Hagerstown. David Segui was playing first base, Leo third. David hit a home run, and this guy hit two, one of them 460 feet. He could hit, but was not a good fielder. Had iron hands.

He went to Rochester and still couldn't field.

Leo came up to Baltimore the tail end of 1990, got into 12 games, nervous and scared. Couldn't catch a ground ball. Dropped a pop fly. They booed him so bad, it made me sick.

He went to Cal Senior and asked for help. Senior would never go to a player, but anybody who went to him got all the help he wanted. The two of them came out early, day after day, Senior hitting hundreds of ground balls and line drives at him. He became a decent fielder. Not the greatest, but a very good fielder. His only deficiency is quickness. He makes the plays, has a good arm.

Leo has great power; in the past I did not like the way he swung the bat—too much uppercut. He seems to have cut down on that some this year, leveling his swing to hit to all fields.

The worst thing that happened to him in '93 was what he didn't do. He was having a good year—ten home runs in less than half a season—and all of a sudden he couldn't swing the bat. He waited too long to report the injury to his wrist and get it taken care of.

The best thing that ever happened to Leo may have been the Orioles' signing of Chris Sabo. I think Leo got a little lazy. When I saw him in spring training, instead of being down because they had brought Sabo in to take his job, he was working harder than I've ever seen him, taking extra BP, extra infield. If he wasn't going to play for the Orioles, he wanted to be ready to play wherever he went.

In March the talk was that the Red Sox wanted him. They were going to trade their third baseman, Scott Cooper, to Minnesota for Shane Mack, and send pitcher Paul Quantrill to Baltimore for Gomez. That was the speculation. There were other deals that were discussed concerning Leo, but the right combination of names never came together.

As it turned out, some of the best deals are the ones you don't make.

Chris Sabo is my kind of guy. He comes in, puts on his uniform, goes out, plays, comes back in, changes, gone. He just does his job. You don't even know he's alive. Usually.

In May he had back problems and lost his job to Gomez who got hot and stayed hot and Sabo made the mistake of taking his frustration and unhappiness to the media. I know how he felt, but I told him, "Chris, if you have a problem of any kind, go to the manager or a coach you like or the general manager and tell them and find out what's what. Don't go to the newspapers."

You cannot do that. You just can't. You know what got Phil Bradley run out of this town? He went to the media and told them the Orioles didn't appreciate him and didn't want to sign him.

You got a gripe? Go to the man in charge. Dauer and Dempsey wanted to punch Weaver out because they weren't playing. They'd go into his office and tell him, "I should be playing. I'm the second baseman," or "I'm the catcher."

"Well, we'll see," Earl would tell them. "We'll let you know."

Then Earl would laugh when they left his office. He was the manager. He made the decisions. But at least they went to him, instead of going behind his back to some writer and saying, "You know what's going on around here? They don't like me." Yak, yak, yak.

If a player talks to the manager or GM and is still unhappy, then it's okay to go to the writers and say, "I just went to Oates or Roland Hemond and I'm not satisfied with what they said," or something. But even with all Sabo's talk, the writers still made up stuff he never said. He never refused to play. Just the opposite. He wanted to be out there earning what they were paying him. I find nothing wrong with that. He's a hard-nosed, blue collar guy—whatever that means. When he and Oates tried to figure out how to get his bat back into the lineup, Chris offered to play the outfield, a position he had never played before. Trying to play a new position in the middle of the season in the major leagues—that takes guts. But he did it, worked hard at it, and helped the club.

I know the other players like Sabo in the clubhouse. There was never any problem there. Forget anything else you read or heard.

Is there a better all-around shortstop in baseball today than Cal Ripken, Jr.? Every manager would like to have a Junior on his club. People talk about his going to his right and making those backhand plays. A lot of guys can catch the ball in the hole, but they can't throw you out. What makes those plays for Cal is his arm; he's got a pitcher's arm. He was a pitcher in high school. And he's so accurate with it. He can throw guys out standing on his head.

Shortstop is the key position on a team, so most shortstops are better athletes than other guys on the club. I'm an oldtimer. I talk a lot about Marty Marion and Eddie Miller and Pee Wee, Granny Hamner, Rizzuto. I've seen all these guys. Tony Kubek was unbelievable. Gil McDougald was an all-star shortstop, second baseman and third baseman—he could flatout play the game.

Cal is a natural athlete, and talk about baseball sense—he picked up on everything and followed the right people: first Brooks and Doug DeCinces, then Belanger, who was unsurpassed with the glove.

Comparing Cal with all of these others in their prime, for an all-around shortstop at the plate and with the glove, I'd take Cal. In his own quiet way, he is a steadying influence on the others; they all respect him. They could take a lesson from him, too, by watching how he prepares for a game.

I admire Mark McLemore for moving back and forth between right field and second base. A lot of modern-day players will yell and scream about being moved around like that. He does a good job, not sensational, but I'm not worried about him out there in either position.

Tim Hulett is a reliable, valuable fill-in man, but you better not play him 20 or 25 games in a row. Every club needs those utility players on the bench, and he's a good one.

When Jim Frey was managing the Cubs, he told me they had a kid in the minors who was going to be a hitter—Rafael

Palmeiro. He didn't hit much in Chicago, but you could see him coming on in Texas, getting better every year.

He's got a great swing, doesn't overextend it, and a great attitude. When he came to Baltimore, I didn't buy all the baloney where they tried to make him say things like, "I don't like Baltimore."

Somebody in the media tried to make him out to be trouble in the clubhouse. That's the furthest thing from the truth I've seen. These writers are in the clubhouse maybe an hour a month, look around and maybe see nobody talking and go write a story that nobody's talking to anybody else in the clubhouse. Dissension!

Palmeiro is a major leaguer. It's a mystery to me why Texas let him go, or why San Francisco let Will Clark go. I think Clark's agent used Baltimore during the winter, knowing Clark was going to Texas all along. I can see a guy feeling hurt with the kind of treatment Palmeiro got after the great years he had in Texas.

With the Orioles, he is a great fit. He knew before he ever came here that he loved to hit in Camden Yards. I don't blame him. It's made to order for a hitter like him.

Palmeiro had an ingrown toenail late in May, and if you've ever had one of those, you know it's a killer. He didn't want to miss a game. The trainer had to talk him into sitting one out. The next day he played hurting. A problem in the clubhouse? No way.

Chris Hoiles has improved so much with his footwork and calling games, he is now the best I've ever seen in an Orioles uniform, and is probably one of the top three catchers in the American League. He was not hitting well as of June, but I think he'll wind up with a good year. I know I'm an old guy, but I don't care what position you play, if you're hitting .220, how are you in the major leagues? Of course, every club these days has them.

I think Chris's troubles at the plate came from swinging at more bad balls this year than in the past. But he knew that, too. He was not as patient as he should be. With his short, compact swing, he should be waiting a little longer before committing to a swing, and see the ball into the strike zone better.

I came away from spring training in 1994 without much confidence in the pitching. I was there when Sid Fernandez walked off the mound with a sore arm. I left Florida not knowing where they were going to get three healthy starters.

Ben McDonald was the only one who showed some consistency. He worked hard, as mentally and physically strong as an ox, and couldn't wait for the season to get started. He was thinking of all those runs the Orioles didn't score for him in '93, and all they could score for him with the additions of Palmeiro and Sabo. I agreed with him; the offensive lineup was one of the best I'd seen in 28 years in Baltimore.

(So what happened? For the first two months of the season, the Orioles were around the bottom of the league in hitting and the top in pitching. So much for *anybody* thinking they know this game.)

I was concerned about Mike Mussina in the spring. He was not throwing as much overhand as he usually did. The scouts noticed that he had dropped his arm down when he threw. That told them something was hurting, and he was compensating for it. But maybe he was just experimenting; that's what spring training is for. Mike's a very quiet kid, doesn't talk much. He was working with Dick Bosman and Johnny Oates, and I guess Oates knew what he was doing when he named Mussina the opening day pitcher instead of McDonald. Ben had a great spring and Mike did not. So naturally the media criticized Oates for that decision; all they go by is the numbers. They said Ben felt hurt by being bypassed, but of course they never asked Ben how he felt. He told me it didn't bother him at all.

And from opening day Mussina was his usual self, which in his case means a guy who looks like he's been pitching for ten years. Mike has learned how to pitch as quick as anybody can. Jim Palmer wasn't that good at that age. Mike's got great stuff, learns quickly and will not make the same mistake twice.

Mike comes close to that trancelike tunnel vision that Steve Carlton had before and during a game. And, like Palmer or Catfish Hunter, you can never tell by his demeanor on the mound whether he is five runs ahead or behind. I've seen Hunter give up a grand slam and I've seen him strike out the side, and his attitude was always the same: give me the ball and let's go.

George Sisler once told me when he was trying to make a pitcher out of me, "Rex, even if you walk ten guys in a row, walk off that mound like you own them. It's hard to do, but put your head up high and act cocky. And act the same when you shut them out. Give them attitude."

Mike's like that. But acting cocky doesn't mean pumping your fist and jumping around when you strike out a guy. That's just putting on a show for television. Like a guy hitting a home run to win a game and pumping those arms in the air. I don't go for that stuff. You know what would happen in the old days? Whoom! Next time he came up, even if it was the next spring, he'd go down. They didn't go for showboating.

I first heard about Ben McDonald in the spring of 1989, before the Orioles made him the number one draft pick that summer. Richard Justice, a Baltimore baseball writer now with the *Washington Post*, had seen Ben pitch for LSU. I had Justice on my radio program from spring training, and he said, "This kid will walk right into the major leagues and blow 'em away."

Well, I have heard that a few times in my life. I said, "Richard, do you know what you're saying?"

"Rex, you gotta see this guy."

"I've seen eight million guys like that."

"He can't miss."

"I understand he could be a very good pitcher," I said, "but he's not going to go to the major leagues right away. High school, college is one thing. Even I could still blow 'em away to this day."

"I watch a lot of players," he said. "This guy can do it."

A lot of writers and broadcasters jumped on the bandwagon. They had Ben going right into the Orioles' starting rotation. And why not? The Major League Scouting Bureau gave him the highest rating ever for a pitcher. Of all the scouts I talked to, only two voiced any doubts about him. He had all the equipment, but they questioned whether he could equal his college success in professional baseball, a whole different ball game.

All of this was based on what we'd heard; very few of us had seen him. But two former major league pitchers agreed that it wouldn't happen. Jim Palmer and I knew from experience that it takes time, sometimes a lot of time, to become a major league pitcher. Sure, there are exceptions, but very few. Palmer and I kept expressing our doubts publicly, on the air. One day the team president, Larry Lucchino, called us aside.

"Why is it you two geniuses are the only ones with all these doubts?"

"We're not geniuses," I said. "But we have played the game, Jim more than me. We may be right or wrong, it's just our opinion. Ben has never had to worry about things like pitching from a stretch and holding men on base because in high school and college they swung at everything and he rarely had anybody on base. We know that. We did the same thing."

McDonald pitched in the College World Series, then, in August, the Orioles signed him for a big bonus and brought him to Baltimore to work out. I'm in the clubhouse early when Ben comes in. Tall, lanky six foot seven, nice kid. They all went out to the bullpen to watch him throw—Frank Robinson, the manager, pitching coach Al Jackson, GM Roland Hemond, Doug Melvin, Elrod Hendricks. I tagged along.

Ben was wearing a big thick gold chain. Hemond said to me, "Look at that thing. I wonder how much it cost?"

"Take a good look," I said. "You paid for it."

With Elrod catching, McDonald threw as hard as anybody can. But he tipped off his pitches something terrible. We all saw it. Jackson stopped him and showed him how he was changing his grip on the ball to throw a curve. I heard Al saying, "You can't do that. You have to use the same grip or they'll spot that in the big leagues."

My impression was, "He could be a major league pitcher, but not yet. He has no idea about holding people on base or how to pitch. He has been blowing people away all his life (as I had done in high school and Legion ball) because he was bigger than everybody else. He's not going to do that up here."

They sent Ben to Frederick and he started two games, did okay, didn't blow everybody away, but did a good job. The ballpark was packed for his debut, and people came away convinced he was ready.

The Orioles called him up on September 1 and he made his

big league debut in relief on September 6 against Cleveland at Memorial Stadium. It's a thrill for me to announce a Ben McDonald or a Mike Mussina or a guy like Jim Abbott for their first game in Baltimore. It may sound like a little thing, but it's a big thing with me. I've announced the debuts of some pretty good guys: Palmer, Brooks, Ripken, Murray, Boog for the Orioles, and visitors like Mattingly, Winfield, Brett. I don't change my voice or my delivery, but inside I feel it. I still believe that to be a major league player is a great thing.

Anyhow, the first pitch Ben threw in the big leagues, Cory Snyder hit into a double play to end the inning. Standing ovation. A couple innings later Joe Carter hit a tremendous blow over somebody's head in the outfield and I thought, "Welcome to the big leagues." These are not college kids up there at the plate. I don't care if you can throw 100 miles an hour; if you can't throw something else and you can't throw it right where you want it to go, you're in trouble.

Ben pulled a muscle in his side in the spring of 1990 and began the season pitching on rehab between Hagerstown and Rochester. One night I went with Roland Hemond and Doug Melvin to Hagerstown to see him pitch. A press circus swarmed around him wherever he pitched, and I told WBAL I would call in and file reports during the game.

His first inning was a disaster. He gave up five or six runs, seven hits, including a grand slam. He balked, made an error, threw a wild pitch—all that in one inning. I called in that report. When the inning was over, I watched him closely as he walked off the mound. You could see he was down. I thought: "now we're going to find out what he's made of."

He pulled himself up, went back out and gave up nothing into the seventh. That takes a lot of heart. There are guys I could tell you who couldn't do that.

When he came out of the game I walked down to the little clubhouse beyond right field to see him. The trainer didn't want to let the press get at him until Ben's arm was iced down. I explained to him that I was not part of the media circus and Ben said it was okay.

He was alone, shaving. "That first inning was sure a nightmare," he said. "Everything just seemed to go wrong at the start. But I finally got it together."

He seemed almost in tears.

"I think you're taking it too hard," I said.

"It isn't that. I was supposed to pitch in Rochester, but they predicted rain up there, so they flew me down here in a private plane to pitch tonight. I'm sick and tired of moving around. I'd like to have one home wherever it is and get settled and be able to stick to my daily routine, and get going on my professional career."

He was also frustrated because he had never had any injuries in baseball or basketball. I can understand that. We talked a little more and then he went out to meet the horde of press people and did a good job. Roland Hemond asked me what Ben had said and I told him just like I've told you.

"Here's a kid," I said, "not long out of Louisiana, and you've got him flying all over the place just to pitch."

They left Ben in Rochester after that until they called him up in July. In his first big league start on July 21 he pitched a four-hit shutout over the White Sox, and won his first five starts. Then he tailed off a little and was 3-5 the rest of the year.

At that point many of those same media experts who had been touting McDonald as a sure thing for the starting rotation from day one were saying, "The trouble with Ben McDonald is the Orioles rushed him." Or he didn't make it right away because he pitched too many innings in his last year at LSU. Or his father ruined him by holding out for more money. Or...or...or....

I think the biggest mistake was made with Ben before spring training in 1991 when Frank Robinson announced that McDonald would be the opening day pitcher. Other managers in the league wondered aloud why the Orioles would do that to a youngster, especially before camp even opened, when who knew what might happen. I think Frank did it to try to give Ben some confidence. In my opinion, you want a veteran pitcher out there with all the hoopla that goes on.

As it turned out, Ben got hurt again and did not open the season in Baltimore. He strained his right elbow, came back in late April, pitched a few times—not very well—reinjured the arm, and was 6-8 for the year.

In the spring of 1992 Ben was still a thrower, not a pitcher. But he grew up in the next two years, aided by the influence of Rick Sutcliffe, and by the spring of 1994 he was a pitcher and a team leader, out front congratulating somebody or greeting the pitcher coming off the field. In spring training he handled interviews with assurance. He's come a long way.

But I worry about Ben's arm, and about this fact of history: very tall pitchers seldom excel. Of course, today just about every pitcher is very tall by earlier standards. Ben is 6-7. He and Randy Johnson may prove to be the exceptions. I hope so.

Ben is a very good fielder and is proud of it. I've seen pitchers fail to cover first base on a ground ball to the first baseman. Jeff Ballard, a brilliant kid, did it twice in one game. I thought Frank Robinson was going to go berserk. Ben will beat the fastest runner over there. He knows how to execute a rundown— Cal Senior taught him. Early this year he took a throw at home plate and tagged out a runner sliding in trying to score on a wild pitch. A lot of guys wouldn't do that. He's into the game all the way.

Why can't they get through to a pitcher that fielding your position properly might win you a game? Fielding is fun. I used to enjoy that part of the game, and fielding swinging bunts saved my no-hitter. But some guys just stand out there and count their change. I don't understand that.

Ben had not missed a game in 80 straight starts when he had to skip one because of a pulled groin muscle in late May. That was the day they brought up Scott Klingenbeck to fill in on the mound. When I saw Ben early that day he looked a little down.

"Are you all right?"

"I'm letting myself and the team down. I should be out there."

"Forget it," I said. "Let me tell you about a guy named Drysdale. There was a ten-year period in his career where he never missed a start. Every fourth day, not fifth, for ten years. You can do it. You might go out after this and not miss a start for another ten years."

I don't know how much it helped. But I think he'll be okay. I like and appreciate Ben a great deal.

Sid Fernandez is an exceptional guy. The media in Baltimore jumped all over this "fat guy, out of shape" and a lot of callers asked, "How can that guy pitch?"

He was not and is not out of shape. He's in shape for the shape he's in, and has always pitched that way. I don't care if he weighs 500 pounds, if he can pitch. Isn't that the bottom line? And this guy can pitch. He always did a good job in New York. He's got that strange delivery, and he's so slow, until his arm gets so far, then—wham!

He proved early with the Orioles that he could pitch nine innings. The club was less concerned with his arm than his knees, and they concentrated on keeping them in good condition to support his weight under the strain of pitching.

When players switch leagues they sometimes have difficulty adjusting to the different umpires. I have never understood why we have National League and American League umpires. Why shouldn't they all circulate among all the teams in both leagues? They mix them up in spring training and in the World Series.

But Fernandez said he found no big difference with the umps. Maybe the good pitchers adjust easier.

Jamie Moyer is another guy who learned how to pitch. I watched him when he was with other clubs and he never showed me much. When the Orioles got him, they went through this dialogue with him:

"Roger Clemens—what's his main pitch?"

"Fastball."

"How many times a game do you think he uses it?"

"I guess 75 or 80 percent."

"What's your best pitch?"

"Change-up."

"How many times do you use it?"

"Twenty percent of the time."

"You just answered the problem yourself. We want you to throw that change-up constantly. Don't be afraid to throw it; it's your out pitch."

Moyer's a bright guy who knows how to pitch, but he's got

to get the ball in his strike zone. Like Preacher Roe, if he's giving up a lot of hits, that shows he doesn't have his control. Walks are not the gauge of pitchers like them. You can't "just miss" when you have that kind of stuff.

Control pitchers often have to pitch to the umpire behind the plate as well as to the hitters. If they don't get the calls on the corners, they're in trouble. A lot of umpires will tell you that's not true, but they have their idiosyncracies, and they get reputations around the league.

Preacher Roe had trouble when Larry Goetz was behind the plate. Goetz would not give him the pitches he needed to win.

Babe Pinelli was a low-ball umpire. He'd give the pitcher below the knee. Pinelli was behind the plate in my no-hitter.

We used to discuss the umpires in our pregame meetings.

"Who's umpiring?"

"Pinelli."

"Keep the ball down."

Our catchers in Brooklyn told me that Scotty Robb could not stay with the curve ball. It would fool him. You could throw the world's greatest curve and he would call it a ball. You had to stay away from it.

Jim Palmer rated Steve Palermo the best of the umps because "he gives you nothing. But he gives the hitters nothing, too."

Pitchers—and hitters—want umpires to be consistent above everything else. Palermo, Dave Phillips, Richie Garcia are a few I've heard players cite for their consistency.

I saw Lee Smith with the Cubs and the word "intimidating" is the only word that fits. Like Dick Radatz and Goose Gossage; when they came in and started warming up, you didn't want any part of them. When Smith strolls slowly in and takes his time warming up, that's for effect. It may not bother all hitters, but it gives them time to think.

Smith was devastating in Chicago. I pitched in Wrigley Field, and it hasn't changed. The stands and walls are so close around the infield you feel like you're pitching from 40 feet instead of 60. (Then we went to Pittsburgh and Forbes Field, where the wall behind home plate was 100 yards away and it looked like you were throwing 120 feet.) It's all an illusion, but that kind of thing can pump up a pitcher. It's like the wind at Wrigley; they always talk about the wind blowing out. That's a fallacy. It actually blows in more than it blows out. But baseball is a mental game, and these are the factors that can affect players' thinking.

Relievers have a different mindset from the rest of humanity, but they are not all the same. Some, like Gregg Olson, are very nervous. That can be good. I think Smith is as calm as he appears to be. That comes from experience. But, calm or jumpy, they all want the ball.

I did some relieving. When you walk in from the bullpen in the middle of an inning, that's a different situation from the closers coming in to start the ninth. Walking in, you see what's in front of you, and you know you have to get the ball over right now with something on it. Then you get to the mound and the manager asks you, "Have you got good stuff?" or "You throwing hard?" What are you going to say, no? Doesn't matter what you say, you've got to pitch to one batter, at least.

One thing all relievers think about is: Keep the ball down. If in doubt what to throw, keep it low. That's the toughest pitch to hit, even for left-handers, whose natural swing is supposed to be more effective for a low pitch. I don't know if that's true, but I think you have a better chance of getting a batter out if you can make him hit it on the ground and not up in the air. Of course, the hitters know all that, too. They also know that the pitcher will be trying to get that first pitch over for a strike. A relief pitcher should be equipped to get a breaking ball over as well as a fastball. If you have to throw a fastball down the middle to get that first pitch over, they will sit on it.

Many great relievers worked fast; grab it and throw. They didn't want the hitter to get set. Others, like Olson and Smith, take their time. Olson took more time, walking off the mound after each pitch, than any reliever I ever saw. That can make a batter a little over-anxious, too. Whatever works for you, go with it.

Most of the late-inning guys wait to go down to the bullpen until the seventh inning. Lee Smith is one of the few who stays out there. I think he belongs up there with Eckersley, Radatz, Gossage, Fingers.

Mark Williamson has been primarily a relief pitcher since he broke in in the minors in 1982. He came to the Orioles with Terry Kennedy in the trade that sent Storm Davis to San Diego in 1986, and he has been a valuable man in the bullpen ever since (he missed most of 1992 with a sore elbow).

A tall skinny guy who throws harder than you think, he's got a live fastball and a great palmball—a change-up that drops. Mark's a very good pitcher in the right spot, that so-called set-up man. He seldom gets any credit in the stats for what he does. That bothers a lot of people, but not him. He knows where he's coming from. A starter may go five innings, then Mark comes in, pitches three shutout innings, and the closer works the ninth. Starter gets the win, closer gets the save, set-up man gets paid. That's all. End of the year, his won-lost record may be 0-0. But he may have been in 60 or more games and did more to win them than the starter or the closer.

I'd love to see them take that save stat out. That would really get the closers' agents up in arms.

Mark has a good arm, but I don't think he can pitch two days in a row. A very quiet guy, he'll do a little walking around out in the bullpen during the early innings. He enjoys classical music and is probably the best golfer on the team.

I think Alan Mills was hurt when the Yankees traded him. He has great stuff, but is not as consistent as he should be. Sometimes he is "conveniently wild,"—as Mr. Rickey sould say, just enough to keep the hitters loose— and sometimes not so conveniently. He can make a mistake and get away with it, but he is basically a one-pitch pitcher—fastball. That prevents him from being a starter.

Mills looked great in spring training. He'll do anything he's asked to do—middle reliever, set-up man, closer, whatever. That can be hard on a pitcher mentally, because they tend to fix themselves into one role.

The day after Johnny Oates became manager of the Orioles in 1991, he brought up Jim Poole and Todd Frohwirth, two pitchers who fit their limited roles, pitching to one or two batters most of the time. Poole might have become a starter, but he broke down and has been a spot reliever ever since. A quiet, reserved, bright guy, he gets a little restless sitting in the bullpen.

Todd Frohwirth's underhand delivery fooled hitters for a while, but his effectiveness gradually decreased while he was here. He is very tough on himself. The Orioles let him go in the spring and he signed with Boston, but he did not do the job there, and they sent him down to the minors in June.

The Orioles signed Mark Eichhorn, another sidearmer, to replace Frohwirth. It took him a while for his sinker to start working, but when it did, he became very effective in middle relief. When they picked up Tom Bolton, it gave them a much-needed second left-hander.

When I left spring training, I liked the fit of the bullpen, and had more confidence in them than the starters. They had a rocky time of it early in the season, but they came around and have been better than most other bullpens I've seen so far this year.

And somebody once said, if you have a real good bullpen, your starters are good.

I love to see the future Orioles play in Bowie and Frederick. Sometimes you see a kid and a light bulb goes on: This guy is something special. It was that way when I saw Mike Oquist pitch; he knew how. Like Rick Forney, Scott Klingenbeck, John O'Donoghue, Oquist did not throw very hard. But pitching is more about getting the ball over the plate where you want it, not where the hitters want it. These kids will never be throwers; they will be good pitchers.

I think Oquist was a little overwhelmed when he made his first start for the Orioles. But he had pitched well in relief and deserved the chance.

Arthur Rhodes had not progressed very much. I first saw him in Frederick and Hagerstown. He could throw hard and had a great curve. They brought him up in '91; the Orioles weren't going anywhere and they wanted to take a look at him. Before each start he was drenched from perspiration, like somebody had put a hose on him, and he left it in the bullpen.

They worked and worked with him, and once in a while he

pitched a good game. He's got the physical ability, but he still isn't doing that much with it. I went through that torture. You know you've got the ability and you see other guys doing well, and you're not. When Rhodes sees guys like Jamie Moyer and Scott Klingenbeck winning games in the major leagues, he must think, "What are they doing up there?"

I know what that's like too. I used to watch Preacher Roe go out there and throw darts and not walk anybody and give up two or three hits and win without breaking a sweat, and I'd go out there and carry on and exert myself and wind up with a handful of nothing. Some pitchers can overcome all that; some can't.

Rhodes may get it together. He looked impressive when they brought him up in July—pitched two complete-game shutouts. Time will tell if he's found the key to consistency.

I've followed Brad Pennington in the minors, too, and he's just got to settle down. If he doesn't do anything this year, I'd try him as a starter. He has balked at that idea in the past, wants to pitch every day, every other day. None of this sitting around four or five days without being in there. But a kid that big and strong— I think he's wasting it.

Brad reminds me of Sandy Koufax in a few ways. It took Koufax several years to get it together, and it drove him crazy to sit around between starts. He hated it.

Pennington also reminds me of Curt Schilling when Curt was with the Orioles. Pennington's not that screwy; he's just loose. The best way to describe him is: too much too soon. That's all. He thought it was too easy. He went up the ladder in a hurry, striking out a lot of guys—and walking them, too. Then he got to the majors and did well his first few times out and didn't think he had to work at it. He got down on himself in '93, didn't think he could get anybody out. I think he's matured this year. Maybe he'll go in a trade and some pitching coach will straighten him out.

As fascinating as it is to watch these kids in the minor leagues, it's equally fascinating to see how their careers turn out. I've been lucky and privileged to have seen a lot of them come and go.

Somebody stopped me on the street one day in Baltimore

and said, "You know what you said on the air the other day? You said, 'I think I know what I'm talking about.' How do you know what you're talking about if you only think you know what you're talking about?"

He's got something there. It's like a guy giving you a definite maybe.

But when I started thinking about it, I decided that I meant what I said. What do I know? What does anybody really know about this game called baseball? Not much. I have my opinions, like millions of other fans, and my memories, again like millions of fans, and that's all I've tried to share with you.

And for all of them, and all of you—THANK Youuuu.

Appendix

All-Time Orioles Roster
1954–1993

Managers (10)
Altobelli, Joe ('83-'85)
Bauer, Hank ('64-'68)
Dykes, Jimmy ('54)
Harris, Luman ('61)
Hitchcock, Billy ('62-'63)
Oates, Johnny ('91-)
Richards, Paul ('55-'61)
Ripken, Cal Sr. ('87-'88)
Robinson, Frank ('88-'91)
Weaver, Earl ('68-'82, '85-'86)

Coaches (45)
Adair, Jimmy ('57-'61)
Appling, Luke ('63)
Bamberger, George ('68-'77)
Bauer, Hank ('63)
Biagini, Greg ('92-)
Bosman, Dick ('92-)
Brecheen, Harry ('54-'67)
Buford, Don ('88, '94)
Busby, Jim ('61)

Crowley, Terry ('85-'88)
Ermer, Cal ('62)
Ferraro, Mike ('93)
Frey, Jim ('70-'79)
Harris, Luman ('55-'61)
Hart, John ('88)
Hendricks, Elrod ('78-)
Hoscheit, Vern ('68)
Hunter, Billy ('64-'77)
Jackson, Al ('89-'91)
Johnson, Darrell ('62)
Lau, Charlie ('69)
Lollar, Sherman ('64-'67)
Lopes, Davey ('92-)
McCraw, Tom ('89-'91)
Mendoza, Minnie ('88)
Miller, Ray ('78-'85)
Motton, Curt ('89-'91)
Narron, Jerry ('93-)
Oates, Johnny ('89-'91)
Oliver, Tom ('54)
Ripken, Cal Sr. ('76-'86, '89-'92)

Robinson, Brooks ('77)
Robinson, Eddie ('57-'59)
Robinson, Frank ('78-'80, '85-'87)
Rowe, Ken ('85-'86)
Rowe, Ralph ('81-'84)
Scarborough, Ray ('68)
Skaff, Frank ('54)
Staller, George ('62, '68-'75)
Starrette, Herm ('88)
Vincent, Al ('55-'59)
Weaver, Earl ('68)
Wiley, Mark ('87)
Williams, Jimmy ('81-'87)
Woodling, Gene ('64-'67)

Players (538)
Aase, Don ('85-'88), RHP
Abrams, Cal ('54-'55), OF, L-L
Adair, Jerry ('58-'66), 2B, R-R
Adams, Bobby ('56), IF, R-R
Adamson, Mike ('67-'69), RHP
Aldrich, Jay ('90), RHP
Alexander, Bob ('55), RHP
Alexander, Doyle ('72-'76), RHP
Alexander, Manny ('92-), IF, R-R
Anderson, Brady ('88-), OF, L-L
Anderson, John ('60), RHP
Anderson, Mike ('78), OF, R-R
Aparicio, Luis ('63-'67), SS, R-R
Arnold, Tony ('86-'87), RHP
Avila, Bobby ('59), 2B, R-R
Ayala, Benny ('79-'84), OF, R-R
Bailor, Bob ('75-'76), IF, R-R
Baines, Harold ('93-), DH, L-L
Baker, Frank ('73-'74), IF, L-R
Ballard, Jeff ('87-'91), LHP
Bamberger, George ('59), RHP
Barber, Steve ('60-'67), LHP
Barker, Ray Buddy ('60), 1B, L-R
Barnowski, Ed ('65-'66), RHP
Bautista, Jose ('88-'91), RHP
Baylor, Don ('70-'75), OF, R-R
Beamon, Charlie ('56-'58), RHP
Beene, Fred ('68-'70), RHP
Belanger, Mark ('65-'81), SS, R-R

Bell, Eric ('85-'87), LHP
Bell, Juan ('89-'91), SS, S-R
Beniquez, Juan ('86), OF, R-R
Berry, Connie Neil ('54), IF, R-R
Bertaina, Frank ('64-'67, '69), LHP
Besana, Fred ('56), LHP
Bickford, Vern ('54), RHP
Birrer, Werner Babe ('56), RHP
Blair, Paul ('64-'76), OF, R-R
Blefary, Curt ('65-'68), OF, L-R
Blyzka, Mike ('54), RHP
Boddicker, Mike ('80-'88), RHP
Bonilla, Juan ('86), 2B, R-R
Bonner, Bob ('80-'83), IF, R-R
Boone, Dan ('90), LHP
Bordi, Rich ('86), RHP
Boswell, Dave ('71), RHP
Bowens, Sam (63-'67), OF, R-R
Boyd, Bob ('56-'60), 1B, L-L
Brabender, Gene ('66-'68), RHP
Bradley, Phil ('89-'90), OF, R-R
Brandt, Jackie ('60-'65), OF, R-R
Breeding, Marv (60-'62), 2B, R-R
Brideweser, Jim ('54, '57), IF, R-R
Briles, Nellie ('77-'78), RHP
Brown, Dick ('63-'65), C, R-R
Brown, Hal Skinny ('55-'62), RHP
Brown, Larry ('73), IF, R-R
Brown, Mark ('84), RHP
Brown, Marty ('90), IF, R-R
Brunet, George ('63), LHP
Buford, Damon ('93-), OF, R-R
Buford, Don ('68-'72), OF, S-R
Bumbry, Al (72-'84), OF, L-R
Bunker, Wally ('63-'68), RHP
Burke, Leo ('58-'59), IF-OF, R-R
Burleson, Rick ('87), IF, R-R
Burnside, Pete ('63), LHP
Busby, Jim ('57-'58, '60-'61), OF, R-R
Buzhardt, John ('67), RHP
Byrd, Harry ('55), RHP
Cabell, Enos ('72-'74), IF, R-R
Carey, Paul ('93-), 1B, L-R
Carrasquel, A. Chico ('59), SS, R-R
Carreon, Camilo ('66), C, R-R

Castleman, Foster ('58), IF, R-R
Causey, Wayne ('55-'57), IF, L-R
Ceccarelli, Art ('57), LHP
Chakales, Bob ('54), RHP
Chevez, Tony ('77), RHP
Chism, Tom ('79), 1B, L-L
Cimoli, Gino ('64), OF, R-R
Clements, Pat ('92), LHP
Coan, Gil ('54-'55), OF, L-R
Coggins, Richie ('72-'74), OF, L-L
Coleman, Joe ('54-'55), RHP
Coleman, Walter Rip ('59-'60), LHP
Connally, Fritz ('85), 3B, R-R
Consuegra, Sandy ('56-'57), RHP
Cook, Michael ('93-), RHP
Corbett, Doug ('87), RHP
Corey, Mark ('79-'81), OF, R-R
Courtney, Clint ('54, '60-'61), C, L-R
Cox, Billy ('55), 3B, R-R
Criscione, Dave ('77), C, R-R
Crowley, Terry ('69-'73, '76-'82), 1B-OF, L-L
Cruz, Todd ('83-'84), 3B, R-R
Cuellar, Mike ('69-'76), LHP
Dagres, Angelo ('55), OF, L-L
Dalrymple, Clay ('69-'71), C, L-R
Dauer, Rich ('76-'85), 2B, R-R
DaVanon, Jerry ('71), IF, R-R
Davis, George Storm ('82-'86, '92), RHP
Davis, Glenn ('91-'93), 1B, R-R
Davis, Tommy ('72-'75), DH, R-R
Davis, Wallace Butch ('88-'89), OF, R-R
DeCinces, Doug ('73-'81), 3B, R-R
de la Rosa, Francisco ('91), RHP
DeLeon, Luis ('87), RHP
Delock, Ike ('63), RHP
Dempsey, Rick ('76-'86, '92), C, R-R
Devereaux, Mike ('89-), OF, R-R
Diering, Chuck ('54-'56), OF, R-R
Dillard, Gordon ('88), LHP
Dillman, Bill ('67), RHP
Dimmel, Mike ('77-'78), OF, R-R
Dixon, Ken ('84-'87), RHP

Dobson, Pat ('71-'72), RHP
Dodd, Tom ('86), DH-PH, R-R
Dorish, Harry ('55-'56), RHP
Drabowsky, Moe ('66-'68, '70), RHP
Drago, Dick ('77), RHP
Dropo, Walt ('59-'61), 1B, R-R
Dukes, Tom ('71), RHP
Duncan, Dave ('75-'76), C, R-R
Duren, Ryne ('54), RHP
Durham, Joe ('54, '57), OF, R-R
Dyer, Jim ('81-'88), OF, L-L
Dyck, Jim ('55-'56), OF, R-R
Epstein, Mike ('66-'67), 1B, L-L
Essegian, Chuck ('61), OF-PH, R-R
Estrada, Chuck ('60-'64), RHP
Etchebarren, Andy ('62, '65-'75), C, R-R
Evans, Dwight ('91), OF, R-R
Evers, Walter Hoot ('55-'56), OF, R-R
Farmer, Ed ('77), RHP
Fernandez, L. Chico ('68), IF, R-R
Ferrarese, Don ('55-'57), LHP
Finigan, Jim ('59), 3B, R-R
Finley, Steve ('89-'90), OF, L-L
Fiore, Mike ('68), 1B, L-L
Fisher, Eddie ('66-'67), RHP
Fisher, Jack ('59-'62), RHP
Fisher, Tom ('67), RHP
Flanagan, Mike ('75-'78, '91-'92), LHP
Flinn, John ('78-'79, '82), RHP
Floyd, Bobby ('68-'70), IF, R-R
Foiles, Hank ('61), C, R-R
Ford, Dan ('82-'85), OF, R-R
Ford, Dave ('78-'81), RHP
Fornieles, Mike ('56-'57), RHP
Fox, Howie, ('54), RHP
Francona, Tito ('56-'57), OF-1B, L-L
Frazier, Joe ('56), OF, L-R
Freed, Roger ('70), 1B-OF, R-R
Fridley, Jim ('54), OF, R-R
Frohwirth, Todd ('91-'93), RHP
Fuller, Jim ('73-'74), OF, R-R

Gaines, Joe ('63-'64), OF, R-R

Gallagher, Dave ('90), OF, R-R

Garcia, Alfonso Kiko ('76-'80), IF, R-R

Garcia, Vinicio Chico ('54), 2B, R-R

Gardner, Billy ('56-'59), 2B, R-R

Garland, Wayne ('73-'76), RHP

Gastall, Tom ('55-'56), C, R-R

Gentile, Jim ('60-'63), 1B, L-L

Gerhart, Ken ('86-'88), OF, R-R

Gilliford, Paul ('67), LHP

Ginsberg, Myron Joe ('56-'60), C, L-R

Gomez, Leo ('90-), IF, R-R

Gonzales, Rene Gonzo ('87-'90), IF, R-R

Goodman, Billy ('57), IF-OF, L-R

Graham, Dan ('80-'81), C-3B, L-R

Gray, Ted ('55), LHP

Green, Gene ('60), OF-C, R-R

Green, Lenny ('57-'59, '64), OF, L-L

Grich, Bob ('70-'76), 2B, R-R

Griffin, Mike ('87), RHP

Grimsley, Ross ('74-'77, '82), LHP

Gross, Wayne ('84-'85), 3B, L-R

Gulliver, Glenn ('82-'83), 3B, L-R

Gutierrez, Jackie ('86-'87), IF, R-R

Habyan, John ('85-'88), RHP

Haddix, Harvey ('64-'65), LHP

Hale, Bob ('55-'59), 1B, L-L

Hall, Dick ('61-'66, '69-'71), RHP

Hammonds, Jeffrey ('93-), OF, R-R

Hamric, Bert ('58), OF-PH, L-R

Haney, Larry ('66-'68), C, R-R

Hansen, Ron ('58-'62), SS, R-R

Hardin, Jim ('67-'71), RHP

Harlow, Larry ('75, '77-'79), OF, L-L

Harnisch, Pete ('88-'90), RHP

Harper, Tommy ('76), DH, R-R

Harrison, Bob ('55-'56), RHP

Harrison, Roric ('72), RHP

Harshman, Jack ('58-'59), LHP

Hart, Mike L. ('87), OF, L-L

Hartzell, Paul (80), RHP

Hatton, Grady ('56), IF, L-R

Havens, Brad ('85-'86), LHP

Hazewood, Drungo ('80), OF, R-R

Heard, Jehosie ('54), LHP

Held, Mel ('56), RHP

Held, Woodie ('66-'67), IF-OF, R-R

Hendricks, Elrod ('68-'72, '73-'76, '78-'79), C, L-R

Hernandez, Leo ('82-'83, '85), 3B, R-R

Herzog, Whitey ('61-'62), OF, L-L

Hickey, Kevin ('89-'91), LHP

Hoeft, Billy ('59-'62), LHP

Hoiles, Chris ('89-), C, R-R

Holdsworth, Fred ('76-'77), RHP

Holton, Brian ('89-'90), RHP

Holtzman, Ken ('76), LHP

Hood, Don ('73-'74), LHP

Horn, Sam ('90-'92), 1B-DH, L-L

Houtteman, Art ('57), RHP

Howard, Bruce ('68), RHP

Hudler, Rex ('86), IF, R-R

Huffman, Phil ('85), RHP

Hughes, Keith ('88), OF, L-L

Huismann, Mark ('89), RHP

Hulett, Tim (89-), IF, R-R

Hunter, Billy ('54), SS, R-R

Huppert, Dave ('83), C, R-R

Hutto, Jim ('75), C, R-R

Hyde, Dick ('61), RHP

Jackson, Grant ('71-'76), LHP

Jackson, Lou ('64), OF, L-R

Jackson, Reggie ('76), OF, L-L

Jackson, Ron ('84), 3B, R-R

Jefferson, Jesse ('73-'75), RHP

Jefferson, Stan ('89-'90), OF, S-R

Johnson, Bob ('63-'67), IF, R-R

Johnson, Connie ('56-'58), RHP

Johnson, Darrell ('62), C, R-R

Johnson, Dave ('65-'72), 2B, R-R

Johnson, Dave ('89-'91), RHP

Johnson, David ('74-'75), RHP

Johnson, Don ('55), RHP

Johnson, Ernie ('59), RHP

Jones, Gordon ('60-'61), RHP

Jones, O'Dell ('86), RHP

Jones, Ricky ('86), IF, R-R

Jones, Sad Sam ('64), RHP

Jones, Stacy ('91), RHP
Kell, George ('56-'57), 3B, R-R
Kellert, Frank ('54), 1B, R-R
Kelly, Pat ('77-'80), OF, L-L
Kennedy, Bob ('54-'55), 3B, R-R
Kennedy, Terry ('87-'88), C, L-R
Kerrigan, Joe ('78, '80), RHP
Kilgus, Paul ('91), LHP
Kinnunen, Mike ('86-'87), LHP
Kirkland, Willie ('64), OF, L-R
Kittle, Ron ('90), 1B-DH, R-R
Klaus, Billy ('59-'60), IF, L-R
Knight, Ray ('87), 3B, R-R
Knowles, Darold ('65), LHP
Kokos, Dick ('54), OF, L-L
Komminsk, Brad ('90), OF, R-R
Koslo, George Dave ('54), LHP
Krenchicki, Wayne ('79-'81), IF, L-R
Kretlow, Lou ('54-'55), RHP
Kryhoski, Dick ('54), 1B, L-L
Kuzava, Bob ('54-'55), LHP
Lacy, Lee ('85-'87), OF, R-R
Landrith, Hobert Hobie ('62-'63), C, L-R
Landrum, Terry Tito ('83, '88), OF, R-R
Larsen, Don ('54, '65), RHP
Lau, Charlie ('61-'63, '64-'67), C, L-R
Lefferts, Craig ('92), LHP
Lehew, Jim ('61-'62), RHP
Lehman, Ken ('57-'58), LHP
Lenhardt, Don ('54), OF, R-R
Leonard, Mark ('93), 1B, L-R
Leonhard, Dave ('67-'72), RHP
Leppert, Don E. ('55), 2B, L-R
Lewis, Richie ('92), RHP
Littlefield, Dick ('54), LHP
Locke, Charlie ('55), RHP
Lockman, Carroll Whitey ('59), 1B, L-R
Loes, Billy ('56-'59), RHP
Lopat, Eddie ('55), LHP
Lopez, Carlos ('78), OF, R-R
Lopez, Marcelino ('67, '69-'70), LHP
Lowenstein, John ('79-'85), OF, L-R

Luebber, Steve ('81), RHP
Luebke, Dick ('62), LHP
Lynn, Fred ('85-'88), OF, L-L
Mabe, Bobbie ('60), RHP
Maddox, Elliott ('77), OF-3B, R-R
Majeski, Hank ('55), 3B, R-R
Marquis, Roger ('55), OF, L-L
Marsh, Fred ('55-'56), IF, R-R
Marshall, Jim ('58), 1B, L-L
Martin, Morrie ('56), LHP
Martinez, Dennis ('76-'86), RHP
Martinez, Felix Tippy ('76-'86), LHP
Martinez, Reyenaldo Chito ('91-'93), OF, L-L
Matchick, Tom ('72), 3B, L-R
Maxwell, Charlie ('55), OF, L-L
May, Dave ('67-'70), OF, L-R
May, Lee ('75-'80), 1B, R-R
May, Rudy ('76-'77), LHP
McCormick, Mike ('63-'64), LHP
McDonald, Ben ('89-), RHP
McDonald, Jim ('55), RHP
McGehee, Kevin (93-), RHP
McGregor, Scott ('76-'88), LHP
McGuire, Mickey ('62, '67), IF, R-R
McKnight, Jeff ('90-'91), IF-OF, S-R
McLemore, Mark (92-), IF, S-R
McNally, Dave ('62-'74), LHP
Mele, Sam ('54), OF, R-R
Melendez, Francisco ('89), 1B, L-L
Melvin, Bob ('89-'91), C, R-R
Mercedes, Luis ('91-'93), OF, R-R
Mesa, Jose ('87, '90-'92), RHP
Miksis, Eddie ('57-'58), IF, R-R
Milacki, Bob ('88-'92), RHP
Miller, Bill ('55), LHP
Miller, Dyar ('75-'77), RHP
Miller, John ('62-'63, '65-'67), RHP
Miller, Randy ('77), RHP
Miller, Stu ('63-'67), RHP
Milligan, Randy ('89-'92), 1B, R-R
Mills, Alan ('92-), RHP
Mirabella, Paul ('83), LHP
Miranda, Willy ('55-'59), SS, S-R

Mitchell, John ('90), RHP
Mitchell, Paul ('75), RHP
Moeller, Ron ('56, '58), LHP
Molinaro, Bob ('79), OF, L-R
Moore, Ray ('55-'57), RHP
Mora, Andres ('76-'78), OF, R-R
Morales, Jose ('81-'82), C-PH, R-R
Moreland, Keith ('89), DH, R-R
Morgan, Mike ('88), RHP
Morogiello, Dan ('83), LHP
Morris, John ('68), LHP
Moss, Les ('54-'55), C, R-R
Motton, Curt ('67-'71, '73-'74), OF, R-R
Moyer, Jamie ('93-), LHP
Murray, Eddie ('77-'88), 1B, S-R
Murray, Ray ('54), C, R-R
Muser, Tony ('75-'77), 1B, L-L
Mussina, Mike (91-), RHP
Narum, Leslie Buster ('63), RHP
Nelson, Bob ('55-'57), OF
Nelson, Roger ('68), RHP
Nichols, Carl ('86-'88), C, R-R
Nicholson, Dave ('60, '62), OF, R-R
Niedenfuer, Tom ('87-'88), RHP
Nieman, Bob ('56-'59), OF, R-R
Nixon, Donell ('90), OF, R-R
Nolan, Joe ('82-'85), C, L-R
Noles, Dickie ('88), RHP
Nordbrook, Tim ('74-'76), IF, R-R
Northrup, Jim ('74-'75), OF, L-R
Oates, Johnny ('70-'72), C, L-R
Obando, Sherman ('93-), OF, R-R
O'Connor, Jack ('87), LHP
O'Dell, Billy ('54, '56-'59), LHP
O'Donoghue, John, Jr. ('93-), LHP
O'Donoghue, John ('68), LHP
Oertel, Chuck ('58), OF, L-R
Oliver, Bob ('74), OF-1B, R-R
Olson, Gregg ('88-'93), RHP
O'Malley, Tom ('85-'86), 3B, L-R
Oquist, Mike ('93-), RHP
Orsino, John ('63-'65), C, R-R
Orsulak, Joe ('88-'92), OF, L-L
Pacella, John ('84), RHP

Pagan, Dave ('76), RHP
Pagliarulo, Mike ('93), 3B, L-R
Palica, Erv ('55-'56), RHP
Palmer, Jim ('65-'67, '69-'84), RHP
Papa, John ('61-'62), RHP
Pappas, Milt ('57-'65), RHP
Pardo, Al ('85-'86), C, S-R
Parent, Mark ('92-'93), C, R-R
Paris, Kelly ('85-'86), IF, S-R
Parrott, Mike ('77), RHP
Patton, Tom ('57), C, R-R
Pearson, Albie ('59-'60), OF, L-L
Pena, Orlando ('71, '73), RHP
Pennington, Brad ('93-), LHP
Peraza, Oswald ('88), RHP
Peterson, Carl Buddy ('57), IF, R-R
Philley, Dave ('55-'56, '60-'61), OF-1B, S-R
Phoebus, Tom ('66-'70), RHP
Pilarcik, Al ('57-'60), OF, L-L
Pillette, Duane ('54-'55), RHP
Pinella, Lou ('64), OF, R-R
Poole, Jim ('91-), LHP
Pope, Dave ('55-'56), OF, L-R
Portocarrero, Arnie ('58-'60), RHP
Powell, John Boog ('61-'74), 1B, L-R
Powers, John ('60), OF, L-R
Powis, Carl ('57), OF, R-R
Price, Joe ('90), LHP
Pyburn, Jim ('55-'57), OF, R-R
Quirk, Art ('62), LHP
Quirk, Jamie ('89), C, L-R
Ramirez, Allan ('83), RHP
Rayford, Floyd ('80, '82, '84-'87), 3B-C, R-R
Reinbach, Mike ('74), OF, L-R
Rettenmund, Merv ('68-'73), OF, R-R
Reynolds, Bob ('72-'75), RHP
Reynolds, Harold ('93), 2B, S-R
Rhodes, Arthur ('91-), LHP
Rice, Del ('60), C, R-R
Richert, Pete ('67-'71), LHP
Rineer, Jeff ('79), LHP
Ripken, Bill ('87-'92), 2B, R-R
Ripken, Cal Jr. ('81-), SS, R-R

Roberts, Robin ('62-'65), RHP
Robinson, Brooks ('55-'77), 3B, R-R
Robinson, Earl ('61-'62, '64), OF, R-R
Robinson, Eddie ('57), 1B, L-R
Robinson, Frank ('66-'71), OF, R-R
Robinson, Jeff M. ('91), RHP
Robles, Sergio ('72-'73), C, R-R
Rodriguez, Aurelio ('83), 3B, R-R
Rodriguez, Vic ('84), 2B, R-R
Roenicke, Gary ('78-'85), OF, R-R
Rogovin, Saul ('55), RHP
Rowdon, Wade, ('88), 3B, R-R
Rowe, Ken ('64-'65), RHP
Royster, Willie ('81), C, R-R
Roznovsky, Vic ('66-'67), C, L-R
Rudolph, Ken ('77), C, R-R
Sakata, Lenn ('80-'85), IF, R-R
Salmon, Ruthford Chico ('69-'72), IF, R-R
Sanchez, Orlando ('84), C, L-R
Saverine, Bob ('59, '62-'64), IF-OF, S-R
Scarsone, Steve ('92-'93), IF, R-R
Schallock, Art ('55), LHP
Scherrer, Bill ('88), LHP
Schilling, Curt ('88-'90), RHP
Schmidt, Dave ('87-'89), RHP
Schmitz, Johnny ('56), LHP
Schneider, Jeff ('81), LHP
Schu, Rick ('88-'89), 3B, R-R
Scott, Ralph Mickey ('72-'73), LHP
Segrist, Kal ('55), IF, R-R
Segui, David ('90-), 1B-OF, S-L
Severinsen, Al ('69), RHP
Sheets, Larry ('84-'89), OF-DH, L-R
Shelby, John ('81-'87), OF, S-R
Shetrone, Barry ('59-'62), OF, L-R
Shields, Tommy ('92), IF, L-R
Shopay, Tom ('71-'72, '75-'77), OF, L-R
Short, Billy ('62, '66), LHP
Siebern, Norm ('64-'65), 1B, L-R
Simmons, Nelson ('87), OF, S-R
Singleton, Ken ('75-'84), OF, S-R
Sisk, Doug ('88), RHP

Skaggs, Dave ('77-'80), C, R-R
Sleater, Lou ('58), LHP
Smith, Al ('63), OF, R-R
Smith, Billy ('77-'79), 2B, S-R
Smith, Hal ('55-'56), C, R-R
Smith, Lonnie ('93), OF, R-R
Smith, Texas Mike ('89-'90), RHP
Smith, Nate ('62), C, R-R
Smith, Roy ('91), RHP
Snell, Nate ('84-'86), RHP
Snyder, Russ ('61-'67), OF, L-R
Stanhouse, Don ('78-'79, '82), RHP
Stanicek, Pete ('87-'88), IF-OF, S-R
Starrette, Herm ('63-'65), RHP
Stefero, John ('83, '86), C, L-R
Stephens, Gene ('60-'61), OF, L-R
Stephens, Vern ('54-'55), 3B, R-R
Stephenson, Earl ('77-'78), LHP
Stewart, Sammy ('78-'85), RHP
Stillman, Royle ('75-'76), 1B-DH, L-L
Stock, Wes ('59-'64), RHP
Stoddard, Tim ('78-'83), RHP
Stone, Dean ('63), LHP
Stone, Jeff ('88), OF, L-R
Stone, Steve ('79-'81), RHP
Stuart, Marlin ('54), RHP
Sundin, Gordon ('56), RHP
Sutcliffe, Rick, ('92-'93), RHP
Swaggerty, Bill ('83-'86), RHP
Tackett, Jeff ('91-), C, R-R
Tasby, Willie ('58-'60), OF, R-R
Taylor, Dom ('90), RHP
Taylor, Joe ('58-'59), OF, L-L
Telford, Anthony ('90-'93), RHP
Temple, Johnny ('62), 2B, R-R
Tettleton, Mickey ('88-'90), C, S-R
Thomas, Valmy ('60), C, R-R
Thomson, Bobby ('60), OF, R-R
Throneberry, Marv ('61-'62), 1B, L-L
Thurmond, Mark ('88-'89), LHP
Tibbs, Jay ('88-) RHP
Torrez, Mike ('75), RHP
Traber, Jim ('84, '86, '88-'89), 1B, L-

L

Triandos, Gus ('55-'62), C, R-R
Trout, Paul Dizzy ('57), RHP
Turley, Bob ('54), RHP
Turner, Shane ('91), IF, L-R
Underwood, Tom ('84), LHP
Valentine, Fred ('59, '63, '68), S-R
Valenzuela, Fernando ('93), LHP
Van Gorder, Dave ('87), C, R-R
Vineyard, Dave ('64), RHP
Virgil, Ozzie ('62), 3B, R-R
Voigt, Jack ('92-), OF, R-R
Waitkus, Eddie ('54-'55), 1B, L-L
Walker, Greg ('90), 1B, L-R
Walker, Jerry ('57-'60), RHP
Ward, Pete ('62), OF, L-R
Warwick, Carl ('65), OF, R-L
Washington, Ron ('87), IF, R-R
Watt, Eddie ('66-'73), RHP
Welchel, Don ('82-'83), RHP
Werley, George ('56), RHP
Wertz, Vic ('54), 1B-OF, L-R

Westlake, Wally ('55), OF, R-R
Weston, Michael Mickey ('89-'90), RHP
Whitt, Ernie ('91), C, L-R
Wiggins, Alan ('85-'87), 2B, S-R
Wight, Bill ('55-'57), LHP
Wilhelm, Hoyt ('58-'62), RHP
Williams, Dallas ('81), OF, L-L
Williams, Dick ('56-'57, '58, '61-'62), OF-IF, R-R
Williams, Earl ('73-'74), C-1B, R-R
Williamson, Mark ('87-'93), RHP
Wilson, Jim ('55-'56), RHP
Woodling, Gene ('55, '58-'60), OF, L-R
Worthington, Craig ('88-'91), 3B, R-R
Young, Bobby ('54-'55), 2B, L-R
Young, Mike ('82-'87), OF, S-R
Zupo, Frank Noodles ('57-'58, '61), C, L-R
Zuverink, George ('55-'59), RHP

Most Valuable Orioles

1954-Chuck Diering (OF)
1955-Dave Philley (OF)
1956-Bob Nieman (OF)
1957-Billy Gardner (2B)
1958-Gus Triandos (C)
1959-Gene Woodling (OF)
1960-Brooks Robinson (3B)
1961-Jim Gentile (1B)
1962-Brooks Robinson (3B)
1963-Stu Miller (HRP)
1964-Brooks Robinson (3B)
1965-Stu Miller (HRP)
1966-Frank Robinson (OF)
1967-Frank Robinson (OF)
1968-Dave McNally (LHP)
1969-Boog Powell (1B)
1970-Boog Powell (1B)
1971-B. Robby (3B)/F. Robby (OF)
1972-Jim Palmer (RHP)
1973-Jim Palmer (RHP)

1974-Paul Blair (OF)/Mike Cuellar (LHP)
1975-Ken Singleton (OF)
1976-Lee May (1B)
1977-Ken Singleton (OF)
1978-Eddie Murray (1B)
1979-Ken Singleton (OF)
1980-Al Bumbry (OF)
1981-Eddie Murray (1B)
1982-Eddie Murray (1B)
1983-E. Murray (1B)/C. Ripken (SS)
1984-Eddie Murray (1B)
1985-Eddie Murray (1B)
1986-Don Aase (RHP)
1987-Larry Sheets (OF)
1988-E. Murray (1B)/C. Ripken (SS)
1989-Gregg Olson (RHP)
1990-Cal Ripken (SS)
1991-Cal Ripken (SS)
1992-Mike Devereaux (OF)
1993-Chris Hoiles (C)

Orioles Standings

Yr	W	L	Pct	GB/GA	P	Mgr(s)
1993	85	77	.525	10	T-3rd	Johnny Oates
1992	89	73	.549	7	3rd	Johnny Oates
1991	67	95	.414	24	6th	Frank Robinson/Oates
1990	76	85	.472	11-1/2	5th	Frank Robinson
1989	87	75	.537	2	2nd	Frank Robinson
1988	54	107	.335	34-1/2	7th	Cal Ripken Sr/Robinson
1987	67	95	.414	31	6th	Cal Ripken Sr.
1986	73	89	.451	22-1/2	7th	Earl Weaver
1985	83	79	.516	16	4th	Altobelli/Ripken/Weaver
1984	85	77	.525	19	5th	Joe Altobelli
1983	98	64	.605	(6)	1st	Joe Altobelli
1982	94	68	.580	1	2nd	Earl Weaver
1981	59	46	.562	1	*2nd	Earl Weaver
1980	100	62	.617	3	2nd	Earl Weaver
1979	102	57	.642	(8)	1st	Earl Weaver
1978	90	71	.559	9	4th	Earl Weaver
1977	97	64	.602	2	2nd	Earl Weaver
1976	88	74	.543	10-1/2	2nd	Earl Weaver
1975	90	69	.566	4-1/2	2nd	Earl Weaver
1974	91	71	.562	(2)	1st	Earl Weaver
1973	97	65	.599	(8)	1st	Earl Weaver
1972	80	74	.519	8	3rd	Earl Weaver
1971	101	57	.639	(12)	1st	Earl Weaver
1970	108	554	.667	(15)	1st	Earl Weaver
1969	109	53	.673	(19)	1st	Earl Weaver
1968	91	71	.562	12	2nd	Hank Bauer/Earl Weaver
1967	76	85	.472	15-1/2	T-6th	Hank Bauer
1966	97	63	.606	(9)	1st	Hank Bauer
1965	94	68	.580	8	3rd	Hank Bauer
1964	97	65	.599	2	3rd	Hank Bauer
1963	86	76	.531	18-1/2	4th	Billy Hitchcock
1962	77	85	.475	19	7th	Billy Hitchcock
1961	95	67	.586	14	3rd	Richards/Luman Harris
1960	89	65	.578	8	2nd	Paul Richards
1959	74	80	.481	20	6th	Paul Richards
1958	74	79	.484	17-1/2	6th	Paul Richards
1957	76	76	.500	21	5th	Paul Richards
1956	69	85	.448	28	6th	Paul Richards
1955	57	97	.370	39	7th	Paul Richards
1954	54	100	.351	57	7th	Jimmy Dykes
Totals	3376	2962	.533			

*First Half: 31-23, .574, 2 GB...Second Half: 28-23, .549, 2 GB

T-Tie in standings ('93 ith Detroit; '67 with Washington)

Members of the Orioles Hall of Fame

Brooks Robinson, 3b ('77)
Frank Robinson, of ('77)
Dave McNally, lhp ('78)
Boog Powell, 1b ('79)
Gus Triandos, c ('81)
Luis Aparicio, ss ('82)
Mike Cuellar, lhp ('82)
Mark Belanger, ss ('83)
Earl Weaver, mgr ('83)
Paul Blair, of ('84)
Paul Richards, mgr ('84)
Milt Pappas, rhp ('85)

Jim Palmer, rhp ('86)
Ken Singleton, of ('86)
Al Bumbry, of ('87)
Steve Barber, lhp ('88)
Jim Gentile, 1b ('89)
Stu Miller, rhp ('89)
Dick Hall, rhp ('89)
Hank Bauer, mgr ('90)
Scott McGregor, lhp ('90)
Hal Brown, rhp ('91)
Gene Woodling, of ('92)
Don Buford ('93)

Major Orioles Award Winners

Most Valuable Player, AL
(BBWAA) Brooks Robinson ('64),
Frank Robinson ('66), Boog Powell
('70),
Cal Ripken Jr. ('83 and '91).

Cy Young Award, AL (BBWAA)
Mike Cuellar ('69 tied with Denny
McLain), Jim Palmer ('73, '75, '76);
Mike Flanagan ('79), Steve Stone
('80).

Manager of the Year (BBWAA)
Frank Robinson ('89).
Manager of the Year, Major League
(TSN)
Hank Bauer ('66), Earl Weaver ('77,
'79), Frank Robinson ('89), Johnny
Oates ('93).
Manager of the Year, AL (AP)
Paul Richards ('60), Hank Bauer
('64, '66), Earl Weaver ('73, '77,
'79), Frank Robinson ('89).
Manager of the Year, AL (UPI)
Earl Weaver ('79), Joe Altobelli
('83), Frank Robinson ('89).

Rookie of the Year, AL (BBWAA)
Ron Hansen ('60), Curt Blefary ('65),
Al Bumbry ('73), Eddie Murray ('77),
Cal Ripken Jr. ('82), Gregg Olson
('89).
Rookie of the Year, AL (TSN)
Ron Hansen ('60), Curt Blefary ('65),
Al Bumbry ('73), Cal Ripken ('82),
Craig Worthington ('89).
Rookie Pitcher of the Year, AL (TSN)
Wally Bunker ('64), Tom Phoebus
('67), Mike Boddicker ('83).

Player of the Year, AL (TSN)
Brooks Robinson ('64), Frank
Robinson ('66), Cal Ripken Jr. ('83
and '89).
Player of the Year, AL (*Baseball
America*)
Cal Ripken Jr. ('83 and '91).

Pitcher of the Year, AL (TSN)
Chuck Estrada ('60), Jim Palmer ('73,
'75, '76), Mike Flanagan ('79), Steve
Stone ('80).
Player of the Year, Major League
(TSN)
Frank Robinson ('66), Cal Ripken Jr.

('83 and '89).
Most Valuable Player, World Series
Frank Robinson ('66), Brooks
Robinson ('70), Rick Dempsey ('83).
Most Valuable Player, ALCS (Leland
S. MacPhail Jr. Award)
Mike Boddicker ('83).
Arch Ward Memorial Trophy for Most
Valuable Player, All-Star Game
(Commissioner's Office)
Billy O'Dell ('58), Brooks Robinson,
('66), Frank Robinson ('71), Cal
Ripken ('91).

Executive of the Year, Major League
(TSN)
Harry Dalton ('70), Hank Peters ('79),
Roland Hemond ('89).
Executive of the Year, Major League
(UPI)
Hank Peters ('79), Roland Hemond
('89).

Roberto Clemente Award
(Commissioner's Office)
Presented annually to player who best
typifies the game of baseball, both
on and off the field
Brooks Robinson ('72), Ken
Singleton ('82), Cal Ripken Jr. ('92).

Joe Cronin Award (AL Office)
Presented annually to an AL player
for significant achievement
Jim Palmer ('76), Brooks Robinson
('77).

Bart Giamatti Caring Award
(Baseball Alumni Team)
For exceptional devotion and
contribution to both Baseball and the
Community
Cal Ripken Jr. ('90—first time
presented.)

Jack Dunn Memorial Community
Service Award
Elrod Hendricks ('87), Ken
Singleton ('88), Brooks Robinson
('89), Jim Palmer ('91).

Orioles Gold Glove Winners

Year	Player	Year	Player
1960	B. Robinson (3b)	1970	B. Robinson (3b)
1961	B. Robinson (3b)		D. Johnson (2b)
1962	B. Robinson (3b)		Blair (of)
1963	B. Robinson (3b)	1971	B. Robinson (3b)
1964	B. Robinson (3b)		Belanger (ss)
	Aparicio (ss)		D. Johnson (2b)
1965	B. Robinson (3b)		Blair (of)
1966	B. Robinson (3b)	1972	B. Robinson (3b)
	Aparicio (ss)		Blair (of)
1967	B. Robinson (3b)	1973	B. Robinson (3b)
	Blair (of)		Belanger (ss)
1968	B. Robinson (3b)		Grich (2b)
1969	B. Robinson (3b)		Blair (of)
	Belanger (ss)	1974	B. Robinson (3b)
	D. Johnson (2b)		Belanger (ss)
	Blair (of)		Grich (2b)

	Blair (of)		Palmer (p)
1975	B. Robinson (3b)	1978	Belanger (ss)
	Belanger (ss)		Palmer (p)
	Grich (2b)	1979	Palmer (p)
	Blair (of)	1982	Murray (1b)
1976	Belanger (ss)	1983	Murray (1b)
	Grich (2b)	1984	Murray (1b)
	Palmer (p)	1991	C. Ripken (ss)
1977	Belanger (ss)	1992	C. Ripken (ss)

Orioles All-Star Game Selectees

1954
Bob Turley (DNP)
1955
Jim Wilson (DNP)
1956
George Kell (ST)
1957
George Kell (ST)
Billy Loes
Gus Triandos (DNP)
1958
Billy O'Dell
Gus Triandos (ST)
1959
Billy O'Dell2
Gus Triandos (ST)1
Jerry Walker (ST)+2
Hoyt Wilhelmn (DNP 1st)
Gene Woodling2
1960
Chuck Estrada (DNP 2nd)
Jim Gentile (DNP 2nd)
Ron Hansen (ST both)
Brooks Robinson
1961
Jack Brandt (DNP 2nd)
Jim Gentile (DNP 2nd)
Brooks Robinson (ST both)
Hoyt Wilhelm (DNP 2nd)
1962
Jim Gentile (ST both)
Milt Pappas (both)

Brooks Robinson (both)
Hoyt Wilhelm*
1963
Luis Aparicio
Brooks Robinson
Steve Barber*
1964
Luis Aparicio*
Brooks Robinson (ST)
Norm Siebern
1965
Milt Pappas (ST)+
Brooks Robinson (ST)
1966
Steve Barber (DNP)
Andy Etchebarren (DNP)
Brooks Robinson (ST)
Frank Robinson (ST)
1967
Andy Etchebarren (DNP)
Brooks Robinson (ST)
Frank Robinson (DNP)
1968
Dave Johnson
Boog Powell
Brooks Robinson (ST)
1969
Paul Blair
Dave Johnson*
Dave McNally
Boog Powell (ST)
Brooks Robinson
Frank Robinson (ST)

APPENDIX

1970
Mike Cuellar (DNP)
Dave Johnson (ST)+
Dave McNally (DNP)
Jim Palmer (ST)+
Boog Powell (ST)
Brooks Robinson
Frank Robinson (ST)
1971
Don Buford
Mike Cuellar
Jim Palmer
Boog Powell*
Brooks Robinson (ST)
Frank Robinson (ST)
1972
Pat Dobson (DNP)
Bobby Grich (ST)+
Dave McNally
Jim Palmer (ST)+
Brooks Robinson (ST)
1973
Paul Blair
Brooks Robinson (ST)
1974
Mike Cuellar (DNP)
Bobby Grich
Brooks Robinson (ST)
1975
Jim Palmer (DNP)
1976
Mark Belanger
Bobby Grich (ST)
1977
Jim Palmer (ST)+
Ken Singleton
1978
Jim Palmer (ST)+
Mike Flanagan (DNP)
Eddie Murray (DNP)
1979
Ken Singleton
Don Stanhouse (DNP)
1980
Al Bumbry

Steve Stone (ST)+
1981
Scott McGregor (DNP)
Eddie Murray
Ken Singleton (ST)
1982
Ken Singleton (ST)
1983
Tippy Martinez (DNP)
Eddie Murray
Cal Ripken
1984
Mike Boddicker (DNP)
Eddie Murray
Cal Ripken (ST)
1985
Eddie Murray (ST)
Cal Ripken (ST)
1986
Don Aase
Eddie Murray (ST)
Cal Ripken (ST)
1987
Terry Kennedy (ST)
Cal Ripken (ST)
1988
Cal Ripken (ST)+
1989
Mickey Tettleton
Cal Ripken (ST)
1990
Gregg Olson (DNP)
Cal Ripken (ST)
1991
Cal Ripken (ST)
1992
Brady Anderson
Mike Mussina
Cal Ripken (ST)
1993
Mike Mussina
Cal Ripken (ST)
Managers: Paul Richards, '61**;
Hank Bauer, '67; Earl Weaver, '70,
'71, '72, '74++, '80; Joe Altobelli, '84.

Modern Orioles in the Baseball Hall of Fame

Robin Roberts ('76)
Frank Robinson ('82)
Brooks Robinson ('83)
George Kell ('83+)
Luis Aparicio ('84)
Hoyt Wilhelm ('85)
Jim Palmer ('90)
Reggie Jackson ('93)
+Veterans Committee Selection

In 1993, Chuck Thompson became the recipient of the Ford C. Frick Award, presented by the Hall of Fame to a broadcaster for major contributions to the game of baseball.

Index